Matt Livingston, You Liar!

Matt Livingston, You Liar!

Matt Livingston

E. L. Marker
Salt Lake City

Felt Hall

Matt Livingston you liar!!!!!!!

This is the first text message Karen Adams, the girl with the cropped Twitter profile picture, sends me.

She isn't a fan of my "pretending to be upset" that a guy called her sister to get her phone number. She followed the breadcrumbs and found me. Yes, it was me. I didn't mean to make it so easy. She figured me out a lot more quickly than I anticipated. I'm smiling so big at all those exclamation points at the end of her text. Which doesn't make a lot of sense, right? Why am I immediately endeared to someone who calls me a liar and uses exclamation points in a text message? Am I that lonely? I don't even know her. This should be a "delete" and "block number" type of scenario. These are both warning signs. But I am sad and lonely and I need attention.

I text her back, and we meet up outside the BYU library later that day. I get in her car because I don't have one, we get shakes, and we quickly launch a relationship built on contrived reactions, rude accusations, and lots of extra exclamation points.

I'm not a liar at the time she calls me one. I'm just teasing, I'm pretending, I'm flirting, but I'm not lying. It's a joke.

". . . looks up my number in the student directory, calls my house, gets my number from my little sister, and interrupts my meeting!" Karen is putting on a show, telling the story to all the other make-up-quizzers when I walk in late.

"Yeah, who *does* that?" I chime in to the girls next to my chair as I sit down. "Call someone's sister to get a phone number? Pffffff. Lame."

Karen's teasing too. We are both enjoying it. She's the TA, I'm the student. She's dialed in and running the show. I'm just home from my LDS mission and a complete mess. She says, "Who does that?" and I say, "I know, right?"

She knows it's someone in the room. Has to be. I don't have long until she finds out it's me.

But *she's* lying for real. I just don't know it yet. Eventually I will learn.

Years later I looked back on these first days with Karen and asked my sister Kelly what she thought of it all. What she thought when her brother married a gal he didn't know. She told me she looked Karen up on Facebook and saw the full picture Karen had cropped her face from for her Twitter picture. The rest of the image was a bunch of beer-toting college football players with their arms draped all over her.

But I don't have a smartphone yet, circa 2009, and I don't have a computer either, so I don't look up Karen on Facebook. I have spent the last two years on my LDS mission learning to see the best in people, and now I plow through warning signs like a daredevil snowboarder. I don't even consider looking into her past before giving her my future. I do have a Facebook, but soon Karen will make me delete it, and we will have a joint Facebook.

Our first assignment in Comms 211 is to set up a free Twitter account, follow Karen's account, and Tweet a few times on our own. I write my first few Tweets from student computers in the campus library. I don't really care to know the truth about her or her picture. I just want her to be the one for me so I can get married like everyone says I should. I keep saying I won't; I say I'll get my Masters and save money before marriage, I say I'll only date casually, I say I'll be twenty-five before I put a ring on a girl. I'm not ready. Not even close. I'm young and immature with no plan or direction.

I lie to myself and say I can do it. Now that I'm in college and am done with my LDS mission, marriage is all I can think about. It's everywhere I look. All my friends are getting married, all my church leaders are telling me to get married, and I can't escape. This girl who calls me a liar all tongue-in-cheek doesn't know how correct she really is. She tells me I'm taking her out again tomorrow. Tells me I'm hers. Gives me an easy way out of figuring out my life. She pulls me in. I can't resist.

In the hours leading up to that fateful text message from my TA, I need to attend a make-up quiz with her, but I can't find where the quiz will take place. I think back on her cute Twitter picture. The one that crops her out of the bar where she's partying and drinking and breaking all the other rules of being LDS. But I can't see any of that. Her cute face and my rushed and troubled search for a mate are reason enough to scroll the university student directory to get her phone number. I email her too, but it's last minute, and I know she won't get it in time to respond.

Only she does get it in time to respond. And she emails me back almost instantly. Why do I try so hard? Why can't I just send her an email asking where the quiz will be given? Or why can't I just show up where I think the make-up quiz will be? Do I really have to call her too? Why can't I just miss a quiz every once in awhile like a regular college sophomore? But since Matt Livingston the liar emails, and calls, and attends, the TA on the other side of the cropped Twitter picture has him dead to rights. Name, email address, phone number, face. No escape. Yeah, I did make it too easy for her. Too many breadcrumbs.

"Hello?"

"Hi, is this Karen Adams's number?"

"No, she is at BYU. This is her sister, but I can give you her cell phone if you want."

"Okay."

I memorize the cell phone number. I have a short-term photographic memory, which is how I memorized a girl's number last week and called her a few nights later to go make out in the park on 900 East in Provo. I'll never call that girl again. I don't even know her name. Just her number. I know my childhood phone numbers, addresses, all my credit card numbers. Numbers are easy.

I find it strange that my TA's little sister offers up her sister's digits so easily. She should have hung up on me. Or just let the phone ring like most teenagers do. She should have protected her sister from a creepy college guy like me. The power could have gone out, a tree could have fallen on their house, an eagle could have swooped through the library and taken my phone out of my hand, lots of things could have stopped our conversation from happening. But Karen's sister Rachel is sort of an overachiever like me, so our subconscious kindred spirits teamed up to connect one liar to another, and now it's time for me to call the number.

"Hello, this is Karen."

"Hi, this is one of your students. Could you please tell me where to go for the make-up quiz at two o'clock?"

"First off, don't ever call me at this number. This is my cell phone, and I'm meeting with the quarterbacks' coach, and this is a waste of my time. But the quiz is in conference room 191B in the news building."

I saunter into the quiz room at two-oh-three p.m. to Karen laughing with her students about the boy who called *her sister* and got *her cell phone number* and most importantly called her when she *was interviewing the quarterback coach.*

Despite the improv comedy show, I still catch most of the female eyes in the room with my well-timed late entrance and flex my bulging arms through my size extra-small Ed Hardy shirtsleeves. I loudly drag a chair out from beneath the conference room table next to a cute blonde freshman girl and fall into the charades.

Bulging forearms slide to rest way out into the middle of the table for all to see. Especially Karen the TA. I work out with two hundred and ninety-five pounds on bench press and do dips and pull-ups with three forty-five pound "biscuits" hanging from a chain belt beneath my waist. I am trying to be my version of Dwayne "The Rock" Johnson, just like all the other dudes I see in the free campus gym. I'm just better at it than most of them. I really am "the hardest worker in the room." I eat tons of eggs and chicken breast and rice just like the Rock. My thirty-five-dollar a week Resident Assistant meal card is dialed in. We eat like The Rock and work out like The Rock, and we strut around like him too, placing our forearms on tables where the girls can see bulging veins and calloused hands.

I love calling attention to myself and then pretending I didn't. Dean's List, muscular, handsome, spiritual. I recently returned from my two-year mission for The Church of Jesus Christ of Latter-day Saints, where I held the highest leadership position for an entire year. Looking at me, you'd think I'm the man. But when I say I love calling attention to myself, what I mean is that I am sad and lonely and unprepared for the regular civilian life I've re-entered.

From the time I was three, I prepared to go to college, serve a mission for two years, and get married. My dad did it. Most of my childhood church and community leaders did it. Mission at nineteen, marriage at twenty-one. Now that the mission is over, all those voices are telling me to get married, but I'm not ready. I feel abandoned by God and a little angry at Him too. On my mission I felt so close to God, and now I can't hear Him at all. I'm confused about everything. Many of my close friends have gone off and married girls they loved before they left on their missions, and the rest are off partying and drinking. I look like I have it together, but I cry myself to sleep almost every night. But I keep building and showing off my body to deflect all that.

So, on this day I finish my quiz before anyone else and hand it in to Karen, making sure she sees my name at the top. I hold the paper in exactly the right way for her to see my name as I hand it to her. Make good eye contact too. Obviously, I know she will find out who I am because of the detailed trail of other information I just left her. Interview interrupter number one.

Karen texts me less than ten minutes later while I'm still walking to my next stop. What she sends me reminds me of something my mom learned from her favorite professor at BYU, where she was a student twenty-five years ago. And yes, of course I only came here to make my parents happy. It's impossible not to. I had full-ride offers to every institution in Utah, but when Mom and I visited BYU, we both knew I would come here. Anyway, the thing Mom learned here, which I would too, is *we can only accuse others of what we ourselves are guilty.*

We can only accuse others of what we ourselves are guilty.

We can only accuse others of what we ourselves are guilty. *Matt Livingston you liar!!!!!!!*

Her text comes from a Blackberry, because Blackberries are the phones sports reporters use. iPhones are for the masses of recreational phone users. People who meet with quarterback coaches use Blackberries because they are professional grade. I have a cheap T-Mobile slider phone. You have to slide it open to use the keyboard. But I love it! It fits anywhere and is indestructible. Karen calls it the brick. You know the expression "shit a brick?" I drop that brick in the toilet once a week. I am always tired, never sleeping, often dropping things and forgetting things. The brick keeps on sliding and dialing just fine. Just like when it dialed Karen's little sister and then dialed Karen.

Years later we will go to Karen's best friend Lauren's wedding at the Biltmore estate in Asheville, North Carolina. Her best friend's "godfather" and ESPN legend John Buccigross will stroll in late, buzzed, in a gaudy suit, slurring loudly like a lawnmower running on oil instead of gas. Bucci would have been one of those reporters using a Blackberry in 2009. Because he was a professional reporter just like Karen.

Karen tells me she has been interested in sports since she was in middle school. Every morning she and her dad would go for a run and talk about sports. She still runs every morning. They would talk mostly about BYU football. Her dad Brian knew all the players, all the top recruits for next season, all the depth charts. When she arrived in Provo, she blew the BYU professors away with her sports knowledge and easily got into the broadcast journalism major. Now she knows all the football players, hangs out with them on the weekends, and goes shopping with their girlfriends. She is the only non-athlete member of the student-athlete Cougar Council. She has tickets to games and events. She's a big deal. She was a big-time tennis player in high school too. She sounds like the one for me.

None of this is what it seems. Karen has daddy-issues. Since all her athletic interests are built on their relationship, once we get married and she doesn't need to impress him anymore, she won't care about any of it. We will never talk about sports. She will never once play a match of tennis with me. She will stop running for good. She will pivot into needing to one-up him and get a PhD like he has. She won't want to be Daddy's little sports reporter anymore. She will want to be the next doctor in the family.

It's all about her. Everything is about her. In the beginning, I am on board with this. She builds herself up and breaks me down the entire time we are together. Starting with that first text message Karen sends me from her Blackberry. The day she sends me that text and I respond so enthusiastically to her accusation is the day I become her handsome little liar. I do it in the name of love, which sounds noble, right? She needs me, and she needs a me I've never been before, but the me I am right now isn't working for me anyway. It's time to go with Karen. For her I will lie to myself, my family, my God, my friends. It's easier than sorting out my emotions and finding my way. I will soon become a prolific and habitual liar for Karen. Anything for her. All my lies become my new purpose: to protect Karen and cover for her. The lies she tells me mainly stem from her cropped Twitter profile picture and what she really did last summer.

Her Twitter picture was taken a couple months before we met at a bar in Gainesville, Florida, with a bunch of drunk Florida Gator offensive linemen. She was there for a three-month sports broadcasting internship, which only lasted a few weeks, but she still stayed all summer. To . . . party! Her best friend Lauren, who's wedding we will later attend at the Biltmore, attends UF, so Karen stayed with her. Sometimes the rest of the picture tries to un-crop itself, but Karen always has an answer. In our church and especially at BYU, we don't smoke, we don't drink, we don't party, we don't have sex, we don't anything. It's called the Honor Code. BYU makes the NCAA basketball tournament for the first time in years, and our star center, who went on to play NBA ball, suspends himself for breaking the Honor Code. We give each other the benefit of the doubt that we all live the same standards. If you don't, you're a liar, which is far worse than breaking any of the other rules. So yeah, sometimes her summer tries to reveal itself to me, but she keeps it out of view.

Why were you at the parties? *I was the designated driver.* Okay.

But that happens at the end of the party, why were you there during the party? *To tell them to come to church on Sunday because the parties were often on Saturday nights.* Okay, sweet! This woman really is my soul mate!

Why did you get fired from the internship? *The coach was a jerk.* Waterworks turn on. How dare I ask? Insensitive boyfriend. Okay.

Why does Matt Patchan the Florida Gator lineman still text you at three a.m. to come over? *He's just drunk. He always wanted me to stay over but I never did!* Waterworks again. I am so insensitive!

But I can't write "Okay" on that one. There is only one reason a 300-lb. college football player with a beer in his hand texts a cute girl at three a.m. I don't bring it up again, but every time he texts her, she gets really uncomfortable and feels the need to bring it up and explain herself to me. She checks my phone constantly, going through my text messages, like I can even send them from my brick of a phone. I could care less about her private conversations, but she always wants to read mine. I have an internship and an RA job and she texts me all the time, trying to become the only conversation I'm having with anyone. Trying to use up all my time so I don't have any for anyone else.

The humidity in Florida gave her acne. She's trying to become a sports reporter, an anchor newswoman, the kind that have their face on the TV screen all hours of the day and night. She constantly talks about how she needs to get rid of her acne. She started taking Acutane to get rid of it, and it's taking an immediate toll. She calls me hysterical from the side of the freeway and says she had a panic attack. She watched a semi-truck run her over. She blames it on the Acutane. We go to So You Think You Can Dance, and she screams at me and hits me all night. Then she cools down and talks to me in a pet voice and blames it on the Acutane. I feel so bad for her.

We get home from the show and she asks me to scratch her back under her shirt because the Acutane makes her so itchy. Back becomes side, then she rolls over, my hand slips, and I accidentally touch her boob. She is so flat-chested I actually don't notice until she yells at me. How embarrassing! But this is exactly why I don't touch girls under their shirts! Why am I doing all this scratching for this itchy girl? To help with the Acutane so she can get a job at ESPN and we can live happily ever after.

She's itchy other places too and needs lots of dry humping. I've never grinded like this with girls before, ever. We call it the law of chastity. It's one of the most important of all the laws of God: no sexual contact of any kind outside of marriage. Catholics believe in it too, but I hear they are a little less strict. Muslims are just as strict as Latter-day Saints. My favorite Bible story is Joseph in Egypt. He forgives and saves his family after they try to kill him. Goes from a homeless servant to second-to-the-king. More impressive than any of that, he turns down the hottest and most powerful chick in Egypt when she comes to him undressing herself. He runs away with his shirt still in her hand. He would not be persuaded to stoop below his values.

We've only been dating a few weeks, and Karen is really getting after it on my rock-solid weightlifter body. This is scary and strange for me, since I still don't know whether I am a man.

I am a late bloomer. All my friends started looking at pornography and jacking off on bus trips by eighth grade. At that time I still had very little pubic hair and no wet dreams. I avoid pornography because when I was eleven I stood over my favorite uncle's grave in the desert of Western Utah and saw very clearly where pornography will get you, because everyone said his pornography addiction had led him down the path to suicide. I don't want to shoot myself in the mouth for failure to appease a pornography addiction, so I stay away from it. I just ran a 5K against pornography in roughly eighteen minutes, and the BYU track team was all over me at the finish line to recruit me. I ran with tears streaming back to my ears because I still miss my uncle. I gave in to peer pressure twice and watched porn with my friends. It felt disgusting and gave me a headache. I also searched on my mom's computer for some sexual thing one of my friends told me about. She and my dad asked me about it. I was just really confused by what my body was supposed to be doing and what I was supposed to know. Or do. Or say. It seemed to me that my body wasn't changing like my friend's bodies were.

Fast-forward to today: I am a twenty-one-year-old returned missionary, and I still have never ejaculated.

One of the covenants adult members of the LDS Church make with God is that we will get married and multiply and replenish the earth. This is a big trial of faith for me. I want to get married and have kids but don't know if I can. I have never told a single soul about this, not even my journal. I journal every night but never write about it. I just stress myself out and believe that one day I'll be a man. But beneath that faith, I really think my penis must be broken and I will never have seed. Don't let me lose you, I'm about to connect the dots. Because now I have my catalyst. This itchy girl is dry humping me like a bunny rabbit and moaning and shuddering and breathing all over me, and I peed. A lot. This has almost happened a few times before, but I always hold it back, but tonight she's really vigorous and I don't really want to hold back. Let's just see what happens. Karen is proud of herself and laughs with me and we clean it up with wet rags. It takes walking back home to realize that I finally just ejaculated! I would have SEED! I thank God in the loudest, most raucous yet sincere prayer. Ironically, that sort of sexual contact, even with clothes on, is forbidden by God. But tonight, God approved it, because this feeling of finally knowing I am a man is a righteous feeling. And since all my other anxieties and insecurities and lonelinesses are stronger than ever, it's a sign that I need to stick with Karen no matter what.

If I were a little more self-aware, I could have used this experience to rebuild my regular relationship with God in the regular civilian world, but I can't. I'm still sad and angry that my mission is over and all my friends peaced out on me.

Now we are back in Karen's bedroom, where I inadvertently touched her boob before gloriously becoming a man on her couch. She hates her bedroom. She hates her roommate. Hates her classes. Hates her church leaders. She hates everything. That's why she needs me: something to love! She hates herself, she hates me too; I just don't know it yet. Her roommate Katie pissed her off, so Karen signed her up for pornographic magazines. This night in her bedroom, Karen tells me about a demon that lives in her closet and cast a spell on her just before we met. I know this game, blame it on the Acutane, the imaginary root of all her evils. But she doesn't blame it on the Acutane. She's serious and starts to cry. She's terrified to be alone with the demon. I don't know the extent of her demons, but I see that she needs me, and I decide to stay no matter what. When she puts her eyes in vulnerable mode like that, I feel so close to her. My empathy for her has no bounds. Whether this is lust, or duty, or destiny, or decision, I will stay and keep her demons away. But I am starting to see that Karen's greatest demon is herself. Hopefully that part of it really is the Acutane like she says. Either way, her needs totally consume me and that is exactly what I need right now. Thanks to her, I won't have to deal with my own anger and sadness. She is my next mission. I am so sad and so lonely, just like her. But my feelings are temporary and will pass with time. Hers are permanent. What will we do down the road? Down the road, two of my siblings will serve and return from missions. Down the road, they will be strong enough to come home from their service and feel the anger of what feels like abandonment by God and ride it out.

When God calls you on a mission, He gives you His power. I got a lot of it. I felt it in everything I did. It has mass and energy and light and love. I became a role model and a leader for scores of other missionaries. When you come home, God takes it all away. I felt so abandoned in the church building where my powers were taken away. That experience exposed deep inner fears of loneliness that I don't know how to face. Filling that immense emptiness is my primary focus now because I am so. Damn. Scared.

Before she went to party in Florida while I was still in Oregon serving God, Karen tells me, she went through therapy for several months. But she didn't finish. Whatever that means. She wouldn't talk more about it. What demons does the therapist know about that I don't? I see clearly very early on it has to do with her and her father

Brian. Our encounters with him are so weird, she becomes a different person. Everybody has issues with their parents. I still haven't really "seen" mine since returning from my mission. They are here, but I don't know them. They are still raising two teenagers and dealing with my sister Kelly's awesomely dangerous napalm cannon of coming-of-age decisions. Damn, I miss Kelly. She's gone too. She dates girls now and thinks I hate her, but I don't. I just miss her. I need therapy too! But I'm the strong one here, so I will never admit it.

Let me explain more about this mission thing and the cold turkey transition of coming home. In Oregon, I spent every waking moment teaching people about the gospel of Jesus Christ for twenty-four straight months. In Bend, everyone walks outside because they are crazy healthy there. Even the bums have Salomon shoes and Columbia coats. Once a week we had a designated hour for "street contacting." One day in one hour, I made over two hundred meaningful contacts with strangers at a river park in Bend. Lots of them are runners, so I run them down, tell them how great the gospel is, hand them a "Pass-Along Card" with lds.org on it, and ask for an appointment to come teach them in their home. Sometimes it worked, usually it didn't. We reconvened with the other missionaries when the hour was up to give our numbers, and I was like Charlie and the Chocolate Factory, only backward.

"How many contacts, Elder Walkenhorst?"

"Two."

"Elder Jarvis?"

"Thirty-two." (He would be smiling pretty big after such a wide margin improvement over the last guy).

"Elder Livingston?"

"Two hundred and three."

"What's that? Two or three?"

"Um, no. Two *hundred* and three."

You get the point.

They called me The Machine. In my one-on-one interviews, my leaders would lovingly encourage me to slow down. I just wanted to do my best. I have that relentless drive to do my best regardless. I am an Eagle Scout. "Do a good turn daily." "Always do your best." I was hospitalized twice on my mission and given an IV because I blacked out and couldn't stand. A midnight IV later, I was back out there like nothing happened. I share this example because it shows how I learned to view people. It came clear for me a few months into my mission when one of the big shots in the Church came to Eugene to speak to us at a mission conference. He encouraged us to see people with new eyes. Don't see them for how they look or what they do, see them how God sees them. See them dressed in white ready to enter heaven. Straight from C. S. Lewis. And the only way they will get in is if we baptize them! So off I went! Just like the little bird in *Are You My Mother?* Except I could baptize all of them, even the Snort! They are all my mothers. Even Jesus said that when his mom missed him. "Who is my mother and my brethren?" he asked. "Them that do the will of my Father in Heaven." Call it brainwashing if you want, but this was what I believed.

That's why members of the LDS Church work really hard to get the word out. We believe we are all brothers and sisters in God's family, and we all have to follow the steps Jesus prescribed to get into Heaven. One scripture passage missionaries often read in the Book of Mormon describes some wayward youth who come back around to share the gospel with estranged relatives who want to kill them. The scripture says, "The very thought that any soul should endure endless torment did cause their very souls to quake and tremble." If what they believed was true, they had to share it with the world.

Around the same time, I am getting all quaky and trembly and trying to do what's right just like these Book of Mormon missionaries.

I read a Goethe quote in Bishop Gardemann's church office in Bend: "See others less in the light of what they do or fail to do, and more in the light of what they suffer." He tried to set me up on a future date with his daughter for after my mission. That happened a lot. I declined the date, but did see people for what they suffered. Empathy, compassion, forgiveness.

Now that Karen and I are together, I see her as God sees her, for what she suffers. She suffers a lot. Everything is hard for her. But how do I know how God sees people? I should be trying to date people who are nice and who I can actually have fun with. But I am too busy doing what I was told, and trying to do my best, and trying to not try to get married, but it's not working. I play along while Karen sets her hooks into some sort of hero complex I have not yet outgrown. It feels good to be her "hero." My dad watches from a distance while Matt Livingston the Liar goes with Karen further and further down a road I do not like. He reminds my mom, "Honey, don't worry about Matt, he's a Boy Scout. He's just trying to do the right thing." Dad's right. He knows the right thing is never to try to make someone else happy. It never works. He will try to reassure my mom for years, but eventually he will give up. By 2014, the reassurance stops, and Dad doesn't know if I will make it. "I think he's dying," he starts to tell my mom. My marriage to Karen will be harder for them than for me.

How my dad knows me so well, I don't know. After all the terrible things I will say to him, all the holidays we will ruin, all the missed family events, I wouldn't be that merciful to me if I were him. He saw what I suffered. Maybe there are some people out there who really do see us the way God sees us. His words and comfort will help my mom through my Liar years.

When Karen explains everything about her demons, which she does constantly, I see what she suffers and how great she could be without her acne medicine. When we meet, she is smart and funny and athletic and loves sports. She has uncanny command of a room. But she just hates everything! She has an explanation for that too. I start to pry, and she has a perfect explanation for everything.

Why don't you go to your church meetings? *My bishop called me the wrong name.*

Why do you seem so depressed? *It's the acne medicine I'm on, Accutane. Stop asking me that! You must not love me!*

Why did you stop going to therapy? *I'll go back one day.*

Why did you start going to therapy? *Instant subject change.*

More important were the questions I didn't ask. Why did you delete your Facebook, why do you hate all my friends, why are you always breaking things, why do you get so pissed at me every time I don't want you to grind all over me and make out?

Before I get to these other questions, her parents turn the tables on me and start asking me difficult questions, making me second-guess who I am. During high school I wrote a news column for the Southern Utah News in Kanab, Utah. We moved to Kanab from Canada just after my eleventh birthday. Some of the news columns I wrote received national attention, and many people made me their poster boy. Among them were many LGBTQ websites who needed an advocate on certain human rights issues. Karen's mom had seen some of the websites, and while she didn't read any of my content or care about my positions, she took issue with the websites who quoted me. She called during the ten-minute break between classes and backed me into a corner. How could I support such sinful people? I had written a certain piece that blasted the Kanab city government for outlawing gay people. Any half-decent journalist would have done the same thing. Julie doesn't actually care about the websites. She's on assignment from Karen's dad, Brian. She's eternally on assignment for Brian. He is the ultimate taskmaster. He knows if he can keep me off balance, he can make me feel lucky to get to join his family.

Karen and her folks are playing me like I used to play people as a high school journalist. I love her, I will propose to her, and I will marry her.

I just have this feeling that I know we will have babies together. I tell my friend Braydon, who also went on his mission to Oregon. "Bro, I can't describe it, I just know we are going to have babies together." I play it off like a spiritual clairvoyant hunch, but I'm just horny, same as every other return missionary. I am blinded by lust and looking for ways to make it work. I see no red flags. But my sister Kelly sees Karen's Facebook page before she deletes it. The drinking and partying from last summer are there in plain sight. I don't even have Facebook. I don't do background checks on people yet. Everything has been explained to my satisfaction. My sister loves me enough not to burst my bubble about my girlfriend. She never tells me what she sees on Facebook.

Felt Hall is the building where I live and work as a Resident Assistant. A few months before my mission ended, Mom called and said that one of my BYU scholarships went bankrupt. I still have my full tuition scholarship and maybe a few other small ones, but I need a job to make up the difference. I don't have a credit card and am not going into debt for my Bachelor's. So, while I wrapped up my mission in Oregon, I applied for and got this RA job at Felt Hall. My writing in high school for the Southern Utah News opened some doors, so I also set up an internship at NPR radio in Salt Lake City for a thousand dollar stipend. I don't have a car, so I get on the bus at five a.m. twice a week and ride from Provo to Salt Lake. While working and living at home, it was easy to save money. I saved ten thousand dollars just during high school to pay for my mission. It feels almost impossible to save money while paying for school.

Writing is my true love. I started writing stories and keeping a journal when I was seven years old. Karen thinks it's stupid and I need to get over it. I called the column I wrote in high school for the *Southern Utah News* "Cowboy Currents." We were the Kanab Cowboys, and I wrote streams of current events. I like double meanings like that. The one that defended unconventional families got me famous for a while. Frommer's wrote about it, a professor from the University of Utah used me in his curriculum, and the *Salt Lake Tribune* put me on the front page twice. BYU gave me a scholarship. The Utah Press Association created an award for me. The only other journalist they *ever* did that for was my editor, Dixie Brunner. I love Dixie. Writing with her was so much fun. She gave me way more leeway than she probably should have! NPR came to my high school auditorium and held a debate between me and the mayor. The NPR guy who mediated the debate gave me this thousand dollar internship in Salt Lake City.

I hate it! The internship, that is. The one bright spot is the guy who announces the breaks and the weather. He's scraggly and looks homeless, but like all radio voices, speaks as smoothly as maple syrup. He looks just like the guy from *A Goofy Movie* who eats the leaning tower of "Cheesa" squirted out of a can onto his cartoon white-gloved hand. I want to squirt cheese into this guy's long scraggly beard every time I see him. There's a female intern from a different department my boss Elaine introduced me to at an evening event last week. I said something kind of rude, and Elaine told me I made her cry. I was just stressed out from Karen texting me and demanding instant responses all day. Elaine eats a carrot every day at ten a.m. like it's life or death. Yesterday she missed her carrot and yelled at me for not reminding her to eat it even though she never asked me to remind her, since I damn well know she eats it every day at ten and she knows I know, and therefore it's my fault. Elaine has red hair and I almost called her carrots in retaliation but hold back! My brain is fully occupied by Karen all day at the internship. The further I am from her, the more needy she gets with me. She wants me with her every waking minute, so when I'm in Salt Lake its texting, texting, texting. We are getting serious, and I can see where it's going, but I already decided not to get married till I am at least twenty-five. But here I am all day every day responding to needy texts from Karen. I am still chickening out of this struggle to reclaim some sense of identity after my mission, and Karen provides a welcome distraction from all the growth I need. Growth sucks! It's so much easier to spend every waking moment giving 100% of my love and attention to Karen, even though I can tell it will never be enough and she will always want more. I love it because I don't have to worry about fixing myself anymore. Boom, problem solved: distracted for life, needed for eternity.

Karen hates it when I play basketball in the evenings. Most of the LDS church buildings have basketball courts, and it's fairly easy to find someone with keys wherever you are in the world. I play and workout most early mornings too, which is fine because she is asleep. But evening is her time. She bribes me not to go and throws tantrums and gets really upset. Tonight I am playing with my best friend Tanner when she calls. Tanner is my best friend, yes, but he's also my idol. I never told him, but I couldn't pick a better one. When I first moved to Kanab in sixth grade, I was a huge Atlanta Braves fan. Tanner and I were on the same bus after the first day of school. I thought his name was "Turner." He was tall, popular, athletic, and tan, and he invited me to come play at his house that first bus ride home. I watched the Braves on TBS, "Turner Broadcast Station," and the move to Utah was hard, so I saw meeting this new friend Turner as God's tender mercy, telling me he was watching out for me just like I watched the Braves. What are the odds I meet a friend with the same name as the Braves' TV station? I still believe it was a message from God, even though his name is Tanner, not Turner. We watched our first R-rated movie together, went to basketball camp together, his family gave me my first job, he gave me my first concussion. Completely by accident. When we were high-school freshmen, I threw him an alley-oop in the first quarter of the game and got benched for the whole tournament. Didn't even care. I believed if I threw it up, Tanner would dunk it. No matter how high. That's how I saw him. Infinitely athletic and anything was possible. He's the first non-family member I will call after deciding to get a divorce. We won our football state rings together senior year. Karen will throw away my state ring during our divorce. Just like she's about to get me to throw away my friendship with Tanner. I need her distractions so bad I'll do anything to keep her around.

So I'm playing basketball at the church when Karen calls, and Tanner picks up my phone because I'm playing and he's sitting this one out.

"Hellllooo, this is Matt's phone."

"Put him on the phone, now."

"I would love to but can't do that right now, he's playing, can I have him call you back when the game is over?"

"No, did I stutter, put him on now, idiot!!!"

"Hey, easy there, woman, he is playing and I'll pass on the messag—"

"All you Kanab people are so stupid! Get him now or—"

Tanner hangs up. Karen never forgives and never forgets. So that's the end of it. Tanner and Matt are no more. I won't talk to Tanner for seven years. He will still sneak into our wedding reception, and I'll bribe Karen to go to his, but we don't get to be friends. I won't get to hug my best friend on my wedding day. That's how dead I am. Dead enough to agree to make Tanner, my hero, dead to me without hesitation.

We've been dating just over a month, and it's Karen's twenty-first birthday. For just over a month, I've consumed myself with making a miserable woman happy, and it's the greatest challenge I've ever faced, but I know I can do it and no other guy ever could. She tells me all the time how poorly she was treated by all the boys before me. Those days are long gone. I use the only forty-three dollars to my name to send roses and chocolate to her work office with the love note, "Get used to it." Huge mistake! For our first date I take her to the nicest restaurant in Orem, the Chef's Table. Another mistake! I eat only canned chicken after because it's all I can afford. At Chef's Table, Karen complains most of the meal that her butternut squash soup is too hot. We've eaten out a handful of times, and almost every time she's burned her mouth on food because she eats huge bites right away without checking the food's temperature. The day after we met, she burned her mouth on the French onion soup at Mimi's Café in Orem. Three years later, we will return to the Chef's Table, and I will use my work Amex to pay for what the Groupon won't cover. Bank account will still be just as empty as it is now. Karen will demand date nights and expensive dinners and new cars and vacations we can't afford the entire time I am with her. And I will say yes, and I will find ways to make it work, and she will still be miserable and complain about the soup and everything else.

I am a server at Chick-fil-A: "My pleasure."

Every Sunday night, I hold a devotional for my freshman boys at Felt Hall. I love these boys. Dallas Yorgason and Devin Larsen from Boise are my favorites. Karen is here with me at devotional tonight. On her cue, we recite this little saying of hers together for the dudes. Since I write poetry and other stupid things, she knows that putting our relationship in a poem helps me convince myself it's a good relationship. I write her poems all the time. I don't think she even reads them. But she loves the fact that they are hers and that I spend time writing them. Here is her poem which we mew out together on cue:

"Love is patient, love is kind, love is slowly losing your mind."

I feel like such an idiot. I don't know how these boys hold their vomit in their mouths. Bless them. None of them even laugh. Although I feel like a fraud and an impostor, I find solace in that little poem Karen recites all the time. It's like, I believe love is patient, I believe love is kind, so therefore it must logically follow that love is slowly losing your mind. It's right there in the poem. I took Philosophy 201 before my mission and learned about enthymemes. If

A equals B, and B equals C, then A equals C. Therefore, if you are in love, you lose your mind. Great, then I am right on track!

Let me explain more about how I am losing my mind. Karen isn't the worst part. She just suffers a lot, and I see she needs me, so I put up with her crap. The real problem is the man who shows up to the BYU-TCU football game in scrubs and takes Karen and her new boyfriend to pizza afterward. Enter Karen's dad, Brian Adams. My shoulders tense up a little and my heart rate still accelerates when I write that name. On the walk to the game, I buy her a white-and-blue necklace of kalua nuts, and she loves it. During the first half of the game, Karen and I hold hands for the first time. I haven't said "I love you" yet, but I will soon. We start holding hands walking around campus now, and I do tell her I love her, and now she loosens up. She is mad and angry about everything: peers, her teachers, her job, her weight, school, her parents. I'll do anything to lighten the mood. She loves violent movies and TV shows, so I play into that. We make a gun shape with our held hands, pointer fingers out, and pretend to shoot people. I also dumpster-dive the Provo Bakery down the street from her apartment to retrieve day-old bread. In the beginning the bread is for feeding the ducks on the south side of campus. Nasty inbred ducks whose colony never leaves the pond, so they all have two heads and four feet and crooked feathers and none of them can fly. But soon we start throwing the bread at people driving in cars, and this amuses her much more, so the ducks go hungry and the drivers and their passengers get bread in the face.

At halftime during the game, we are still holding hands for the first time. Karen and I walk over to see her parents. They are in "Grandma and Grandpa's seats" at the forty-yard line, where I will be several times in the future. These seats are spoken of in the Adams' home as if they are seats at the right hand of God in the kingdom of Heaven. Brian is wearing doctor scrubs. Only he's not a doctor. Well, he is, but not that kind of doctor. The point is, he wants me to ask if he is a doctor. Why, yes he is: a psychologist. Cool. I am taking a psychology class. At BYU, the class called Psychology Statistics, Psyc 201, double counts as a social science credit and a statistics credit. I find and take all the double-dippers because I am efficient like that.

Brian compliments me on everything: my mission, my athleticism, my grades. I don't know it yet, but he has already decided I am to marry Karen, based on conversations they have been having. He's been coaching Karen how to lead me along. He buys us candied cinnamon almonds, gives us hugs, and invites us to pizza at The Brick Oven afterward. His wife Julie, Karen's mom, is there too, but she says very little, mainly smiles.

The Brick Oven is the king of pizza at BYU. It's right down the road from the duck pond where we misappropriate the defunct duck's dough. His offer to take us there is an act of endless love. I am so poor and eat out so little, though that's changing because Karen wants to eat out every meal. But I can't afford it. The only eating out I am doing on a regular basis begins in a trash can. I grab Wendy's receipts out of the trash can and write a fake survey code on the back to get free never-frozen Wendy's Singles after working out for free in the Fieldhouse student gym. Dinner at the Brick Oven was a godsend to a poor college couple like us.

Over dinner, Brian showers praise on me like I am riding into Jerusalem on a colt. This is weird because he doesn't even know me, but he's a psychologist, so he must absorb my life's work within a few minutes of us meeting. He tells me how amazing I am for taking so many credit hours, that I don't have student loans, that I am working full-time, that I still work out so much. My flailing sense of self make me fertile soil for his seeds of flattery, just like my loneliness makes me ripe for Karen's plucking. Brian tells Karen that night I am the one for her and she must marry me. This is her chance. Julie continues her quiet attitude at dinner. Brian sneaks in several snide remarks to deprecate his wife in just the right way to include her but make sure she remembers her place as his subordinate, and she blushes and laughs just like she is supposed to. She does that every time he hates one of the meals she cooks, every time he reminds her that her parents and siblings suck, and any time she tries to wear makeup or perfume. He keeps her on a tight leash. He does it to Karen too. But he will never do it to me. I am his chosen one. The one he chose to offload his greatest burden onto. His oldest daughter, his wild child, Karen.

Brian visits me several times in the coming weeks. Watering all the seeds he planted. We play basketball, work out, hell, he even sleeps in my dorm room on the floor. We are bros. He is left-handed, overweight, and a little cross-eyed, so it's strange that he wants to join in on my exercise routine. Leading up to Thanksgiving, I prepare to ask him if I can marry Karen under his tutelage. She refers to it as the all-important "Talk." The Talk becomes all I think about. Will Brian find me worthy to marry Karen? I have no money, the job market sucks in the wake of the housing market crash, and my family is not well-established in his eyes. I know that's a problem. While she coaches me for The Talk, Karen tells me how poorly she was treated by the many boyfriends she had last year: Joe Semanoff, Alex Wolfe, Jayden Wagner, Jonathan Tavernari, a few others. Athletes. Jocks. Jerks. I am her Superman here to treat her right after they all treated her wrong. I see Alex at the iconic Orem 24 Hour Fitness near the BYU campus. I dunk on his fat ass there on the same court where Tanner and I played pick-up ball all night after a BYU football game we watched with Tanner's dad when we were in eighth grade. It's the first time I've ever dunked during a game. I am Karen's high-flying hero here to soar over her old boyfriends and save her from herself. That line comes from her favorite song she listens to in her Toyota Corolla every day, Evanescence "Bring Me to Life." In the song, the singer laments losing her soul and asks to be saved from the nothing she has become.

All the emotions are coursing and mixing and jacking me up about our relationship. I'm doing it, I'm making Karen happy. At least a little bit, I can see it, when I stay with her so she can ignore me and watch TV and I write her nice poems she doesn't read and make her food she won't eat. Everything works cool. Her dad gives me one hundred dollars in one dollar bills he saved just for me. I use it to get a boot off my car outside my friend Justin's house, make that booter count every dollar, in the dark, on the sidewalk. Life is awesome. I am Karen's final destination boyfriend.

When baseball season starts, Karen and I will go to one BYU baseball game. Her old boyfriend the big jerk jock Alex Wolfe hits three home runs. In the same game. He will win an award for his performance that day at the annual BYU Cougars award banquet. I am so impressed I'm almost speechless but act like it's no big deal. But that was amazing! Three home runs! In the same game! Nobody does that! I console myself, thinking with a smirk, *Dunked on his fat ass.*

Thanksgiving rolls around, and we roll in that little Corolla down to Twin Peaks where the Adams live so Brian and I can have the long-awaited Talk. This is where I get knighted as Karen's forever boyfriend. I have swatted my friends out of my life like flies, still haven't rebuilt much of a relationship with most family members after my mission, and am ready for my new family to bring me on board full-time. Karen has explained most of my friends and family are "unhealthy" people, so I can't have relationships with them or I will be "unhealthy" too. My mom, Tanner, my sister Kelly, all unhealthy people I need to leave behind. Brian and I go into his office and close the door around seven p.m. and won't come out till ten. If I am already Matt Livingston the Liar, then I am about to become a traitor too.

I figure Brian will tell me mostly about *Karen.* Nope. He starts with an analysis all about *me.* Brian has been asking around and doing his homework and now has me and my family all figured out.

The Adams live in Twin Peaks, which is only an hour away from my small hometown of Kanab. Brian explains how since my dad works far from home and I have four younger siblings, they all look up to me as their dad. I was the one who took them places and helped them with problems, right? Right. Brian explains that my mom is too emotionally dependent on me and that's not my place. Coming home from my mission has been hard and confusing, right? Right. This is why. I have unhealthy relationships with my parents. Brian knows people who know my parents and *e*veryone (he holds the first "e" extra-long and raises his bushy unibrow for effect) knows my parents' marriage is in trouble and they are messed up in the head. In the most cunning and sensible way, Brian leads me to decide that my family is unhealthy and they need to be out of my life for good. Out of *our* new life. Brian is my replacement dad and his family is my replacement family. If this is what it takes to be Karen's Superman, which I know is my destiny, I accept. I will cry a lot but never look back. "For this purpose shall a man leave his father and mother and cleave unto his wife." Easy. I know the Word. Time to be a man. "No man, having put his hand to the plough, and looking back, is fit for the kingdom of God."

Next we talk about money. He has a ton of money in a safe in the basement. It's bolted to the floor so a bunch of Polynesians can't come in and take it. He shows me a gun and tells me he has lots of guns in case someone who's not as strong as a Polynesian comes for the money even though it's bolted to the floor. If it's a Polynesian, forget the guns, that will just make them madder. Trust the bolts if they are Tongan, otherwise ya shoot 'em. I will be one of the few people who knows the combination to the safe and where all the guns are hidden.

I sit silently and listen to his intricate detail and contingency plans. I am a little lost but also nervous and keep myself engaged and listening. I imagine a Maori in his lava-lava picking up Brian's thousand pound safe like it's a waste basket and carrying it outside to his friends. He wants me to shoot this guy?

More money talk. Brian loves to talk about money. He is giving me twenty-five hundred dollars to pay for Karen's engagement ring, and later he will help me pay for our honeymoon because we are going to the Florida Keys just like some good family friends of theirs. It's the perfect getaway. We need to stay on Key Marathon just like their friends did, and I love to snorkel and SCUBA so I will love it, and Karen just returned from Florida so of course she needs to go back and she will love it! Brian must really love me because look at all this planning he has done for us, wow. I have no idea how much of Karen's prior-summer Florida shenanigans Brian knows about. Does he know she didn't finish the internship? Does he know she can't hardly talk about Florida without crying? As easy as it would be to take Brian' money, I can't. I respectfully decline because there's always a catch. I will be in debt to no man. I don't say that, but he reads my mind.

Brian won't take no for an answer.

Now Brian talks about God, his second-favorite topic. He explains that God works in only one way: you give God all you have, He gives you all He has. He recites a bunch of scriptures that teach this but he knows I already know them very well. I have several chapters of Isaiah committed to memory. I love the scriptures. I timed how long it took to recite the Isaiah chapters in my head so I could hold the plank position while keeping time without a watch. That's how I knock out both my daily scripture study and my workout before six a.m. I'm trying to revitalize my relationship with God by connecting it to my fitness routine. My fitness routine, *there's* one thing I know I can depend on forever. Even Brian won't ask me to stop working out.

In conclusion: as long as I do my best for Brian and his oldest daughter Karen, he will do his best for me. This is the order of the kingdom of God. Surely I don't want to defy God! I take my forty pieces of silver from Brian as he hands me a check to pay for his daughter's ring.

We emerge from the office and Karen is bawling her eyes out. She thinks it went terrible and that I am leaving for good. She thinks she has been found out. Her guilty conscience has nowhere to hide during The Talk when she's without me longer than any other waking moment in November. She hugs me to say goodbye.

Her mindset this whole time has been to make Dad happy, to use me to cover up what she did last summer, to get married to a returned missionary in the LDS temple just like they have told her to do her entire life. For weeks she has been telling people "she met her list." I am her list. The list of things she has been taught to look for in a mate. So it's not her list, it's her dad's list. I get it. I'm in a similar boat. I acknowledge the reason I went to BYU was to make my folks happy. All oldest children like Karen and I have some mommy and daddy issues. Regardless, it feels good to hear that Karen, who has dated all the best guys, has finally met the greatest of them all and that I am her list! I am the perfect man. Strong, honest, handsome, smart, funny, hardworking, loving, kind, righteous, blah blah blah. Eagle Scout. State champion. Sterling Scholar. National Merit Scholar. All-State. I would have been paraded onto the field at halftime of our state championship football game as an Academic All-American too, but my football Coach Bucky Orton forgot to fill out his part of the paperwork. I didn't care at all because we won the game where I got the ring Karen will throw away one day. But now, whenever Karen calls me her "list," inwardly I think, All those things are not me! And lists aren't real, anyway! Relationships are hard! I have a self! I am not a piece of meat! But I never say any of that out loud. All the things I think I am are from a past life anyway. Now I need Karen to think I'm her list so Brian can lead me into the future.

She asks me to tell her five things I love about her all the time.

So I do.

My teenage brother comes up one weekend to visit me in Felt Hall. We go to the football field and I lift him up so he can do a pull-up on one of the uprights in the endzone at LaVell Edwards Stadium. I am so happy to see his pride at being lifted up on that upright. This is the last time I am a big brother to a teenager. After The Talk, I know my time with Kyle is winding down. By the time I come back home to my family and myself several years later, Kyle and my youngest sister Lindsay will have moved out of the house. After The Talk with Brian, I am ready to step out on all my "unhealthy" family relationships.

That same Thanksgiving weekend, Karen and I take both our parents to Chili's in Twin Peaks to meet each other for the first time. Karen is on my left, her parents on my right, and my parents across from me. Far away, like they should be. Karen has us in matching sweaters. Her dad hates them. He chews her out right in front of me afterward, right outside the restaurant. Then he adds insult to injury, tells her to never ask me to carry her purse again. Rattles off this whole list of her offenses for the evening. I'm thinking, what the hell, dude? Stop yelling at her on the sidewalk by the take-out parking. Must be one of those God things. If thy matching sweater offend thee, cut it off. I say nothing.

The parent dinner meeting is strange. I got hurt a lot before the age of eight, so my dad decides now is a good time to tell my future in-laws that I am a total kamikaze, have been since I was two. At age two I jumped into a bonfire and went to the hospital with third degree burns all over both forearms while my mom went to the maternity wing and gave birth to my sister Morgan. At five I almost lost my eye in a car accident. At six I fell through an icy river surface only to be rescued by my dog. At eight I tried to flying-squirrel from a tree branch to a rope and spent the next twenty-four hours in a coma. I'm not mad about what Dad's saying, I think it's hilarious, but I'm nervous because I know Karen will yell at me about it later. She has been yelling at me every night since we met. Her yelling at me is our nighttime routine. She yells, storms off to the freezer for ice cream, then comes back to the couch as if nothing happened and asks me to get her seconds from the freezer. I brought her car to her three minutes too late and the wind messed up her hair while she was waiting. When we walked between classes I said something too loud. I let her leave lunch with a piece of something in her teeth. I must not care about her at all. I need to tell her five sweet things about her right now to prove that I still do.

So when my dad says I am a kamikaze, I tense up, anticipating the yelling that will come later that night, knowing it will be loud and annoying. Her parents tell my parents how well connected they are and how they know everyone. I snicker inside. Hey, we are staying at Karen's parents tonight, she won't be able to yell very much or very loudly. I thank them silently and chill out a little and listen to how they know the car guy, the sports guy, the church guy, the lawn guy. For years to come my parents will laugh about that meeting. My mom will joke to my dad, "Oh yeah? Well, I know so-and-so." My dad will reply curiously, "Oh really?" And then she will say, "Yes and so-and-so and so-and-so." Dr. Adams loves when Karen and I take our picture with Jimmer Fredette, the BYU-basketball-star-turned-NBA-player. He loves saying he knows public figures. A year or two later, we bring some of Karen's BYU rugby player friends over, and for Brian that's like having POTUS in the house. He will smile his biggest scrunchy-face, slitty-eyed Adams' smile the whole time.

Brian and Julie also make sure my parents know Brian has a PhD. That's actually the first thing he says. "Hi, I'm Dr. Adams." Same as when he met me. All people must know Brian Adams is a doctor. When Karen and I marry a few months later, the first draft of the wedding announcement will say: "Mr. and Mrs. Brian Adams."

Brian takes it out on Julie, how dastardly a deed has been done to omit the "Dr." from his name and replace it with the diminutive "Mr." such as the one preceding my dad's name. This comes after we hold a long discussion over Christmas break about what goes on the wedding announcement. During said wedding announcement discussion, Brian says that he thinks my dad is a really smart guy, and that he might be in school his whole life, he is so smart. Brian has this huge distinction between brains and decision-making skills. He says there are plenty of smart people, but the people who get ahead don't have to be smart, they just need to have good judgment. Being smart is worthless without having good judgment. When he calls my dad "smart" he is really calling my dad an idiot, and we both know it. I nod gravely. The month between Thanksgiving and Christmas, I am mentally preparing to limit all contact with my family. It's sad, but I am so occupied taking care of Karen, it's not like I have time for my family anymore. The things Brian told me in The Talk are constantly swirling around in my brain. Is my mom really in love with me? Is my dad really a loser? Do all my younger siblings expect too much of me? I don't hardly talk to them; they all grew up into other people while I was away on my mission.

These facts and questions bother me. I haven't given any of my parent or sibling relationships enough time in the six months I've been back from my two years away. But Brian is the expert, the clinical psychologist, the PhD. People are his thing, so who am I to argue? It's time to move on with Karen now. Gee, thanks, Brian!

The week of our wedding, my dad sends me a telegraph to meet him in Hurricane for a few minutes. Hurricane is a neutral ground halfway between Kanab and Twin Peaks. I say telegraph because it wasn't a text message, and wasn't a phone call, my phone is under constant supervision from Karen. I don't remember how he got me the message, but it must have been a telegraph. Before we go to Twin

Peaks for our wedding week, Karen forbids me from going to Kanab or seeing my family at all. She begs and cries and yells at me when I don't think it's fair, but I keep the peace and solemnly swear not to go to Kanab and then tell her five sweet things. But I don't specifically say I won't talk to any of my family members. The thing is, even though I've been enlightened and know they are all unhealthy and hold me back, I love them. I miss them. I don't understand anything about adulthood or how this works, but I am sad and lonely and not nearly as mad at God anymore. I'm feeling a lot better and starting to wonder what I'm doing. I'm more stressed out than ever taking care of Karen, way worse than any of my family members ever made me. I bury these feelings under the promises I have made to Brian, whose cell phone plan I am now on and to whom I have sworn I will make Karen the apple of my eye. He's the king of hookups. He also gives me guns. Lots of guns. He gives me BYU swag from 2003 that still has the tags on it. He even gives me some of his old LDS underwear we call garments. No joke. The underwear has no tags. The tags are long gone. These garments are used, and he gives them to me. What a gift. Don't worry, I don't wear them! I have never been a notch past waist size thirty and these are size thirty-six. Which is also confusing. Why is he giving me his old used garments that will never fit me in a million years? He hands me a stack of these girthy garments in front of both our wives, so I stay straight-faced and gracious and hold my hands out like I am receiving a sword from a king. He places his used underwear in my outstretched hands.

I defy my containment order and commandeer a vehicle and drive to Hurricane. Getting away from Karen feels like getting fresh air, and I must admit I look forward to seeing a friendly face. Dad.

On the way to see my dad, I want to cruise through Hurricane and drive all the way to Kanab one last time to be with my family before I marry Karen and leave them all for good. But it won't make it any easier, I have already left for good. I already chose Karen. And she forbade me to contact them. But I still meet Dad in the parking lot across from Taco Bell on Main Street in Hurricane, where's he's sitting behind the wheel of his Kia. I climb into the passenger seat. No hugs, no pleasantries, now is time for me to be strong and prove my resolve to myself. Dad talks about the danger of getting into a relationship with someone who is controlling and abusive. I hear him out and quickly say goodbye. He's no people expert. No PhD. I get out of his car and drive back to Twin Peaks.

Dad sees that I need saving. I am in trouble and I do need my dad. Dad knows something is wrong. All of it was wrong. But I have a new dad now. When I took Karen to that SYTYCD concert, the best couple danced to Leona Lewis, "Bleeding Love." They danced an impressive and emotionally charged dance. That was one of the songs Karen and I played and sang in the car or wherever. My dad sees it as one more garbage influence in my decision to love where there is pain, tradeoffs, agony, sorrow, all those other things he feels in my presence that were not there before and do not belong. He knows I am under a spell, just like dancers fall under the spell of the music they dance to. Only with them, it's just a dance, for me this is my life. I'm not on a stage or in front of a crowd, this is my reality behind closed doors when nobody is there to talk or see or hear. When we meet in Hurricane, he reaches out to save me from all that bleeding love garbage he can see, and I say no. He watches me start to bleed out and die right there. He purses his lips and looks down at his steering wheel as I walk out on him and his little Kia for the Doctor with the big Camry. Maybe I am already dead.

For years after meeting me in Hurricane, my dad and my mom go to therapy as they watch me die. They need someone objective with whom to talk about me. My parents don't know what to do, so they start dying too. I will finally see it clearly after calling and telling them I am getting a divorce six years later and hearing them immediately burst into tears of rejoicing. As things get especially hard between now and then, my dad tells my mom, "Matt's dying." Mom asks, "What should we do?" And then they cry.

My dad asks his therapists that question over and over for years. "What should we do?" I put them in an impossible situation. How do you love someone you aren't allowed to love? There is nothing they can do.

When I first talk to my dad after Karen and I separate, I tell him I am sorry. I am so, so sorry. I am the most sorry for walking out on my dad that day in Hurricane than anything else I did. And I did some really shitty things to a lot of really great people. But that was the worst. Dad and I raised cows together in Canada when I was young. We skipped rocks together on the Kootenay River in British Columbia the first time I heard him use a swear word. He said "bitch." I loved it even though he was literally using it to describe a female dog. That time he took the day off to skip stones with me and tell me about bitches, I was struggling with a bad friend.

I was in homeschool and didn't have a lot of friends. My mom had me write a book report about every country in the world that year. My favorite was Morocco. I'll take Mom there one day. This was third grade, age eight. One of the only two friends I had kept telling me weird sex stories. Once he told me about a guy who would visit a girl at night and rape her with a buttered carrot. Me and this friend hid in the woods behind his house and smoked something. The only something I ever smoked. Another time he was driving with my family and me in our van and was telling me a story about a cocker spaniel, but the kid changed the name to "cock and spank it." Mom didn't send me to his house after she heard him say that. I had no idea what it meant.

That day while we skipped stones and I heard my dad swear, I thought, I don't need that weird friend telling me naughty stories anymore. I can get my fill of naughty while hanging out with my dad talking about the bitches!

He took me to see my favorite team play hockey when we didn't have enough money to buy decent tires for our van. This was in Alberta, Canada, before we made the move to Utah. We may drive off the road en route but we will see the game! We may have set the record for most off-road ditch ice slides in a family vehicle. I have a C-shaped scar under my right eye from windshield glass from one of the ice slides that turned into a near-fatal crash. My "C" scar is shaped just like the flaming "C" in the Calgary Flames hockey team logo. They are one of two hockey teams in Alberta. Hockey is everything up there. When I will take my kids camping, the heat of the fire reminds me of the flames they shot into the air when the Calgary Flames scored a goal that night. Dad took me on tractor rides when I was just old enough to spot goose nests in the alfalfa fields to make sure we didn't destroy the nests and break the eggs. He gave me a tomato soup bath the first time I was sprayed by a skunk. He came to all my football games in high school and read all my newspaper articles. He taught me how to throw a baseball, but I never learned how to hit very well. He's the greatest man in my world, and now I get to be just like him, and nobody is going to stop me, and he's the one I turn to when I don't know what to do. And then there's my brother Kyle, who is already like my dad, and he never has and never will let anyone come between him and family. My dad reminds me that I am the master of my fate. I am the captain of my soul. Back from the night that covered me, black as the pit from pole to pole. I thank God for my dad!

Dad was there for me when I arrived at BYU as a freshman and all my insecurities surfaced. Everyone at BYU was a valedictorian, just like me. Everyone was on scholarship, just like me. Everyone got a thirty-one on the ACT, just like me. One kid on my floor got a perfect thirty-six! I was average now. I wasn't secure enough in myself to be average. Just a few weeks into my first semester, I wanted to give up and move into my dad's office and write books. One night we were talking and my dad quoted me Julius Caesar:

> "There is a tide in the affairs of men,
> Which, taken at the flood leads on to fortune.
> Omitted, all the journey of his life,
> Is bound in shallows and in miseries.
> 'Tis in this vast sea we are now afloat.
> And we must take the current when it serves
> Or lose our ventures."

I may not have it perfect, but that's the way I remember it, and I'm not going to look it up to make sure I have it right. With this quote, my dad stirred my Scottish soul, and the Livingstons that fought with William Wallace welled up in me, the same way they welled up in me as a newspaper delivery boy long ago.

Dad took me to the thrift store to get the suit I wore to the interview for my first job delivering those newspapers. The interview was short. The newspaper man looked at eight-year-old me, looked at my dad, slammed a bound stack of papers on the desk, handed my dad a printed paper route and said, "What are you waiting for, get to work!" One time when I delivered to a house, a dog chased me. My dad, who was still in the car, shouted, "Run, Matt, drop that paper and *run!* Big dog might bite!" I dropped the paper and ran back to the car. I could hear the beast chasing me, but I did not turn and look, I kept my eyes on my dad and leapt into the safety of the car. What must have been as big and wild as a timber wolf slammed into my car door just after I closed it. Dad sped off. My dad retold that story with pride to as many people as would hear it. When I hear my dad, I am strong. That day in Hurricane I do not hear my dad, and I am weak.

After the Superbowl in 2019, when Tom Brady tells the small boy quasi-reporter that his hero is his dad, I cry for hours. Every kid's hero is his dad. I sold mine for a honeymoon in the Keys and some old underwear. But when I come back around, Dad brings me right back into his number one spot. We will hike the Grand Canyon together a month after my divorce. He and I and my mom and my sister Kelly. My sister Kelly is the only part of my true life that will stay with me through my entire liar life. Brian will never ask me to get rid of her, and she will never leave. In these days leading up to the wedding, she's the only member of my family who comes around, and the only one the Adams treat with any decency. Our reception will be at the Adams' house, of course.

Doctor Adams' house.

The wedding is at the temple, and after the wedding we all have lunch. After lunch Karen and I follow Doctor Adams' plan and head to our resort honeymoon suite for the few hours before the reception. Meanwhile my family goes with her family to the Adams' home. While they are all busy not getting along, I am busy not fitting my genitals into my new bride's, which is weird and frustrating. Brian had several sex talks with me but never mentioned this part. If there's a third topic he likes after money and God, it's sex or guns. My parents never told me anything about sex. One of Brian' sex talks was with Karen's younger brother Markell at Goodwood Barbecue in Orem. He was like, "If you want to have sex, you ask, and if she says no, then she has to come ask you later that day. And if she asks you for sex and you say no, you have to go ask her for sex when you're ready later that day. You never go to sleep with an open sex invitation. And your first time," he smiles really big and squinty and unibrowy at this part, "you get to be two kids playing in a sandbox just like when you're young." We have this same talk several times. With Karen there, with her teenage siblings there, with church people there, with Julie there. Totally casual sex talks. So while the sex is not happening and the sand in the sandbox is more like cement, Grandma starts playing the piano for all the grandkids to sing and dance.

When we get back from our honeymoon a full week later, the Adams are all still talking about my terrible grandma. They have a beautiful piano at the Adams' home, and my grandma quickly found it on the afternoon of the reception. Piano has always been her thing, from primary songs to classic sing-alongs, I have hundreds of memories of skipping around Grandma playing the piano. But on the afternoon of an important wedding reception! At *Doctor* Adams' house! Entertaining the little ones! Impudent woman! How dare she! She was the devil. I am numb during these conversations. They are beyond ridiculous. I can't disagree, because Brian is the Doctor and the people expert and everything, but really? This was a week ago and you all are still upset and can't move past a grandma playing piano for her grandkids? Really? My grandma is evil for *that*? For such an expert, Brian sure causes a lot of drama. Every friend or family get-together includes a recap from Doctor Adams about everything everyone does wrong. Brian's parents and Julie's parents both live in Twin Peaks, so these gatherings are frequent, and the recaps are harsh and exhausting. This person didn't set the table the right way at Grandma's house, this person didn't put the cat in the office the first time they were asked, this person didn't remember to bring this thing they were supposed to buy. Julie takes the brunt of the heat. Brian doesn't criticize me often, but even I get reprimanded. When I say, "Be there in a minute," and I don't come for three or four minutes, I am wrong. A minute is sixty seconds, and if I'm going to be longer than that, I need to specify better.

The caterer at our wedding makes us a delicious box of sumptuous snacks for the first night in Twin Peaks and our drive to the Las Vegas airport the next morning. Crème brulee, fruit and cheese, good stuff. We are only about an hour into the drive to Vegas the next morning when Karen has me stop at McDonalds so she can get a McMuffin. When we first met, Karen was up at five a.m. every day running and working out. Those days become sporadic and then screech to an abrupt halt the moment we get married. Out with the exercise, out with the alarm clock. In with the McDonalds and the Yogurtland and the Taco Bell.

Our honeymoon is in the paradisaical Florida Keys. I have this bad habit of taking advantage of situations and assuming I can get away with it. It's part of the reason I am good at sales, which I will learn in a few weeks after Karen and I move to Southern California for my summer job selling pest control contracts. We get to our little hotel-bungalow and I see the one that's ours, a dinky hotel room in a four-plex right next to a huge standalone villa. I try the door to the villa just for kicks and its open. I direct Karen into the villa instead of the room I know is ours, the room Brian paid for with his credit card after he paid for our flights, and we settle into the good life. I walk back to the office with a request awhile later and they say, "Oh, I am so sorry, that one's not yours!" I am the sneaky one and Karen is the angry one. This makes us the perfect tag team to get what we want. She storms in like it's their fault and lays down some searing insults. We keep the villa. I smile and laugh like, "Yep, knew it would happen." I am learning how to play her craziness as a strength to keep other people off balance too. But she already hates our trip to paradise, and the complaints are mounting.

This is our first vacation together and I have no idea what I am in for. Every vacation with Karen is absolutely miserable for the first forty-eight hours: travel takes a toll on her, being in unfamiliar places messes with her sense of control, she thinks everyone is judging her and looking at her funny. Before we get married, she constantly talks about how she hates being home and wants to go on vacation as often as possible, but now that we are in arguably the most perfect beach in America, all she can talk about how much she hates it because it was the wrong one. She hates the beach, hates the sun, hates the water. Hates her bathing suit, hates the fresh squeezed orange juice, hates trying to have sex. We just got here, and now she wants to leave.

For months Karen has been singing songs to me about birthday sex and sex on the beach. My birthday is only a week away, May eleventh. She adds the tempting epithet "in bed" to the end of all my sentences like some people do with "that's what she said" or "your mom." Now that we are married and on a beach and it's May, the answer is: No! She hides in the villa and watches TV. What??? When she does emerge, Karen wants to drive two hours away from paradise to a crappy Miami shopping center and buy Coach purses. So we do. I love the beach and the ocean so much I shipped my speargun in a gun case from Brian to the hotel. But I sigh goodbye to days of adventure and become the shopping bag cart.

Her misery on our honeymoon sets a pattern. When we return to life at home, immediately we start to plan another big beach trip. Her misery at home isn't so bad when she has social media pictures of a vacation to look forward to so we can go there and be miserable and then come home and be miserable again. This will become the cycle of our lives. Karen wants to be anywhere but here. I will play along because I want to believe one day we will be in the right place at the right time. All we have to do is find a way to get there. We will go to Thailand, Bali, Seattle, Oahu, Kauai, Puerta Vallarta, Cancun, Grand Cayman, Hilton Head, Amelia Island, La Jolla, Disney a bunch of times, etc. We go to all to these beachy paradises and once we arrive, Karen gets upset about something, frowns at me, waddles away and threatens me that she never will return. Or she sits in her beach chair and snarls at me while I frolic in the waves. We are a beached whale and a spinning dolphin.

Let me explain beached whale. When we first met, she was in good shape, but starting with the stress of the wedding and from there on after, Karen will always be overweight. But that's not why I say "beached whale." All Adams women are overweight, and Dr. Brian has a big problem with it. We first visit the Adams for Thanksgiving, then Christmas, and soon we are in a pattern of visiting at least once a month. During every visit, Brian extends to me an open invitation to join him on his six a.m. runs. I don't run much, but I am a lot faster than most runners. After I beat half the BYU track team in that 5K a few months ago, their coach walked up and tried to recruit me. I pointed to the cast on my arm and told him I would love to join but couldn't since I was hurt. That was awesome. Still healthy enough to beat most of your runners with no training! I had crashed this girl's moped at a stoplight a week or two earlier and broken my right wrist. Wrote two midterms left-handed, then went and got casted with my parents' health insurance.

On the mornings we run together, Brian heaves himself through his wickedly easy three-mile runs and tells me how sad he is that his heavy girls never join him. Three teenage daughters and a wife but none who run. They are all overweight and he hates it. Karen seems to like running, but on her days off from work and school, she sleeps in. The running was part of her being single and trying to attract a mate. Nothing more. I don't get it. On my days off, I work out all day if I can! To Karen, exercise is a burden, not a release. For me it's a pathway to euphoria. Endorphins don't discriminate whether you are sad, angry, or lonely, endorphins will lift you up and make you feel good.

Brian's commentary on his girls never running with him comes full circle when we play cards in the evening. Rook is his game of choice. He has all these fat jokes he tells. His favorite joke is a story he tells about when he was at BYU, something something about this girl and then they called her a "*beach*ed whale!" I have heard this joke several times and will hear it many more times. Brian aims his squinty eyes and unibrow right at his large wife and then redirects his attention to his large daughters, and they laugh till they cry because that's what you do when Brian makes a joke, especially when he makes it at your expense and you know it but pretend you don't, because he does as he pleases and everyone else holds in their feelings and plays along.

Karen *used* to run with Brian. When she was in high school. That's where her love for sports reporting comes from. He would tell her all about the cool famous football players and she would memorize their height and weight and how much they could bench and their favorite childhood cartoons.

Halfway through our first year at BYU, Karen got some sort of internship at ESPN headquarters in Connecticut. She and her Blackberry were going places, and me and my Nokia brick were coming along for the ride. I am going to hang out with Carmelo Anthony and Lala in NYC! None of this will pan out. Now that we are married, she's self-destructing and it's all my fault. I'm guessing she made up the whole internship thing. None of our mutual professors ever said anything about it. I never saw any emails. She uses words like "department" and "contacting" and "background check," the vague sort of language you use to string someone along a made-up pipe dream.

Jeffrey Road

I ONLY HAVE TO DIG THROUGH THE BUSHES FOR HER engagement ring once. We have been back from our honeymoon a week and this is our nightly routine: Karen yells at me for being poor, then throws her ring at me and drives away, never to return. While I am getting scratched by the bushes, my brain starts to scramble, and I have two questions.

First: I don't wonder whether or not she will come back, but whether or not she will have a small mountain of frozen yogurt in hand when she does.

Second: why am I the one looking for this ring? Her dad bought it. She wears it. Sure, I threw another thirteen hundred on top of his twenty-five hundred, but that still makes it mostly his. After I bought it, I had one dollar left to my name.

I proposed to Karen at Chef's Table, where we went for our first dinner date. I had the piano man playing her favorite song from *Phantom,* I even got the same table as our first date there. I wore a puffy Sean John jacket the whole meal so I could keep the ring in my breast pocket without her noticing the lump. I was so sweaty and dizzy. She scream-cries at me when she sees other proposals on Instagram because mine sucked so bad. No hot air balloon or helicopter? I am such a dumbass!

All I have to give Karen, even down to my last dollar, will never be good enough. I think Brian married himself through the two of us . . . he's the one that I married, she was just his puppet; and he's the one who married her, I was just his puppet. Now I am her puppet, lifting my arms up and down digging around in the hedges looking for the engagement ring my new bride Karen has once again cast aside in a fit of rage and driven off "for good" in our little Corolla back to her family in Utah . . . and I do. Not. Care. Go back to Utah. My life is a lot quieter with you gone. I feel like a puppet because I have no control over anything in this marriage. Nothing I am doing is working. I am constantly reacting to Karen's complaints. While we were dating, she woke up early to run, she had a full-time job, she attended church with me. Now she is changing all that and blaming it on me. She says she won't go to church at all, she refuses to exercise, she won't get a job. But I know things will get better. She will bring our Corolla back with a mountain of fro-yo like last night and the night before.

I say our little Corolla. It's hers. Well, Brian's. He bought it from the people at Newby Buick in Twin Peaks because he knows the owners there. That's what he told my parents at Chili's, anyway. I have no car. I haven't had a car since before I left on my mission four years ago. It broke down on 900 East in Provo, so I sold it for a hundred and fifty dollars to a junker. I have no car and I have no money. Karen reminds me all the time. All those other boyfriends had cars and money. She should have just married one of them.

One of my mission friends introduces me to Matt Kennedy, my new boss, who doesn't know I am working maintenance digging for diamonds in my off hours. The first time I meet Matt Kennedy, he invites me to lunch at The Training Table in Provo right on the Provo River that divides Provo from Orem. I am sold on him before he says a word. I just like him, from that very first moment, at The Training Table across the street from Bon Losee hair school where I get cheap haircuts because I am poor.

Matt likes The Training Table because each table has a landline phone you use to make your order. Just like an agent making a last-second trade during the draft. During business hours I sell pest control contracts door-to-door in Orange County CA for Matt's company Guardian Pest Control. I set a summer goal to make forty grand. I will actually gross fifty-two thousand in commissions, not counting all the tens and twenties Matt gives me along the way because I will win every single daily or weekly sales contest he holds this whole summer except for one. Tyler from Twin Peaks will win one. Only one. And only because he sneaks into one of my neighborhoods and works one of my streets. I will win every other.

I went to the apartments on Jeffrey Road once before, while passing through for my best mission buddy's wedding last summer. Right before I met Karen. His name is Ryan Leet. I idolize him like I idolize Tanner.

While on my mission, people called us Bubba (him) and Leroy (me). He was charismatic Bubba from Valdosta, Georgia, and I was the country bumpkin Leroy from Kanab, Utah. We were straight out of a Mark Twain novel. He had all the experience and credibility and personality; I had all the work ethic and tenacity and youthful exuberance. We complemented each other like only the best teammates do. When people would try to close their doors on us, we would break into song, and usually the same ones, without having to think. We were in sync. One time a lady with a huge mole on her lip grabbed his face after we sang to her and in slow-motion pulled his head toward that mole and those lips until she planted a smooch the size of a Zen garden right between his eyes.

He's another one I disowned during that first year of dating Karen. He told me to break up with her when she gave me the ultimatum the previous fall. A night or two after I told her I loved her.

"Marry me or break up with me."

I called Ryan that night. I said I liked this girl, but I didn't like the ultimatum. He said straight up, "She's crazy, man, don't do it. Break up with her. I've seen this kind of thing before. It's never good. Do you want to marry a crazy person?"

Ryan was twenty-six when we served our missions together, and I was twenty. He had a college degree, had worked for a mortgage fraud company just as everything came crashing down in the mortgage industry, and had developed an extremely acute worldview. He understood life. He saw what motivated people and why things worked and didn't work. Ryan saw things as they were. Unless they were sweets.

He saw all those as equally small and edible regardless of size or quantity or calories. One evening we were chilling with our mission president (the volunteer leader of our LDS mission headquartered in Eugene, Oregon) at his house after scripture study, and he examined the label of one of those giant individually wrapped gas station sugar cookies with extra frosting and extra-extra sprinkles.

"Serving size: half a cookie?" said President McDonald. "Who eats half a cookie? What is this crap? Four hundred calories! Per serving! Half a cookie!"

Ryan looked at him with this blank look. His look said, "It's a cookie, not a book. Stop reading it and eat it."

Then President McDonald said, "You know what FAT stands for, Elders? Flavor And Taste." And then he ate exactly half of the cookie.

Ryan went home just a few months before me. To get him fit for his bride-to-be, we woke up every morning at exactly five-forty a.m. and went to the YMCA, where he ran like ten miles until his face turned green and his legs shook like the drunks on Sixth Street as we shared the gospel with them. A couple of times I thought he was going to pass out. A couple of times he did. But he kept on running anyway. For his final birthday, just a few weeks before going home to his Heather, one of our close associates made Ryan a cake with their couple picture on it and the inscription, "Porky and His Georgia Peach." Heather is from California, which is why we stopped by the Jeffrey Road apartments to pick up some of the other mission buddy groomsmen last summer. Ryan and Heather married in the San Diego LDS Temple on July 18, 2009. I wanted him to look his best, so we broke mission rules and went tanning too. It was winter in Eugene, Oregon. You would tan too.

The streets got so icy our Chrysler minivan couldn't make it up the hill to our duplex after the YMCA some mornings. We would drive way back down the street and get our speed up and pray with all our might to the God we served that the light would turn green before we blew through the intersection and up that hill and slid into our driveway with the e-brake. Our timing was good, or we wouldn't be here today.

Before Christmas that final winter, President McDonald tipped us off that all missionaries were soon going to be banned from buying gym memberships. We went straight to the YMCA and paid for the next six months in advance. That Sunday when he made the announcement generally across the mission, we smiled and shrugged. Sorry, guys. If you had a membership, you didn't have to cancel, you just couldn't buy or renew. That was the rule. Effective immediately. We had passed on the tip to those who we wanted to know and gave them time to buy. We withheld it from those who we didn't want to know. We had absolute power, and we were absolutely corrupt. We also led the entire mission in baptisms and lessons.

The last night I talked to Ryan, I bawled my eyes out as I walked home from Karen's house to my little RA dorm in Felt Hall where Brian Adams came and slept over because we were bros. I didn't know what to do. I saw myself giving myself up for what I thought was the greater cause.

Like most LDS kids, Karen and I were primed our whole adolescence to save ourselves for marriage and to get married young. A lot of times it lasts, like with my parents and with Karen's parents. As long as you are focused on the same goals and building your foundation on the gospel of Jesus Christ, you will be fine. Karen's foundation was not on the gospel. And I didn't let myself see that. I just saw someone who needed me and who suffered a lot, and I thought God wanted me to step up and marry Karen and have a quiver of children. That was my conclusion after the night Ryan told me she was crazy. I had been trained to think, "college, mission, marriage." That was the plan. I served my mission, I am flying through college, and now all that is left is marriage. Any decent woman should do. My focus was on *marriage* when it should have been on *wife*. I was so worried about getting into the temple and saying "yes" (we don't say "I do," we just say "yes") that I kind of rushed the whole "But who am I really marrying?" part.

I pray about it, but this is long before I learn to let God answer my prayers. I make up my mind and find my own way of justifying marrying her. God didn't really need me to marry Karen. He wants me to marry whoever I want, not for Him, not for her, but for me. Or to marry nobody at all until I am ready. There are many great things about the Church, but one thing that's not so great is the pressure on young people to get married. I was Percival, taking all this advice too literally on my grail quest. President Macdonald gave me an exit interview and letter all about the importance of getting married soon. After my divorce, my mom will write a bunch of letters to Church leadership saying they should stop encouraging that kind of advice. Or better yet, forbid it! Don't push young adults to get married before they even have a credit card.

I inherited from my mom and my dad a belief that doing the right thing always has to be hard. They both came from difficult households and had to leave them behind to form their life together. It was a long road. My mom's parents were verbally abusive alcoholics. My dad's father robbed him blind and made advances on my mom.

So they came together to make a new family, and they left their old families behind. Just like Abraham in the Bible. My parents built their whole lives around helping my siblings and me succeed. When we moved to Utah, my Mom started working in the school district so she could learn the college game inside and out and help us get grants and scholarships and college degrees. Then she got a job at SUU, which provided all of my sisters subsidized tuition so they could get their Bachelor's degrees debt-free.

For me, doing the right thing didn't have to be so hard. I didn't have to leave my family. But I thought I did, so I did the hard thing and married the crazy girl whose manipulative dad told me my family sucks. I did what so many of us do in times of heightened emotion and drew closer to the distraction that took up all my time until I was so gone from myself that I didn't feel pain anymore.

The next day I told Karen about my conversation with Ryan. That was my invitation for her to sever my last link to "me" and become forever "us." That was it. Bye-bye Bubba. "Matt, don't you ever talk to him again. Right?" She made me agree and tell her how disgusted I was with his advice. I lived right next to Ryan that whole summer on Jeffrey Road, and I never once reached out. Ryan and Heather go back to Eugene and visit the folks from our mission just a few months before Karen and I go in the fall. While he is there, Ryan gets me good. He understandably doesn't like Karen very much, so he tells everyone I married my cousin. When Karen and I go to Eugene, we are confronted with that rumor a few times, and Karen gets fuming mad. Fuming red sizzling mad. She gets even more mad at me for not getting mad at Ryan with her. She gets so pissed that I'm not pissed. It's an ongoing thing for us. One night she tries to give me a lesson on why I ought to worry more and the importance of worrying.

His prank is pure genius, how can I be mad? He got me. But really he got her, and then she got me, and I will never hear the end of it. He knows she's a crazy narcissist and that a jab at her fragile image will be good medicine for her. He's already gone. How can I be mad at him? This is his way of saying goodbye to an old friend. A classy move from a classy man. It's a funny message in a bottle to me from a guy who knows I will need all the laughs I can get.

I start muttering things to myself in these bush-digging-ring moments because this new life of mine doesn't make any sense to me. What is going on? Why does she throw her engagement ring at me every night and threaten to leave me? Why is she so mad at me all the time? Are all women like this? I never had a muttering-self prior to living on Jeffrey Road. This muttering makes me different. I am starting to go a little crazy myself. I am stuck in my head. Karen starts calling me "the absent-minded professor, just like your dad." She's right. It's impossible for me to be present in most moments because I am off in whatever space she put me, trying to pacify her, trying to reconcile my life to myself, incapable of coping with any of it.

I find the ring. She comes back with an armful of yogurt with two pounds of gummy bears on top. Then we go to an R-rated action movie. She won't say sorry. She can't say sorry. It would shatter her. The first time I will ever hear her apologize to me will be after we have been divorced for over a year. I, on the other hand, apologize to her for everything. All the time. By taking all the blame, I keep her fragile shell around herself from cracking. The smallest crack, and she will shatter. Any time any person points out any mistake she makes, or disagrees with her, any time she loses at anything, any time she's wrong, she goes on the offensive and attacks until her being wrong is not worth pointing out anymore. Then she moves on like nothing happened even though she insulted your mother, sisters, cats, shoes, and everything else in the process.

The day we got home from honeymooning in the Keys, we drove straight to this apartment on Jeffrey Road in Irvine, California. Super stressful. My response to stress is to sweat it out. Run, jump, lift, bounce, push, pull, throw. Karen eats and shops. Her grandparents gave us a thousand dollars to pay our first months' rent. Instead, Karen puts on her snarly driving face and road-rages us to the AT&T store next to Costco in Irvine, using that money to buy new iPhones on the Everything Plan. I'm down to my last dollar again. I'll figure it out, I tell myself, just like I always do. My hardest task is keeping Karen happy. Get that done, and everything else will be easy.

My first two days selling, I suck. The homeowner answers my knock and I freeze. But it's starting to click. By day ten, I am making over a thousand dollars a day, often more. My professional self becomes a huge part of my identity. I am the best. I will sell more than my boss Kennedy. He is ecstatic. So am I. Matt Kennedy takes me aside a lot to coach me and plan our next summer together when I will return to Irvine and sell for him again. He tells me his plan for us to sell out to Terminix and he wants me in for the ride. After we sell, we will use the money to buy boats and mansions with no mortgages and get whole life insurance instead of term life insurance and lots of other investments I know nothing about. But I will not return next summer because Karen will get hurt by something Matt says to someone else about something unrelated to her and she will never forgive him. He tells his office manager in his own office something Karen doesn't like near the end of the summer, and that's the end of it. "I will never talk to Matt Kennedy again," she says. And she makes me promise to leave at the end of the summer and never bring her back.

Kennedy can tell I am struggling with my marriage. Even before Karen throws a fit over something he tells his office manager. We finish some late-night work and park the white Chevrolet Colorado Guardian Pest Control service truck under the tall and dim parking lot lights for the little Mexican dude to detail it the next morning for twenty bucks. Killer deal. Karen and I even have him detail our little Corolla because it's so cheap. Every couple weeks we all park our cars in a row for him, and he brings his mobile car detailing truck around and makes all our vehicles clean and shiny. Instead of getting out when we park, we stay in the cab and just talk. Kennedy sums up by saying, "The first year is really hard. Just keep going and you'll be fine." Kennedy has a way of getting my adrenaline going. He makes everything sound like an adventure. When he says it, I do it. No matter what it is. Sell a hundred accounts this month, sell ten accounts today, survive a year of marriage.

Mission accepted.

As Kennedy is telling me the 1-year rule, I see these moths buzzing around one of the parking lot lights with a broken housing that exposes the light bulb. Each of the moths gets inside the housing to be closer to the light and each one gets zapped and killed, one by one. I watch them plummet to the ground in slow downward spirals.

The odds are stacked against me, and I know a lesser man wouldn't make it with Karen. Even I am likely going to end up plummeting down in a moth-like death spiral with her. I smile that kamikaze kid smile my Dad loves so much, the hope against hope kind of smile, and change my outlook to see marriage as a challenge and an adventure. One year, and then it gets better. One year to dance near the light but not get zapped. After a year, a new light cover goes on. After a year, it all gets better. Just one year.

I was a journalist and an athlete in my former life. Deadlines make things click for me. I am against the clock. Just like the one that ends after twelve minutes in a quarter or at five o'clock. Make it to next May, buddy, just make it to next May. Just survive. You've got this.

There are times I'm not sure I will.

Whenever I hear or see the word "glint," it takes me right back to Jeffrey Road. A week after I dug in the bushes. I am fast asleep in the middle of the night and catch a glint of something shiny through my eyelids, so I open them. Someone will later ask me what

I think would have happened had I *not* woken up that night. I never thought of that before. The answer is I don't know what would have happened. But I do wake up. And there stands Karen, at the foot of our bed, wielding one of the thousands of wedding gifts Dr. Adams' friends purchased for her from our wedding registry: a meat cleaver.

I have been figuratively back on my heels with Karen for just about a year now, preoccupying myself with her problems to cover up all my loneliness and sadness that have mostly faded by now. Now I am on my heels literally, digging them carefully into the mattress to push myself back and sit upright on the headboard. She holds the knife upright, in the strike position, while the streetlight dances on the blade by way of wind blowing the tree branches just outside our window. How many moths are being zapped tonight? Is tonight my night too? I keep a straight face and sit tall as I can against the headboard. I have no words, no movements, no feelings. I am completely bewildered.

What is she going to do?

I still say nothing. It's only been a handful of seconds, but she's still holding the knife.

Our word "wilderness" comes from frontiersman Daniel Boone's use of that word, bewildered. He crossed rivers and met natives, saw sights and heard sounds that no "white man" had ever seen or heard before. He got lost, a lot. In his journal he wrote that he was "bewildered." It meant "lost." I am bewildered too. She's got me thinking of another frontier explorer, Jim Bowie, namesake of the Bowie butcher knife. He survived a couple gunshots and several stab wounds in his famous duel. I'll be fine.

Karen is wearing the most complex emotions on her face. A few more seconds pass, and they melt into something more discernible, and she begins to cry her usual pathetic cry as she lowers the knife. She walks out of the room, returns unarmed a few moments later, and lays down next to me. I am not allowed to touch her in bed. She is completely repulsed by me: I stink and my breath smells terrible, like rotten eggs. I say nothing. No chance I am falling back asleep. Far too bewildered for that. She sobs herself to sleep and doesn't mention the knife incident for five years. From the moment I sit up against the headboard, I don't move for the rest of the night until I head to the gym extra early.

All of this happens without either of us saying a word. The next morning it is like nothing happened.

The knife incident teaches me the person I married will never be happy. Ever. She is way off in some other place. I feel so bad for her. What the hell is going on? She wants to kill me? I ask myself since I can't ask her. "What did I ever do to you? I have gotten rid of all my friends and family for you and I don't do anything outside of work other than rub your feet and buy you purses. And you come at me with a knife? When I'm sleeping?" I know she has no answers for me. She is long past being rational.

But I have an answer for myself.

I tell myself that this will end one day, because she will die. God loves me, and God loves Karen: God wants me to be happy, and God wants Karen to be happy. I like being alive, so I will live; Karen doesn't like being alive, so she will die. Then she will go to heaven where she can be happy and I will stay here on earth where I am happy. I talk to myself all the time now, and this sounds great.

I think back to myself, okay, Karen is going to die one day. How? Is her depression that bad? Is she going to kill herself? Will she get hit by a truck? I'm not going to do it. I'm not the knife-wielding type. I reply to myself that I don't know how, but I do know for sure that she will die. This is the only way I can reconcile my situation. I am a happy person, and she will never be happy, but I have made her the apple of my eye anyway. So, as long as I am with her, I will never be happy. So she will die one day and then I will be happy. This still doesn't completely work, because in the Church you marry for eternity, and we believe the same way you are when you die is who you will be when you go into heaven. That's why suicide can be so tough; whatever state of mind you are in during life stays with you after you die.

For now, I am taking this problem one lifetime at a time, I suppose. I also am in denial about me not being happy. I convince myself I am still happy. So I make do with a smile. But the people who know me see through that smile and pray for me because they know I am not okay.

Karen tells me on Sunday that she hates the Church, and now that her parents aren't watching, we will never go again. I can just forget about it.

I think it will get better. It won't.

The anger and pain I felt after returning from my mission has all but dissipated. I love going to church and learning about Jesus, but it's more important that I do what Adam did and bite the apple I am given, stick with Eve. Emotionally I am back to normal and feel pretty well adjusted to regular, non-mission life. The angst and agony I felt after my mission that Karen mirrored so well when we were dating is now only hers and put such a wedge between us that I enter a permanent state of denial. Nothing will ever be right. I just have to wait around for this poor, poor soulmate of mine to die.

When we were first dating, Karen called my mom one day and asked how to curb my inexhaustible optimism. It was a brief phone call. Some questions have no answers.

I am becoming more and more numb and muttery. Numb to her complaints. Muttery to myself, frustrated all the time. Trying to make the most of it. We have been married coming up on a month, and it's already more than I can bear. I am only keeping myself going by convincing myself this will end one day because Karen will die. I hesitate to say "soon," but there's definitely an implied "soon" here. Muttering, "Can't you just die already?" while getting her a second bowl of ice cream from the freezer. "What was that, Matchu?" "Oh, nothing."

Every night I come home to the apartment on Jeffrey Road and my scrotum shrivels up as I slide and click the shifter into Park because I know she will launch into yelling at me about something and make me feel like less and less of a human. It isn't sustainable. I shouldn't be this scared to come home to my own apartment.

So although I don't tell myself she will die *soon* and I don't put a timeline on it, it's absolutely implied. Like when you decide you haven't had Oreos in awhile so you're going to get some Oreos, you don't have a timeline in mind but it's going to happen *soon*. You can't stop thinking about Oreos until you've had some. The tire on every car and every pair of sunglasses and everything else that's round becomes Oreos until you buy some and put a dent in a sleeve of them.

Karen stops taking Acutane and starts taking her blue pills "again." I ask her, "What blue pills, *again*?" Oh, it's the medication she was on after she went to therapy last year. Happy pills. She tells me it's headache medicine at first, but pretty soon admits Elavil is for more than headaches. I Google it on my spanking new second-generation iPhone we bought with our first month's rent money, and I find out it's an antidepressant.

This is the first time I learn that Karen is clinically depressed. It makes a lot of sense. This helps me rationalize the fact that she is not rational. Over the next few years, most of her family will join her on Elavil.

By June, Karen decides she doesn't like sports reporting, doesn't like going to church, and now more than anything she wants to be a mom. And now she wants babies ASAP. I'm not ready to be a dad. She starts taking prenatal vitamins. I feel some relief when she stops taking birth control pills because of the extra moodiness they bring on. Something like, *at least now I can sleep through the night without wondering whether I'll wake up with my throat slit.* Like that scripture in the Bible that says when they awoke, they were dead. I guess that answers the earlier question about what would have happened had I not woken up that night. I still have no idea how you wake up dead. It's a weird scripture. Just glad I didn't have to find out the hard way.

Karen's dad, Brian, and her brother, Mark, come out to visit in June. Somehow we screw up the sleeping arrangements, and when Brian has to go pee in the middle of the night, he cannot. He walked into a closet instead and couldn't find a light anywhere, and it's my fault and he's very disturbed all the next morning. I want to laugh and call him a whiny little princess, but he's very serious and I would never do that. He goes on and on about how badly we hurt his bladder. It is *ridiculous*. Brian and his dramatic do-better reports. When I run with him, he usually has to stop halfway through the three miles to go potty too. The keeper of the beached whales needs his bathroom breaks.

Up until Jeffrey Road, I keep a daily journal for the prior twelve years of my life. I have only one journal entry from that entire summer in Irvine. Here is most of it:

"7 June 2010. Karen quote: 'I believe in you on Wavering Lake!' What a supportive wife! Karen got her prenatal vites today and she has started exercising and shopping healthy and just being a great wife! She even bought me another five dozen eggs for the next few weeks."

She was really funny at times. Transposing "unwaveringly" to "on Wavering Lake." Little glistening moments like that carried me through months of her screaming manipulation. I don't know what I mean by "has started exercising." She probably walked around the block that day and encouraged some wishful thinking on my part.

I will write a total of four journal entries over the next two years.

She has so many "things" with her parents. Like at the beach, she loves to wear a bikini, even though she's big now, but her parents can never know. No pictures, no talking about it. And Sundays are the only days we can go to the ocean, because the rest of the week I am working, but her parents can't know we are going to the beach on Sunday. They have to think we are at church. Even though Karen will never go to church again.

Karen, chill out. Your dad vents on me about how fat you all are and your mom always checks on me and asks me if I'm okay because she secretly knows I'm not and never will be, just like she isn't and never will be with Brian. It takes one to know one. But stop worrying, I won't tell them jack squat.

Karen is so scared of them seeing her in her bikini on Sunday. What if a stranger takes a picture and posts it on Facebook and somehow her mom or dad sees it? I'm like, what? Even after we finally get divorced, Karen will still text me things not to tell her parents about. Listen, lady, I don't talk to your freaking parents anymore, and haven't in years, and never will again.

Then Karen's Uncle Snooper from San Diego wants to have us down and teach us to surf. I don't know his real name but have never heard him called anything but Snoop or Snooper. He's an awesome dude. He gave me a disc golf putter with his name "Snooper" in marker on the back that I will keep forever.

Matt Kennedy and I play disc golf a bunch, at least once a week. During one of these games with Kennedy, I got my first hole-in-one. Today Kennedy throws his disc into a residential lake thick with algae and duck poop and strips down to swim in after it without thinking twice. I watch dumbfounded as he swims to the middle of the lake and submerges in search of the disc. He quickly surfaces, all green and slimy looking like Swamp Thing, frisbee in hand. I have seen some incredible athletic feats, but few compare with Swamp Thing's disc dive. I love working for this guy. Who does stuff like this? I've never met anyone like him. When we sell together, I feel like myself again. Working with Matt is nirvana.

Snoop wants to teach us to surf on Sunday. I tell Karen we shouldn't, because I know the chances of her parents hearing about this are high since this is in the family. Karen wants to anyway to make Snoop happy. So we go, and then she yells at me for days afterward that we shouldn't have done it. The night before surf lessons, we go on a booze cruise, and Snoop and his wife Laura get hammered. It makes me super uncomfortable. I am a private introverted person anyway, but it's also really lame being around them when they are drunk. When we go surfing the next day, everyone is already on bad footing. Karen more than me. I must take it to my grave that we went surfing on a Sunday. Karen's conscience is killing her.

In the Church, it's very important to rest on Sunday and keep it holy, but generally any sort of family activity is fine. Especially if you are with someone who doesn't attend, like Snoop, then you're just being like Jesus pulling oxen from the mire. Hanging out with the Publicans. The point is she is terrified of her parents when it comes to certain things. Right or wrong, she's just terrified.

The whole time I know her, there is a save-me-from-my-parents thing going on that I buy into because I want to be the hero. But it's coupled with an I-love-and-respect-my-parents-more-than-you thing that I don't see at first but becomes ever harder to reconcile as time goes on.

I become invincible at work. I learn that since I can turn on the gift of gab at a moment's notice, all I have to do is keep talking to these homeowners, and most of the time they will buy from me just to shut me up. It is like interrogation; everybody breaks in the end. Only it's a very nice interrogation, and all I want is your credit card and all your neighbors' credit cards. I am good at getting them.

I meet a beautiful lady named Nicole, and she invites me into her home to sign the paperwork. This usually just takes place on the doorstep, but maybe one in five will bring you inside. Offer you water, maybe a snack.

There are *Playboy* covers of her all over the inside of her home. Cool! I just sold a Playboy Bunny! She refers more Bunnies to me too. I take a picture of two of her framed magazine covers to show off to the other guys. Karen finds them on her nightly phone audit. She never stops auditing my phone. I just don't have a guilty conscience, so I don't think twice about it. It's just business. A funny story. Karen doesn't think so. She almost leaves for Utah again. Makes me beg her to stay and tell her what an awful person I am and how lucky I am that she doesn't tell her dad.

I have a knack for sneaking into gated HOA neighborhoods. The two biggest obstacles in knocking sales are competition and customer's budget, so the gated communities are perfect. Here no other "bug guys" dare sneak in, and everyone is super wealthy. Here the obstacles shift. They all become security related. When I jump these gates or fences I am jumping over both regular obstacles at once and right into a big pot of money, as long as I can hide from the cops.

In a different neighborhood, the HOA president sees me and has his lawyer call our office with a cease-and-desist threat. Kennedy calls me and says that's the coolest phone call he has ever gotten. He politely declines the lawyer's offer. He *brags* about that call rather than getting pissed like a regular boss. He's fearless. One time this lady says she will call the cops on me. They always say that. But she's rrrrrrrrreally pissed. Her daughter swung the door wide and let me in with her still wearing a bath towel over her massive silicon chest. Of course it's my fault for being invited inside. Not five minutes later, this police cruiser rounds the corner. I dive behind a hedge, take off my Guardian Pest Control shirt and turn it into a towel, and vigorously begin doing crunches and push-ups on the neighbor's lawn. The cop parks right by my car with the obvious Utah plates and stays there in his car. I work out on the lawn for awhile trying to wait him out. Not gonna happen. This lady must be an important resident! I'm still going back to sell her tomorrow. I text Matt Kennedy my location, run right past that cop and my car to our rendezvous point, and come back and retrieve my car the next day. No boot, no ticket, no fine. I sell the same neighborhood the next day, but towel lady doesn't come back to the door.

I carry the Kennedian invincibility with me all summer. Just make it through the first year, like Matt said. His confidence in me at work makes up for the self-doubt I have at home. I am picking up momentum every day. I become more and more outwardly strong and confident, but inwardly starving and broken. I know Matt can see it, at least a little bit, but he doesn't pry.

Matt and his wife, Melanie, have two adorable kids, a boy and a girl. They will go on to have a few more. Karen and I do a lot of things with them. We are the only other couple on the summer sales team. We play Rook with them in the evenings, get dinner every few weeks, go to the beach together on Sundays. Matt and Melanie argue a lot like all good couples who don't bury their feelings, but I don't ever argue with Karen. Matt gets pissed that I don't ever stand up for myself to my wife like he does, but that's my choice and he respects it. I'm jealous that he has a wife who can be criticized without tearing a hole in the universe.

Melanie has season passes to Disney and often brings Karen along with her and her kids. Melanie's daughter, Maddie, says something Karen doesn't like at Disney, so Karen bops Maddie on the mouth. I can't believe Karen does that. I can't believe Melanie still talks to her after that. Karen hates Matt for all eternity because of something he said to his office manager in his own office that has absolutely nothing to do with Karen, but when Karen hits Melanie's daughter in the face, Melanie forgives her without pause. Melanie is scared of Karen like I am. Matt sees through it and isn't scared of her at all.

Karen always wants to shop. What girl doesn't, right? We fight about money every waking moment of *our entire marriage.* The first thing I will do after we separate is remove her name from my credit cards, pay them off, and close the accounts. This will give me so much relief. I won't get another credit card for six months, just to have a breather. The first time we will go to court after the separation (her request, she won't want to settle), I will have already given her thousands and thousands of dollars, but she will have piled up another four grand in credit card debt in just two months.

I come home to our apartment on Jeffrey Road, and we start arguing about money like any other day. Then she pulls out her second generation iPhone she bought with our first month's rent money and orders a Nintendo Wii on Amazon just to prove it's her money and she can do what she wants with it. She says, like she always says, that I am lucky she married me instead of one of her rich athlete boyfriends. The same ones she asked me to save her from. This woman is nuts. I Google search her old three a.m. texting boyfriend Matt Patchan and see he did play in the NFL for several years. I want to look him up and find out what really happened in the summer of 2009. I want to ask him why her best friend Lauren, with whom she stayed all summer after getting fired from her internship later, said he and all the other Florida Gators called her "Krazy Karen."

Salt Lake City 1

SURE, I WILL BE SAD FOR AWHILE AND BECOME ONE OF the youngest widowers around, but I will still thank you, God, so so much for finally taking Karen home to heaven where she can be happy.

We knew not to eat or drink fresh produce in Thailand because it might kill us, but Karen did it anyway. She loves to eat. Karen started to turn green on the flight home. We just got home to Utah, and now I've left Karen at the hospital, where she will die of dengue fever. My best friend Dan's buddy Eric Queathem with the gimpy arm has extensive international travel experience and he diagnosed her yesterday. Karen is a goner. It's actually finally over. Karen is going to die. Right on the one-year mark. Just like Kennedy said. I made it! Things are about to get better!

Eric's wife-to-be, Candi, Dan's wife-to-be, Sarah, and my wife, Karen, are all broadcast TV girls at BYU. Eric and Dan are both rich boys with Beamers who take their girls all over the world all the time. At BYU, boys like them are called "Belmont Boys." Karen reminds me about Candi's and Sarah's travels every chance she gets. Other than to make my parents happy, the other reason I took my journalism scholarship offer at BYU was to meet all the pretty girls in my department, like these three. All the reporters on TV look like dating material. Tall, smart, beautiful. Before I dated Karen, I was trying to date one girl from every sports team at BYU. Including our national champion dance team, of course! The Cougarettes. Rrarr! I had gotten through gymnastics, dance, tennis, and was working on volleyball when I met Karen.

After she texts me "Matt Livingston you liar," it's only twenty-four hours until our first date, two weeks until she gives me the marriage ultimatum, and two months until we decide to get married. I never got around to dating the girl from the volleyball team.

The only girl I dated for any length of time before Karen was another Resident Assistant who lived near Felt Hall named Kelly. After a few dates, I made this elaborate plan for our first kiss. I had kissed several girls in the few months since I returned from my mission. The first girl I kissed was Ali Cooper in Kanab.

The kiss happened on a dirt road by the water towers. Near the water towers, at the edge of Kanab civilization, you can see ancient hieroglyphs on a cliff. I had brought a picnic table and my little grill to that picturesque spot so I could cook salmon for our date and kiss Ali. But she was dating someone else, so she never texted me back after that.

Now back to choreographing that kiss with Kelly, the RA Kelly. Not my sister Kelly. Last I checked she was still some sort of RA at BYU, even now ten years later.

On the lawn by the Museum of Art on campus, I hid her favorite dessert, I want to say it was a coconut cream pie. Something went wrong, and before I could make a move, she ran away screaming and crying and flailing her arms like she was covered in mosquitoes. I looked up at the telephone wire lit by the parking lot lights and saw a few birds sitting there on the wire. Just sitting. Not running away or screaming or swatting at bugs. Were they sleeping? It was late. Or were they really that cool that they could just sit there? I wish girls could be calm like sitting birds. I walked up to the pie where it was hidden and hurtled it against the wall of the MOA. That helped me feel better, like only splattered pies can.

When we move back to Utah after the summer in Irvine, we have some money to take some trips. We take our first trip to Oregon where everyone thought Karen was my cousin and Karen met Tim Stanger. Oh Timmy.

I met Timmy on my mission in Bend the day after he flushed all his cocaine down the toilet and decided to come back into the fold of the Lamb of God. We were inseparable for awhile. As a young undergraduate, he had been studying at the University of Idaho in Moscow and got a B one semester, and his parents cut off his funds, so he started dealing drugs. We met him twelve or so years later. After we got him going to church again, he moved to Eugene during the last year of my mission when I was pretty much stationed there. He served me my first dish of Phad Thai. Straight out of a to-go box. These were the days before UberEats, when you had to call and order from someone who didn't speak English and then just hope that (a) the food was edible and (b) you actually got what you ordered. Tim fed us missionaries all the time, and it was usually take-out Thai. He told me one day we needed to go to Thailand. I agreed and we shook on it.

Even before I met Karen, Tim came to visit me at BYU. We took dates to Sundance, Robert Redford's ski resort which shares its name with the annual film festival, for a full moon ski lift ride. It's a cheap way to make a girl snuggle with you because it's *cold* up there in the fall.

When Karen and I visit Tim in Oregon, he has recently gotten engaged to Shawna Flatten. They are great together. The first place we take Karen is downtown Eugene to the renowned farmer's market, where clothing is optional and hygiene is optional and gender is optional.

We buy tie-dye shirts and spoon rings. The tie-dye shirts are twenty dollars apiece and Karen must have one, so I try to convince the dye lady to give me a deal on the second shirt. She gets really mad and says no. I reply that if I walk away spending twenty dollars on one shirt, where I could have spent thirty or maybe thirty-five dollars on two shirts, she will be missing out on good business because as long as I pay more than her cost on the second shirt she will still be better off. Emotional intelligence is not my strong suit. These are basic economics of supply and demand. Sometimes I don't know when to take a hint and stop. She gets even more pissed. This dye lady is a hippie, not a capitalist. I gladly pay forty dollars for two shirts.

Karen eats a brownie next and gets high as a kite. I told her not to do it. They really do fill everything with weed here. Sixteen-year-old Mikey Garcia, also from back in my mission days, tries to take us on to the next spot, but Karen wants him to do parkour so she can hit on him some more. It's hilarious. Soon her headache hits, so we sit down at an Asian restaurant for lunch. While we are sitting in the booth, Karen slumps over and falls asleep. She dozes for over an hour and sleeps off that brownie weed high while Mikey and I reminisce over spring rolls and chili paste.

Back at Tim's house, Karen suggests we have sex in the bathroom tub upstairs in the guest bedroom. She does this a lot. We will be on a date and she will say we should have sex when we get home and then she changes her mind. She says her anxiety pills kill her sex drive. She only goes through with sex when she's ovulating so she can get pregnant which pregnancy she wants to distract her from her misery. Later that night, while watching Soul Train videos, Karen still has a weedache, so Tim gives her a Soma (muscle relaxer) and she gets all loopy again and calls me a "dirty dog." We all laugh about it and all the other ridiculous things Karen is saying for hours that night and for years to come. Tim pushes it and tries to convince Karen that she needs a nose ring. I prefer Tim's nose ring idea to Karen's idea of getting a tattoo of the rose in the jar from Beauty and the Beast. In the LDS Church, women don't generally pierce anything besides ears, and tattoos are a no-no. Karen is always saying how badly she wants a Belle rose-jar tattoo. Soon I won't be allowed to talk to Tim anymore. This may be for the best.

As long as we are traveling, Karen will go to church with me. At home there are expectations and relationships and commitments and those are hard for Karen. But while traveling, we can just pop in and pop back out again. She knows I want to see the people from my mission, but she doesn't know the false information they have already been given about her. We go to church with many of my old friends, and Karen finds out Ryan Leet told half of Eugene that Matt Livingston married his cousin. She's not amused at all. We leave Eugene and head to Seattle.

Karen's mood has irreparably soured and Seattle is a bust. I don't have enough things planned for us to do and "I'm not taking care of her." Again. Just like last Christmas in Kanab and just like such and such a time and such and such a time. Karen says over and over wherever we are, "You aren't taking care of me." And then she lists her complaints about me. She's griping and crying and waiting for me to tell her I am not worthy of her. I feel so bad for her. I will try harder.

She asks me to tell her all the sweet things I love about her and then she rattles off more lists of all my numerous misdeeds. I am carrying her around all the hundreds of November Seattle rain puddles, distracting her from her anxiety, buying her things, blowing on her food so she wouldn't burn her mouth, telling the managers it's her birthday so we can have free dessert, complaining to the waiters for her, but nothing works. Nothing makes her happy.

She needs a couple dates a week minimum. A date is almost always dinner and a movie, just like how Brian does it. Movie theater at least once a week regardless of what's playing. And she must have a Coke and popcorn and usually snuck-in Taco Bell too. The dates aren't about us or fun or togetherness. They are her collection to brag to non-date couples that I take her on dates all the time.

In Seattle I have to make up ground fast, so we go to Tiffany's and buy one of the three items in the store priced under my new credit card limit of five hundred dollars. Most of the money I made last summer in Irvine doesn't get paid out until January, and tuition and rent and deposits are expensive, so we are still poor.

When we were first dating, I only argued with Karen on two topics. I lost both arguments, so I just stopped arguing and accepted that her opinion would rule. The first was immunizations. The second was credit cards. Karen had a credit card when we met, and I didn't. She wanted me to get one for spending money when we need it. I asked her what she meant by "need," and she danced around the question. I told her credit cards are only to use for building credit, or for emergencies. She said that was stupid and that credit cards are for buying things you don't have the money to buy. I lost it and told her that's the most ridiculous thing I have ever heard. If you want something, you save up for it, you don't use a credit card! If you use a credit card for things you cannot afford, you won't be able to pay it off because you can't afford to, then you'll just end up paying interest *beyond* the amount you already can't afford, now you're too strapped to buy things you actually need!

Then she started to cry and said that's not what she meant, credit cards are for emergencies when you can't access your savings. I gave up. She bought my wedding ring on a credit card. I paid it off with pest control money. I don't remember when I paid off the Tiffany's ring I bought for Karen as an acceptable apology for not planning enough activities in Seattle. Before long I would learn the games of interest-free balance transfers just to keep everything afloat every month. We have no business buying anything from Tiffany's.

Karen has a friend named Tiffany too. Tiffany has a job. As soon as Karen and I get married and she stops working, she will never have any meaningful work or income ever again. A few odd jobs here and there, like in the Guardian Pest Control office, but nothing much more than minimum wage and never for more than a few months. Yet somehow, when good honest hardworking women like Tiffany tell Karen about their jobs, Karen makes them feel dumb. Like, "Oh, you work at a hospital? I would rather die than do that. But I'll come take you to lunch!" Because Matt has a credit card now! We can have all the lunch you want. Come with me, I'll buy.

Tiffany married Karen's dad's friend, Louie from Twin Peaks. Louie has an Xbox and a huge TV and I can't believe he has enough free time in marriage to have a hobby. Right behind my disbelief that he has a hobby stands my dumbfoundedness that of all hobbies, he chose video games. What a waste of precious hobby time! Louie works for NuSkin, the Utah global skin care company that turned a lot of guys into millionaires and a few into billionaires. We go with them to the NuSkin Christmas party and laugh together at the performing comedian Brian Regan. He tells the cleverest joke I've ever heard:

"What's it called when you have second thoughts about calling ahead to reserve a table at a nice restaurant on tribal lands? A reservation reservation reservation!"

We are moving from Provo to Salt Lake City to be closer to Karen's curriculum-satisfying internship at a radio station. Not TV news, radio news. Before we move, I have to kill my professional relationship with Matt Kennedy. After all the people I have cut off from my life, Matt is my only new friend since I met Karen. Now he's going to be gone too.

Kennedy and Karen had a disagreement at the office while I was out working. Karen was so lonely and bored while I was working that Kennedy invited her into his Guardian Pest Control office to help set appointments and kill the time. He even paid her. It was a small office with just a few other people working at their desks. One was a really nice young lady named Kellie doing customer service and collections.

Karen is very particular about how people talk about our church. Her feelings about religion are super complicated. Like she doesn't want to keep Sundays holy or pay tithing or read scriptures or go to church, or any of the things we do, but she can't bear the idea of her parents possibly catching wind that she takes surfing lessons on Sunday. Kellie asked Kennedy a question about the Church and

Karen did *not* like the way Kennedy answered it. And from what I learned, he answered with candor and honesty, and Kellie appreciated and understood his answer. But Karen, who wasn't even part of the conversation, quit on the spot. She hated Kennedy's guts from that moment on. Really, she just didn't approve of how much I liked my boss, and this day she found her excuse to start dividing me from him like she tore me from all the other things I love. She hated him all along, and now she had her ammunition to take him away from me.

She quits and walks outside and has me stop working and come pick her up at a gas station. She barks at me about his perfidious actions, and I daydream about going back to work tomorrow. I am sure it will blow over, and Matt will get immunity from being outlawed because he is my dream boss and he pays me so well. She rants and rails while we drive but I am sure she will get past it. It's just a minor spat.

But there are no minor spats with Karen. We get to our apartment and she starts packing. She wants us to pack up the Corolla and move right now in the middle of my summer job. Pack up and leave in the morning and never come back.

Somehow we stay. But when the summer ends, she makes it very clear I am not to talk to Matt ever again, and *absolutely not* to work for him again. No question.

When we move back to Utah in Fall 2010, the economy sucks. I just spent the summer developing a recession-proof skill (that's what Matt calls door-to-door sales) and securing an immediate future with Matt, but this is no more. I secretly meet with Matt right when we get back to Utah after the summer ends for what he thinks is a planning session. I am going to have to say goodbye instead.

We meet at Legends Grill on the BYU campus. He launches right in and offers me a business partnership at Guardian. He and I will recruit college kids like he recruited me and we will grow big enough to sell to Terminix and become millionaires. What an adventure!

This is the most special anyone has ever made me feel. I'm usually the one trying to make people feel special. Not today. My stomach is full of knots and lumps as I realize how good a thing I'm about to throw away. I didn't know Matt had this much planned for us. I choke on every shitty word that comes up my lying throat and out of my lying mouth, telling Matt that I can't work with him anymore. I feel like a slimy piece of shit with no heartbeat. The enthusiasm in his eyes doesn't dim. He thinks I just need time and that I will come around and accept his generous once-in-a-lifetime offer. Matt keeps in touch over the next few days and sends me recruiting plans and other details, but soon he realizes I am gone and he stops communicating. Sometimes I stare at my phone wishing he would send another text I can't reply to. But he stops. And that's it.

I cry after that meeting. Not so much about missing out on the business opportunity, that won't be a regret until later. That's totally worth crying about too, because Matt will find another partner and execute his plan and became a millionaire. But today in Provo, I cry because I felt the love and admiration in Matt's voice when he offered to share his business with me. The business he had spent his best years and his best work building. He took the best thing he had to offer and offered it to me.

When he looks me in the eye and offers to partner with me, I want to feel like I am made of pure gold. But I can't because I am casting the gold in my life aside like dross to obey someone who I want to die. What a sad, sad day. A sad month. For the next year I struggle to find a different boss I will like who pays well. Impossible. Matt Kennedy set the bar impossibly high. I'll find something that's just fine and make plenty of money next summer, but it sucks compared to working with Matt. I can't believe I lost Kennedy.

All my role models are gone. My dad, Tanner, and Ryan. Now Matt is gone too, and I am plumb out of role models. Brian is many things to me, but I will never look up to or admire him. I can't talk to him about the things of my heart. I just obey him. He may be my master, but he is not my role model.

Years later, Matt Kennedy will hire me as the first sales manager for what is now a billion dollar company. I will tell him my greatest regret in life is turning him down that day in Legends Grill. I didn't want to do it. I had to do it. The way he runs his home and his relationship with Melanie is different than how I did things. He told me he chooses to be a jerk when he needs to be because it keep things in balance. He's right. He and Mel argue all the time and never hide their feelings from each other. They are honest.

Karen vilifies him and tells me how great I am for always supporting her and never putting her down. To a people pleaser like me, this praise feels good enough to keep me suppressing my feelings and opinions. Kennedy understands that creating real love and building a healthy honest relationship often means arguing and disagreeing at times to get there. I don't dare do this with Karen. After the knife and all the screaming and crying and talking down to me, I am afraid. I know I will never have an honest relationship with her and we will never be in love. But I am strong enough to fake it until she dies.

I could just pick Matt Kennedy over Karen and be done with her. But I am still doing my duty to God and still waiting for her to die. A far more rational response. In movies, they always die. I never once think about leaving her. We are married. We are bound together. She threatens to leave me all the time, that's partly why I think leaving is so petty and weak. I never allow the possibility into my mind. I don't want to reduce myself to the status of a quitter. And Karen makes me feel good for doing things the way she wants them done. Sometimes as a reward, she even lets me sleep in the same bed as her, repulsive and stinky as I am.

Karen's good friend Jessica, whose little sister Miss Las Vegas will later be one of our plethora of babysitters, just got divorced. Jessica's husband was addicted to pornography and he pushed her around.

Their marriage only lasted a few months. We didn't know them as a couple, but we did go to their wedding. Karen tells me their divorce story often, and she tells it to a lot of other people too. She retells it to new couples we meet on campus like some people talk about pets or weather. I wonder why she talks about Jessica's divorce so much. Probably reinforcing that the only reason couples get divorced is that the man is a wimpy abusive pervert. That's exactly how I feel: only lousy men fail at marriage. But I am strong, so I will stay strong for Karen and wait until God takes the miserable wench home and saves me from her just like I saved Brian from her.

Every day Karen thinks she has gotten pregnant. She drives to Walgreens to buy disposable pregnancy tests and takes them all the time. She thinks she accidentally peed out the baby. Now she has convinced herself she will never be able to have a baby. We see a doctor who has nothing to say, and Karen tries to convince him she had a miscarriage and she screams and cries and I don't know what to do. She wants me to yell at the doctor to make him take her side of the story. "Everyone is out to get me!" she says. All Karen cares about is whether you are on her side. Am I on her side? Is the doctor on her side? I have no other side to be on.

2011 is a big year. We will graduate this year, and in March we are heading to Thailand. I don't know it yet, but we will also get pregnant for real. First, it's finally January and time to attend Tim and Shawna's wedding at the Mission Inn in Riverside, California. The wedding guests all take a party bus to Disneyland and everyone gets wasted except Karen and me. The rest of the wedding party are so tipsy they can't even step onto the rides. Karen and I ride Space Mountain four times all by ourselves.

We spend some time with Tim and Shawna finalizing plans for our Asia couples' trip, now only two months away. Tim's idea of a plan is: "I'll send you our flights in a month or so, and we will live on the fly." I love it. Vagabonding just like the old days in Oregon. Karen and I are going to take two weeks out of our second-to-last semesters at BYU to join Tim and Shawna on their Honeymoon in Asia.

Karen worked at the only Thai restaurant in Twin Peaks during high school. She introduced me to Tom Kha there, my favorite soup. She worked there with a kid named Alex. After she broke up with him, he turned gay because if he couldn't have her, then no woman was worth having. He wasn't the only guy who turned gay after he couldn't have her. That's what she told me when we stood in line at *Thriller* in Salt Lake City that year, where ex-boyfriend-turned-gay Alex and the other zombie freaks performed the coolest Halloween show in Utah.

Alex turning gay because he couldn't have her is one of the strangest ideas I have ever heard. I have my own theory about how she may have scarred Alex in a slightly different way, possibly the same way she wanted to scar me with that butcher knife. Perhaps it's not, "If I can't have this woman, I will never have another." Maybe it's more like: "If women are capable of this, I will never date another one ever again!" I talk myself up about how tough I am. Weaker men can't handle her, but I can. I won't turn gay! I will cleave unto my wife no matter what and I will love it. Until she dies.

Her Thai restaurant background makes it relatively easy to convince Karen to go with Tim and Shawna and me to Thailand. She wants to tell Benja, the owner of the restaurant, that she's been to Thailand. She wants to go to Bali because of *Eat Pray Love,* so we throw it in the plan. A week in the Gulf of Thailand and a week in Bali. Maybe a couple days in Singapore or Australia.

By the end of the trip, we will have been married for just about a full year. Kennedy's prophecy that things will get better after a year resounds in my head. Maybe something will happen on the trip and I will come home . . . alone.

Asia

I CLIMB UP THE LADDER TO THE LOFT IN OUR TREEHOUSE on Ko Tao and see, to my surprise, hundreds of Vicodin on the hardwood floor. I know Tim has a past. He still knows people who deal drugs. Some of these prescription meds are for him, but most of them are for sale. Tim was in a horrible car accident that broke his neck last year. He's been hopped up on really strong pain pills the whole time we've been in Thailand. He went through his entire two-week supply these first few days. I prayed a minute ago that he won't overdose and die here on his honeymoon. A few times I already thought he did. Die, I mean. He passes out on a bus or a boat and won't wake up. He keeps calling Shawna by his old girlfriend's name, whom he brought to Thailand years earlier last time he needed a drug run. He keeps mixing up his memories of the two trips. On the last island, he kept trying to take us "back to the hotel," a hotel that doesn't exist anymore. It was from his trip five years earlier and has since been turned into condos.When Karen hears all the "clink, clink, clink" noises our first night in Ko Tao and asks me to investigate, I realize why Tim went to the pharmacy so many times back on Ko Samui.

I think since Tim's memories of the two Thailand trips have merged, so has his identity from the two time periods. He has become the drug dealer he was the last time he was in Thailand. When I climb upstairs to check on the strange repetitive clinking noise, he has all his pill bottles stacked on the floor, methodically clinking into their bottles the thousands or tens of thousands of dollars' worth of prescription pills he picked up for around fifty bucks. He mumbles on to me about his buyers, his prices, his quantities. I cling to the thought that he mixed up the two trips and that these ramblings are misplaced memories, that this hadn't been his intention when he invited us to join the honeymoon. I could be mistaken. Perhaps the Asia couples' honeymoon was a drug run from the get-go.

Although the hotel Tim was searching for was gone, his pharmacy remains right where he left it. We stay right across the street from it next to the French bed and breakfast with the buttery croissants. Tim goes to the pharmacy again and again and again. We get these little menthol nasal inhalers that cleanse your nasal passage from that little pharmacy. One time a police officer comes in while the guy behind the counter goes in the back to grab a bunch of pills for Tim. The officer brings his Tiger Balm and leaves. Tim's favorite movie is *Blow,* and he loves the scene when Johnny Depp struts through the airport with a briefcase full of cocaine. He's a changed man, but he's still that guy.

Shawna gets so mad at Tim for calling her Teasha over and over that she refuses to have sex with him. She tells him the news in this little store while we are all getting some groceries, and Tim gets a little handsy in his drug-induced state of mind, so Shawna pushes him away. He reminds her she owes him later and she again refuses, shouting loudly, "Tim, we are not having sex the rest of this trip, I don't care if it's our honeymoon!" So right there in the middle of the store he whines loudly, "Aawwww, but you told me I could break a piece off that ass!" and throws his hands down like a defeated toddler. Karen and I walk out of the store and down the street and away from these shenanigans.

Before we get to the treehouse with the hidden drug-packing loft, we go to a place recommended by Lonely Planet. Don't ever read those books! This place has a *litter of newborn* kittens in our closet. I recognize the kitten mewing sound from the time one of our cats in Kanab gave birth in my parents' box spring under the mattress. It took us forever to find them. These closet kittens are not hard to find. It's like the second thing we see, after the jimmy-rigged misting fan dangling near the window. The kittens are noisy and stinky and some of them are either dead or sickly and dying. We don't bother asking for our money back, just depart quietly and find the treehouse where Tim will clink his capsulated pills tonight.

While snorkeling, Shawna gets sunburned really badly. She won't stop talking about how badly her poor bum hurts. She can't sit. Bums stick up just right when you are lying flat out on the water to snorkel, like hamburger buns on a plate. The sun hits them, but then, since they are three-dimensional, the water reflects the sun at them from every side, and that's where the real danger comes from. Reflected sun becomes focused into tighter beams, and they scorch even worse than direct sunlight. Shawna's bum rumps get roasted from both direct and reflected sunlight for hours while Tim and I are scuba diving. Tim rubs Tiger Balm on her, and Shawna adds some comic relief, reminding him that will be the extent of the action he gets on the trip. When Shawna gets back to California, she will get skin grafts on both cheeks. As bad as a sunburn can get.

We spend most of the second half of the trip with Wayan Poulos. I find him bartering for taxi passengers outside of our hotel. He's a hard-working guy with a minivan and plenty of room for four. We quickly turn Wayan into our private tour guide. For a real tour guide you pay exorbitant tour prices; to reserve Wayan for the entire day, he charges far less than the cumulative taxi rides would have been and knows Bali frontward and backward and takes us to all the beautiful places he knows. His two children both dream of working on cruise ships and touring the world, so they are in school learning English and towel-folding.

The whole time, we are on the lookout for "opium pipes" for Brian. He has a strange obsession with them. When we play Rook, opium pipes are his go-to risqué foreign pronoun. He's always joking about opium pipes. Karen's is similar: "black tar heroin." They would joke, "Remember Uncle so and so with his opium pipes?" And then, "Man, they protected that stuff like it was black-tar heroin!" Karen and Brian loved to talk naughty nonsense that made them the center of attention while making their audience feel uncomfortable and forcibly laugh at their strange and obscure jokes. They have no idea what they are talking about, but they talk about it over and over and over again.

We find Brian a bunch of opium pipes and I buy them all for him. I know he will be so proud of my digging and haggling and smuggling on his behalf! But when I take them to him after the trip, he doesn't even want to touch them. He loves talking about them and asking for them, but of course it's all just a joke. Duh.

After one outing to scour caves in Bali for opium pipes, we are in the back of Wayan's van, all four of us. Karen has gotten herself really mad about something. As usual.

Sometimes she gets madder than she can bear. Before we left, she spiked her MacBook on the floor of our apartment because she stubbed her toe on the wall. She cracked the plastic screen backing, but it still works fine. A different time, we played kickball with her family, and Karen ran into me while trying to run the bases. At first she was just trying to be cute or something, but instead she fell down, really hard. In our ensuing scuffle, she got a wild animal look on her face and bit me in the arm. Hard. She bit my arm through my shirt sleeve. My sleeve wasn't enough, she needed flesh. The same way a toddler will bite in anger. She has done it more than once.

This day in Wayan's van, I am looking out the window at the beautiful lush scenery of volcanoes and rice fields, imagining myself Tarzaning through the jungle trees, and then all of a sudden we are back in that kickball field and that wild animal look roars back into Karen's eyes. She grabs me by the shoulder and bites me, and once again she gets my flesh in her teeth and this time she draws blood. I looked down and see the wound. She has bitten me other times, but not this deep.

Did Karen just bite a chunk out of me?

I don't flinch. Don't move. Skin blood doesn't bother me too much. Bone or organ blood gets me every time. My kids know their birth stories and they say "placenta" at me when they want me to give them something. It's my kryptonite. Flesh wounds, on the other hand, are no big deal. In high school football practice, a teammate hit me so hard he stuck his helmet in that same arm Karen bit.

That was junior year. I played wide receiver, and one practice leading into the playoffs, I caught like ten passes in a row and exploited all the holes in our varsity defense. Our star safety, Brandon Brown, got pissed. He knocked my lights out, and the very next play, I caught the ball through all the stars I was seeing and when he tackled me, his facemask stuck in my arm. He went to get up and my arm went with him because his helmet was stuck in me. I see the scar right next to Karen's bite. Now, like then, I am full of adrenaline from the moment and feel nothing. I say nothing too.

Tim does.

"Whoa, easy there, tiger!"

When I finally open my lips, it's to laugh. Karen the tiger! We have been looking for the mythical Bali tiger our entire trip. Wayan assures us it doesn't exist. But we have brought the creature of lore right into his van!

Wayan does what any responsible driver would, tilts his rear view mirror at my face and asks me as professionally as he can, "You need to go to hospital?" I shake my head no, he nods in the affirmative like Alfred when Batman says he will do his own stitches this time, readjusts his rear view mirror to its normal position, and drives us back to Ubud village. I pull out my Tiger Balm and smear it on my tiger bite with another snicker. How can I be mad? Tiger bite, Tiger Balm. It's all good. I'm on vacation. She's probably going to die soon anyway.

Tim starts talking about their new travel plans as if nothing happened. He and Shawna decide to extend their honeymoon a couple days to come back to that spot and take Thai royalty pictures dressed in traditional garb. He shows me the flyer, and it costs thousands of dollars. Shawna has money. The pictures are hilarious. I won't think of the tiger bite for years until I call Tim with divorce news. After he tells me he and Shawna are going down the same path, which everyone tells you when you tell them you are getting divorced, he reminds me of the Bali tiger bite. Then he tells me he still knows people from his old life and asks if I want him to take care of her.

"Take care of her? What do you mean?" I ask.

"You know, take care of it. Her. Get rid of the problem."

Tim wants to euthanize the Bali tiger.

Am I ready to put her down? Tim wants to know. He can have it done for free too, a favor.

I reluctantly decline his offer for a hit but mostly because that tiger will have taken all of my money and I can't afford it. Or should I say her money and "Wii" couldn't afford it.

Wayan drives us through the most awkward drive of my life. I am bleeding from my shoulder, exhausted from keeping Tim alive on one side and Karen alive on the other, and all I can think about was how badly I want to jump from the balcony of our hotel into the pool when we get back. Karen stays in our hotel room at Tegal Sari in Ubud for something like thirty-six hours straight after that. She will not leave for anything. I meet two girls from Australia who are backpacking during this unexpected break. They are nice and pretty and don't want to bite me.

When I was sixteen, my dad took me with him on a business trip to the Gaylord Palms in Orlando. I found two cute girls there to ride with me on the bus to Disney and explore the park. It started raining hard like it does every afternoon at Disney, so the cute girls bailed but I stayed all day until I had to catch the last ferry back to the shuttle at midnight. That ferry floated me magically along the lake beneath the Disney fireworks. When I got back to our room, Dad was snoring. I loved that he trusted me enough to sleep even though I was nowhere to be found. And I took pride in being the kind of son and teenager who would not betray that trust.

However, I made an unauthorized room charge while he slept. It was from the vending machine down the hall. I don't know what led me to try swiping my room key in the vending machine, but it worked and let me buy all the snacks I wanted. I didn't tell Dad about my room key vending machine trick, not because I didn't want to share, but because I thought he would turn off this magical slush fund room key feature. Disney was magic but this was better! I shared my snacks and Dad asked no questions about where they came from because he loves snacks.

The Australian girls in Bali remind me of the Disney girls. I want to go with them. But I stay.

After my final walking break, I return to Karen and we decide to switch hotels. Our new place has Wi-Fi and a library. I read a book about the history of the Dutch East India Trading Company in Hong Kong. When I check my email, I see one from Tim. He has been looking everywhere for us. Shawna kicked him out of their hotel room too and he's holed up in an Internet café down the street.

The homepage of the Internet browser I am using teems with news of the tsunami tearing down Japan not too far from where we are. The same tsunami gets so bad it will delay Honda and Toyota production for six months. This comes in handy for us in January when we are able to get a killer deal on a new 2011 CRV still on the lot in early 2012. But at the time, I wonder if the tsunami will come through Bali and be the thing that sweeps Karen away from me. I daydream about all three of my traveling companions getting swept away in the tsunami. Those whiny punks would die, but Super Matt will swim to the neighboring island and live out his days with the Komodo dragons.

Karen's misery knows no bounds. Tim and Shawna are miserable too. They are rain clouds, but I am like sunshine. The ultimate optimist. Sure, Karen bit me, but it's just a flesh wound, and I have Tiger Balm to treat the elusive Bali tiger bite. Yes, my best friend is a drug dealer, but we aren't in jail yet. Yes, these people suck, but at least I have a tan. Everything has a bright side.

I am not doing a very good job explaining Karen's misery. I try not to worry about it because I'm trying to salvage the trip. I don't think she smiles once during the whole trip. On the beach back in Thailand, I pay someone to spend two or three hours giving her corn rows because she needs them really bad and it will make her happy, and then she hates them anyway. Now we are playing with monkeys, riding elephants, exploring pristine beaches, swimming under waterfalls, really cool stuff. None of it works for her. She does have some completely legitimate gripes with Tim's drug abuse and drug running. Tim asks us to split up his stash pills between our bags before we fly home. Luckily Karen isn't part of that conversation, or she would have snapped worse than ever before. I draw the line there, we will not be smugglers.

At the second hotel in Ubud with the computer and library, something magical happens. Karen has gotten pretty big at this point and weighs either the same as or more than I do. When we first met, I used to sweep her off her feet and carry her around, but with her weight gain, it's been awhile. The pool at the hotel is just deep enough that she can jump back into my arms like when we first met, and the buoyancy works just right so I can hold her there using the surface tension of the pool. We start playing like this in the pool, and it starts raining pixie dust all around us with sunlight twinkling through the rain clouds. The twilight shining just right, the rain falling just right, the pool rippling just right. Everything sparkles perfectly and we are twirling in pixie dust and floating in the pool. Whatever else happens this trip, this moment has healed us. We can go home now and we are good.

We stop over in LA to join the Adams at Disneyland before we go back to Utah to finish our semester at BYU. We pack into the small Costco-special Disney room that came with the vacation package they bought, but the A/C doesn't work and I can't sleep. I sneak into the resort pool at around two a.m. and float there like we floated in Bali. Around six a.m. when it finally opens, I head to the gym. Water is soothing to me. And grass. And weights. I'm a Taurus. If I am lying on grass watching clouds pass by doing leg raises, nothing can upset me.

I didn't sleep much on our Thailand/Bali trip. Can't sleep now. Haven't slept in weeks. In Asia there were hours upon hours when Karen was going down with dengue fever and catching up on sleep and I went off to swim or read or explore.

At breakfast, Aladdin keeps hitting on me. The Street Rat has always been my favorite Disney prince. This Aladdin on this morning makes it his mission to ruin my affinity for Aladdin forever. He bops his head in and out all around me like a fruit fly. I want to swat him in the face like a fruit fly between bites of French toast.

I am in a weird place. I don't want to be around Aladdin or the Adams or Karen. Karen has turned green with dengue fever. We head back to LAX and I start group texting pictures of her with her symptoms to BYU friends and the word starts coming back to me that she has this deadly Asian sickness called dengue fever.

We head straight to the big hospital in Millcreek just down the street from our apartment. By now Karen knows she has the dengue fever, I know it, all our friends know it. This is the end. She's bawling. Eric is the smartest and most well-traveled guy in my circle. He saw it take a life once before, and Karen has all the symptoms.

We didn't take any of the recommended pre-trip international inoculation cocktails for visiting third-world countries. I never do. I roll around in their dirt and their waterfalls and let my body acclimate but stay away from anything raw. Karen ate and drank things, smoothies and fresh fruit, while glaring at my warnings from across the table. Now it's too late and soon she will be dead. There is no known cure for dengue fever. We are quiet on the drive to the hospital. I am towing the line of trying to look hopeful that she will be okay instead of looking hopeful that she won't.

The doctors draw her blood and have her poop on a tray and say something about needing to wait for the blood work and her stool sample examination before we know what she has. But she's a goner. Can't sleep, can't eat, stomach hurts, body hurts, migraine headaches. Karen is dying. She has dengue fever.

I leave her there hooked up to the IV to go home and feed our cat or something feeling elated and torn. Is this the end of my suffering? Could it be? Is this murder since the thought had entered my mind that perhaps Thailand would kill her before we went? Jesus taught that adultery works that way, does murder too? Like if you wish someone will die and then they die, is that the same thing as murder? Regardless of the moral implications, I am certain she will die, and now everyone will feel bad for me and I will be free and loved by everyone for my loss.

I need the peace and relief that will only come with freedom from this woman. I graciously accept the gift of her death. I scream and cry and hallelujah my way through a prayer of thanksgiving that my wife of just under a year will be taken home to heaven where she can be free from depression, free from her parents, free from herself. And I will be free too. When I get home, the omelet I made her the morning we left for Asia remains there on the counter, right where I left it three weeks ago. But it doesn't stink at all.

I really do want what's best for Karen. I think. Her boundless misery makes it completely logical to me that death will be better for her. I believe in a loving Heavenly Father who doesn't want anyone to suffer mentally every minute of every day as much as she does. God loves us and wants us to be happy. Karen is not happy. God still loves her, so the problem is with the other side of the equation.

Karen must be allowed to be happy, as that is the point of God's love and the sacrifice of his Son. Karen has to die so she can go to paradise and be happy. Right?

I go back to the hospital. The doctor says it will be several days before we get the results back from her stool sample. Otherwise she has the stomach flu but seems fine. Apparently they just set her poop on a counter and wait to see if any fungus grows out of it.

It won't. She's completely fine.

She's sitting in her usual spot on the couch, and I ask her how she feels and she says, "Better." I reply in my mind, "What do you mean, better?" Like better as in the small sense of euphoria you get when you say you see a light before you pass? When she says she feels better, my brain shuts down. She's going to live.

I go back-and-forth from feeling dumb that I thought she was going to die to still wondering if the virus will sneak up and take her in the night. I feel too awkward to go back and ask Eric Queathem, "Shouldn't she be dead by now, dude?" I research dengue fever for myself for the first time and see this can't be an accurate diagnosis for her. I sit out on the steps to our apartment and just look at the stars for a long time.

I call my high school friend Caleb Vincent who scored a touchdown on the third play of our state championship football game. The one where I didn't get Academic All-American honors because Coach Orton forgot to do his part on my application, yeah, that one. Before the game, I got a letter from the Dean of SUU congratulating me on my success in journalism and wishing me luck in the game. After Caleb's touchdown, we knew we would win. We did.

I call Caleb, and we talk for several hours. We started doing some day trading and each lost thousands of dollars in one day on a penny stock called Kunekt. Tickersymbol KNKT. If you look back on it in Spring 2011, you'll see this huge spike and then a flatline. We bought during the spike and didn't sell till after the flatline.

After talking to Caleb, I go inside, and Karen is still on the couch watching the Kardashians like she does every night. It's always either the Kardashians or calling her sister to talk about "juicy dish." Anything to distract herself from her miserable life, which clearly is *not* about to end. Damn you, Eric Queathem!

Eric and his wife rave about their trip to Kauai that summer. I will take Karen there next Christmas. I do not ask Eric for any trip advice.

If dengue fever won't take Karen to heaven, then what will? I made it through the first year of marriage, Matt Kennedy, but now things are far worse and not any better. At least last year I had you. Karen was supposed to die. Nothing is working the way it's supposed to.

A lady comes over from Ohio National Life Insurance to draw my blood while I sit on the other couch one day when I am home alone. I sit and think how I don't want her to die for money and that I don't need life insurance on her, yet she demands life insurance on me. It's pointless for her to get life insurance on me because I am indestructible. If marriage to her for a year can't kill me, nothing ever will. There are a few questions on the life insurance form that can jack up your premium:

1. Do you smoke cigarettes? N-o.
2. Do you regularly skydive? N-o.
3. Do you regularly SCUBA dive? *pause . . .*

Why are they asking these questions instead of "Do you walk on sidewalks?" "Do you drive cars?" "Do you have a heart?" All of these things will kill you much faster than sky or SCUBA diving. I used to be a regular SCUBA diver but also a cheapskate, so what do I do? Do I lie on the application? I am not a liar, well, other than living a lie. Being a lie. I don't even want life insurance because we don't have any assets! But as soon as Karen hears about life insurance, I have to get it.

How do I answer this stupid question? How much more will it cost if I answer "yes" anyway? I'm so frustrated by this one question I want to cry.

I only went diving once in Thailand. In Ko Tao with Tim, where I found a moray eel while Shawna was getting her bum cheeks burned off. I didn't dive once in the year before Thailand.

It blows my mind that anyone considers diving to be dangerous. If Tim can do it with two weeks of opiates in him and survive just fine, it must be pretty safe. All these thoughts are my defense mechanism distracting me from the reality that one more activity I love is on the way out. SCUBA is another thing I will need to give up for Karen.

I love diving and accomplished several dives in the years before we met. I always have a diving trip on the calendar. But now I have no plans to dive next year or the year after. I am in fact not a regular SCUBA diver anymore. It's not a lie when I write another n-o. I don't have basketball, don't have SCUBA, don't have friends, and don't have family.

It's an especially lonely morning here alone in my head space on my couch filling out insurance forms for this sweet old medical examiner who takes my blood and my forms with her as she leaves.

Houston

THIS SUMMER, SINCE I AM BANNED FROM WORKING IN southern California with Kennedy, we are in Houston, where I am selling pest control contracts for a different company. This time I recruit a small team so I can earn extra commissions on their sales. I yank the offer on one recruit when I find out he has a criminal record, including robbing the Smith's pharmacy in Provo.

He broke in through the Smith's roof in the middle of the night and left boot prints in the snow, leading the police straight to his dorm within just a few hours. This makes him a convicted felon. I know by now the importance of doing background checks on people before getting into bed with them. He tries to get me to give him a signing bonus to sweeten his offer. I check around and he's done the same thing with a handful of other companies, too. He wants to take the money and run. I string him along enough to get back at him a little bit and bring three other recruits with me to Houston who have no felonies to speak of.

I am working this summer with my old Oregon mission buddy, Clay Cooper. We met when we were high school students. He was an amazing basketball player I witnessed first-hand many times when our schools played against each other. His Millard Eagles beat my Kanab Cowboys every time. Even though we had Tanner, we still weren't as good as Clay and the Millard guys. Clay's brother, Cade, owns a branch of a pest control company based in Dallas, Texas.

Since I can't work for Kennedy anymore, Barrett Pest Control in Houston is a great alternative.

Houston is far enough away that Brian won't visit this summer. Since we are suddenly out of Brian's jurisdiction, my dad will bring my sister to visit! There's a lake full of alligator gar called Lake Livingston, our last name. It's nice to have a fishing outing with Dad to plan and look forward to.

Cade co-owns the Houston branch of Barrett with a nice guy named Seth Watson. Clay introduced Karen and me to Seth and Cade at the Applebee's in Orem. Early in the meeting, Cade pulled up his leg and slammed his Millard-Utah cowboy boots on the table and asked if I liked them. These two are just funny enough to not be obnoxious. And they are smart.

Barrett Pest Control has lots of market share in Dallas, Texas. Cade and Seth convinced the owner Nathan Barrett to let them grow into Houston, Texas. I only speak with Nathan once when I start killing it with sales. I get to a hundred sales before most guys have twenty, so Seth and Cade call and put him on speaker. He's just a rich boy who inherited his wealthy family business. I don't want his praise. I want to ask him when's the last time he went door to door and sweated it out like me.

Here in Houston, I get some space from Karen for the first time in our marriage. I never do things on my own like I used to. This was a huge part of the reason I fell for Karen. She made it so I never had to face myself and spend time alone. When I met her, I couldn't stand myself and was terrified of being alone. When we met. Not so much anymore. Now I am dying to have alone time. I need it.

She makes me promise that we will never be apart and teases me with lingerie if I ever try to leave her at home to do anything. Even if I am leaving to do something she asked me to do. She teases me with lingerie, yes, but doesn't put it on, or does put it on and then gets upset at how bad she looks and hides in our bedroom and locks the door. This pathetic game drives me nuts. I feel so bad for this poor lady. But oh, how I love going on errands for her! She usually sends me to get Mcflurries. These precious minutes of peace and quiet driving by myself are invaluable to me.

She always needs me. I say I don't like it, but it does feel good to be needed. I drive to Houston alone with her cat, Sprite, and she flies out a week or two later after going home to spend some time with her family. She tells me over and over on the phone how she hates being apart, and that we won't ever do it again. I reply like, "Oh yeah, totally, I can hardly stand it. Barely making it over here."

The first year of marriage is over and just like Kennedy told me last summer, things actually do get better. Karen hits a reset button when she goes home before joining me in Houston. She dyes her hair, loses some weight, and we kind of start over when I pick her up at the George Bush airport with a big elaborate welcome poster I made for her. Karen agreed we needed a reset. Just like we practiced on the phone, we pretend we are meeting for the first time, and it seems to work. Karen stops bringing up every past misdeed every time she is mad. In the midst of our restart, she gets pregnant with Rex Matthew Livingston.

She put in work to make that happen. After sex (which works at this point, probably because she is finally relaxing a little bit), Karen lays on her back with her legs up the wall to help the Xs and Ys find each other. She still takes pregnancy tests all the time, so she sees the blue plus sign appear before any biological signs. She bakes cinnamon rolls and writes me a cute note that we have a "bun in the oven."

Any mother deserves all the love and credit in the world for being a mom. For Karen, motherhood gives her a new purpose that she so badly needs. She turns into a complete badass the first trimester with Rex. She's so tough she has me excited. "This is what I'm talking about! I knew there was a real Great One in there somewhere." She makes me call her The Great One to feel better about herself. She calls me the Whiny Boy. In the summer of 2011, she finally earns her self-given title, the Great One. She pukes her guts out almost every day and only asks me to hold her hair so it doesn't get flushed with the chunks. Rex drains her of all her fluids and nutrients, so pooping becomes nearly impossible for her.

After a bathroom break of extreme effort and agony, a ball of poop comes out as big as a grapefruit and hard as a softball and it plugs the toilet. I quickly wrap my hand in a trash bag and take it to the dumpster. On the walk back, I am ready for Karen to yell at me and say this is my fault and she doesn't want to be a mom. She doesn't even complain. If this poop can come out of her, childbirth will be no big deal. Total badass future mom. I will always love and respect Karen as the mother of our boys regardless of what she did to me, does to me, or will do to me. Watching her puke every day for two months with a smile because she will be a mom has to be one of the greatest things I'll ever be lucky enough to take part in. Moms rule.

She's super sick one morning and asks me for a blessing. In the LDS church we believe Jesus sent Peter, James, and John back to the earth to bestow His Priesthood on men just as they once got it from Jesus. The Church teaches that by that time, in the early 1800s, these three apostles had been resurrected, and they helped restore Jesus' original church by returning the Priesthood to the earth. I didn't get my priesthood from Peter, but I can trace it back to him and from him straight to Jesus Christ. We call that a "line of authority," and it's very similar to a family tree. When Karen asks me for a blessing, I ask my summer recruit and fellow Church member Ryan Spille to assist me. After the blessing, he touches me on the shoulder and looks me in the eye and says, "Wow, man, you really love your wife."

Ryan does improv comedy and theater and he auditioned for Mr. BYU while we were both RAs at BYU last year. I usually sell alone, but I like Ryan, and we often sell together. We play off each other really well and we usually make a lot of money when we work together.

A homeowner rolls up on us just as we clamor over the eight-foot brick fence to get into his gated community. Our keen sales instincts kick in together in absolute synchronicity. As the car rounds the corner toward the garage, I am already over the fence standing next to their driveway. I motion Ryan to a spot on the grass beneath him while he holds his balance on the thin brick wall. Then his acting skills take over. He slips his shirt off and holds it taut like a choke rope, intently looking at the spot I motion to on the grass, not blinking, not losing focus. He rocks his hips back and forth like a cat about to pounce on an unsuspecting mouse and coils up and even I am unprepared for what he does next. (It is a really good thing we are right next to my parked car or this unspoken impromptu plan never would have worked.)

Before I am even ready for it, I watch Ryan the velociraptor leap high from the fence in slow-motion. While he soars, his eyes never lose focus on our chosen spot of ground. He hits the ground, dodges one way, then darts the other way, then goes down into the thick weeds. While his body remains hidden, the polo in his hands writhes up from the weeds straight into the air, possessed by some reptilian devil we can only imagine, and then disappears back into the weeds. We see nothing but a rolling mass of skin, shoes, dust, and grass while Ryan fights for his life. Half my attention stays on him to my left, the other half monitors the homeowners in their car to my right. No way they are going to buy this. My heart pounds just as much from watching Ryan's incredible performance as it does from our illegal activity.

They say what made Shakespeare great was what he *didn't* show on stage, leaving the audience to fill in the beheadings and bear maulings with their imaginations. So it was with the demon snake Ryan held in his polo. It fought him so aggressively that no actual snake could have been more vicious. The dumbfounded homeowners come to a dead stop in their driveway as we watch the spirit of

Steve Irwin the Crocodile Hunter take possession of Ryan Spille the Snake Catcher.

Ryan finally comes up bare-chested and bleeding with his Barrett Pest Control polo covering the imaginary snake he just wrangled from our onlookers' side yard. He's actually cut pretty bad. He leaps to his feet and runs quickly toward my car while the "writhing snake" fights like hell. I whisk over to my car and pop the trunk as he throws the snake and polo inside. I slam it shut and we hunch down behind my car to debrief, hearts thumping out of both our chests.

We just don't want them to call the cops.

"Ryan. That was amazing."

"Dude, I think my back is bleeding."

"So are your arms. I'm gonna sell this family a fat contract now. The commission is all yours. Are you okay?"

"Never better. I'll be in the car."

Still nervous that the homeowner would be suspicious and call the cops on us, I walk up to the car. *Fake it until you make it.* Here we go.

The dad parks his car in the garage and comes to meet me with his credit card in hand. First, he thanks me. Then he asks what kind it was. That's how amazing Ryan's acting was. I have never seen anything like it. The guy doesn't even ask for our pricing, just hands me his Amex and asks when his first pest treatment will be. I give him the standard answer: tomorrow, along with all his other neighbors.

The experience reminds me of the first contract I ever sold with Kennedy. The guy just reached in his pocket and handed me his Amex. We tell all the people in all the neighborhoods we are their bug guys. Eventually it always works.

One weekend Karen decides to brave the morning sickness and takes a weekend away with our friends Dan and Sarah. The apartment gets so quiet I read the entire *Hunger Games* series. Before I finish the first book, I know the girl from *Winter's Bone* will play

Katniss and the movies will be huge. Jennifer Lawrence. If you look at some pictures of Karen and pictures of JLaw, they could be twin sisters. My favorite JLaw movie *by far* will be *Silver Linings Playbook* because it allows me to laugh about my wife in what feels like a really healthy way.

Jennifer Lawrence's costar in *Silver Linings* will be Bradley Cooper. Before we have our second child, Karen will tell me I need to grow my hair out long like Bradley Cooper first. No babies until I have Bradley Cooper hair. I also have to bulk up my trapezium muscles like Tom Hardy in the movie *Warrior* because he looks so hot to her. She licks her lips and moans when she sees these guys in movies to let me know I'm not as good as them.

I will do the same reading thing with the *Divergent* series. Read them all in a weekend and tell Karen her girl from *Secret Life of the American Teenager* will be the lead. And again I am right. In our marriage, I am never allowed to be right. That's why I remember being right on those two occasions.

After she returns from the weekend with Sarah and Dan, Karen tells me when she and Sarah were out shopping, she tried using her debit card to buy some designer shoes but it declined since she was out of state. I don't know anything about it, but it's all my fault. I care nothing about designer shoes and am just glad the purchase didn't go through. I am probably too tight with money, but I feel like I need to be because Karen spends way too much. Even with all the money "Wii" made these last two summers, we aren't saving much.

It's hard to believe Dad and Lindsay are coming to visit. Brian is the one who said I can't spend time with my family, and I don't know if he told Karen, but since we are far enough away from Brian and it's just a couple days and Karen doesn't mind, it looks like it's actually going to happen. I haven't talked to Dad much since before my mission, and I'm kind of mad that he messed up all our family dynamics the way Brian said he did, but it will be great to forget all of that and just fish. I got the alligator gar fishing trip all booked and everything lines up perfectly. This will be just like the old days, skipping stones and talking about bitches. Matt and John Livingston are going fishing with fishing guide Jeff Livingston on Lake Livingston an hour north of Houston.

While we fish, my youngest sister, Lindsay, stays at our apartment with pregnant Karen. Karen pretends to be interested in Lindsay's life, asking her questions, and then making Lindsay feel like her responses are not good enough. Textbook Karen. Who's your best friend? Lame. What music do you like? Lame. What do you want to study in school? Lame.

They go out to lunch, and when they come back to the apartment, Sprite the cat has puked all over the carpet. Karen quickly starts yelling at Lindsay for not cleaning it up because pregnant women shouldn't use cleaning chemicals. When Lindsay tries to help clean it up, Karen gets mad and tells her to forget it, it's too late. Lazy lousy guest. Then Karen leaves her at the apartment with no explanation. Lindsay is a sweetheart and doesn't get yelled at very often. Then Karen comes back with slices of cheesecake for both of them and they watch Kardashians as if nothing happened.

We only leave Houston together once to join Karen and her family for a reunion on a mountain lake in Utah. I don't want to go and leave money on the table that I should be making while knocking all these doors in Houston. The trip to Utah doesn't last long, and soon I am back to knocking.

July in Houston gets really, really hot. Ryan and I find spots closer to the ocean where it's a little cooler and breezier just so we can last the day. I get so hot while knocking a neighborhood I fall down on the sidewalk from heat exhaustion and stay there until a guy in a State Farm Insurance truck pulls over and gives me some water. He lives around the corner, and I sell him our pest control. He knows lots of people, so I give him a discount for a bunch of referrals.

I love selling. It distracts me from having to plan ahead about graduating and getting a real job in a few months. Karen and I are both about to enter our last semester at BYU. Then we need to graduate, get off our parents' health insurance, and I need to get a real job for our new family. We will need that new and bigger car the tsunami back in Asia helps us get a deal on. I will have to give up this pretend high-paying job for a real job in Utah. But I don't want to. I want to keep selling door-to-door. I don't like structured jobs with desks and tasks and managers. But no respectable husband does summer sales forever. It's almost time to grow up.

I don't know why the money is always gone. As we head back to Utah, Karen gets us on the government-subsidized health insurance for new families. With all our education and living expenses and since I am a 1099 employee, my pest control money doesn't show as income. Karen hates the idea of being on Medicare, but she's being a responsible proactive mother and does it anyway. I'm impressed and grateful. It won't last very long, but it will get us through most of the hospital bills of having baby Rex in February.

1600 South

Karen gets so mad at my dad on Christmas that he and my mom aren't allowed to come see their first grandson Rex when he's born two months later.

Lucy the Chihuahua has been with us since we picked her up near the end of the summer in Houston. She comes with us when we visit my family for a day or two over Christmas break in Kanab. When Lucy sees the red desert cliffs in Kanab, they tug at her Mexican desert dog heart strings, and she runs out the front door to join her long-lost pack. Then third-term Karen, who's great with child, ventures out of my parents' red-cliff home to retrieve Lucy.

My dad is standing in the kitchen gazing out the window washing dishes, thinking how nice of us to visit on Christmas and that Karen hasn't yelled at anyone yet. That's all about to change. Karen sees my dad smiling out the window and thinks he is making fun of her, a pregnant woman in a Mumu who really could use some help catching this peppy puppy. She storms in screaming at him.

My softest-spoken sister Morgan steps in from her bedroom down the hall and says, "You can't yell like this at us anymore. You need to stop." Karen storms off and packs our bags in Brian's Corolla from Newby Buick where he knows the owners. She drives to the high school weight room where Kyle and I are working out. She seems calm and cool around Kyle because he's a ripped teenage athlete and she wants his approval, but she quickly gets me to come outside. Then she breaks down bawling and says my dad made fun of her and treated her like shit and that he will never see his first grandson and we are never going back to Kanab. The car is packed and we need to leave right now.

Now she's yelling at me over and over again the same as she always does: "You're not taking care of me!" This makes me feel terrible. I want to scream back: "What do you want me to do?" but I already know the answer. No matter what I do it will never be what she wants. Like when the miller's daughter starts spinning gold for Rumpelstiltskin, it was never enough. He always wanted more. Karen will always want more of me. And since I'm not writing or playing basketball or spending any alone time or getting any love from anyone, my tank hovers pretty close to empty all the time. I am losing my sense of self and I can't be my best self no matter how hard I try. Trying to conjure up more to give her from my empty stores has become a self-defeating cycle.

A few weeks after Christmas, Karen writes my parents "the email." She's on the computer all afternoon composing it. My parents and all my siblings will read it. I will never read it; I just can't do things related to drama or games. She writes it to prove her supremacy. She is always right and they are always wrong. Just like the doctor she tried to convince she had a miscarriage. She addresses the email to my mom and says, like Brian told me, that she and my dad didn't do anything right. They didn't raise their kids right. They don't have a healthy relationship. They don't even fold the laundry right. That's actually in the email. She and my dad are bad examples to their five kids, and Karen therefore cannot allow our baby to be around any of them. They are banned. She leaves some hints in the email that if they shape up they might have a chance to visit baby Rex, but no promises. The night Rex is born on February nineteenth, the Provo hospital sets a record for baby births. We watch out the window as the clear black night suddenly turns white with thick snow that raises the atmospheric pressure and pushes baby Rex and all the other babies down and out into the cold dark white world. I felt the pressure change too. In my wrist. I have a half-moon of titanium in my wrist from surgery after we won our football state title senior year. It always feels drastic changes in the weather. I broke my wrist the third game of the season. We started 0-3, and then we won nine straight, including the title. Half of us had something broken by then.

Baby Rex gets a visit from Karen's whole family that afternoon. It's four hours from Twin Peaks to Provo, but they come right away like they have so many times before. Rex is the first grandchild on Karen's side too, and his arrival is a big deal for everyone. My family knows they are uninvited from the hospital. Karen reminds me to make perfectly sure.

The dichotomy of trying to do the right thing tears me to pieces. I'm not even ready to have a baby, Karen decided we have to because she gave up on everything else and just wants to be a mom now! Brian already convinced me my duty is to his daughter, my wife, but this baby boy is not ours to keep back from his family. I don't even know if we can legally tell them not to come. It's so wrong. My belief that Karen will die hibernates for the time being because Rex needs her to nurse him into a healthy life.

My parents are so sad not to see Rex. They have each been in therapy for almost two years trying to cope with the problem my marriage has been since the beginning and trying to be good parents through it all. They hire a lawyer to see if they can sue for visitation rights to see their grandbaby. The lawyer tells them they can't, but they get a second and third opinion that they might be able to. My parents love to walk together. It's not uncommon for them to walk ten miles together any given day. During the long cold lonely winter of 2012, they walk and they cry. They will do anything to see Rex. What can they do?

My mom has a good friend in Salt Lake whom she sends to our town home with lunch for Karen. Karen says no to the friend and sends her back home with the food and asks her to tell my mom, "How dare you try to sneak your way into my home using your friend!" After that my mom sends a gift package for Rex, and Karen complains for days that the UPS man woke Rex up from his nap when he brought it. But she eats all the snacks in the gift box without complaining.

My dad calls me a month later in March to arrange a meeting so he and my mom can see their grandson. Since the day we met, Karen and I often remarked on the similarity of our life flow and family situations. We are both the oldest of five kids; we are both attending BYU in the Salt Lake Valley; both our families live in Southern Utah where we can easily visit on holidays. Family members are constantly passing by us and we are constantly passing by them, and it's very easy to see everyone frequently. These days, regardless of the similarities and geographical closeness, there can be *no* contact with the "unhealthy" Livingstons.

After several weeks of not seeing baby Rex, my mom and dad reach a tipping point. I'm out walking Lucy the Chihuahua and my dad calls. I pace around our town home listening as he tells me how strange I am acting and that we have no right to keep them from their grandson. He has had enough. He hints at getting a court order and I laugh. Karen coached me for this. She knew he would call and threaten to involve the law. Karen always coaches me on what to say to my parents, just like Brian coaches Julie on what to say to hers. I tell him it's his own fault they can't visit. What does he want me to do? He's the one who sleeps in the master bedroom closet and is completely emotionally unavailable to my mom. It's not my fault they are unhealthy, but they aren't welcome with us. I am so sure of myself telling off my dad like that and finally taking care of my wife like she always asks. I brag to Karen about the conversation. In that moment I am the person she wants me to be.

She's so pleased with me reaming my dad she changes her mind on the spot and decides they can visit and see Rex. I just spent an hour telling my dad off, and in two minutes she changes her mind. My joy at her concession is clouded by my anger that I have just been someone else toward my dad. They make the four-hour drive that same weekend. Before they come over, my mom, dad, and youngest sister Lindsay sit in the nearby Olive Garden for two hours to mentally prepare themselves.

Heaven and earth align when the woman now affectionately known as Gramalisa and the baby boy named Rex look into each other's eyes for the first time. Rex makes a noise we have not heard before, a noise that becomes his signature noise, something between a coo and a chuckle. Then he starts snapping his hands with excitement. We call them his crab hands. These two motions become his excitement indicators, and they start right here during his first time laying on Gramalisa's lap. It will be rocky and messy, but Gramalisa will do whatever needs to be done in coming years to see her first grandson Rex.

The economy still hasn't fully recovered from the housing market crash. The age-old Daily Universe BYU newspaper folds, along with all the others. There are no jobs in writing or journalism. Most of my classmates apply to law school. I have a wife who needs cars and clothes and 'cations, so I take the first job I can find, working remotely in sales for a company based in Chicago. My salary: $36,400.

I had made that much in my best *month* the previous summer.

I am drained from the stress of graduating, the stress of preparing for a baby, the stress of losing my family and friends, the stress of being back in Provo. I hate my job from the first day because I am so poor! I'm making barely more than minimum wage! But I get to work from home so I can keep taking care of Karen and protecting her from the world. We have health insurance and they pay me back for my gym membership as long as I go ten times a month. No problem there.

Before I sign the offer, my only special request is for a week of paternity leave to take care of Karen and Rex. When I tell Karen about my new job, she reminds me she should have married a guy who went on to play semi-professional basketball in Europe so she could be rich and not worry about money.

A week after I accept the job offer, we graduate from BYU. During graduation when I read my name in the commencement flyer, I realize that I am not him anymore. I am not Matt Livingston. Not the one I used to read about, anyway. The one I used to read about won championships and set records and set things right. The one I see in this graduation announcement is poor and rude and sad. I am disgusted with myself.

We buy Karen's first new car ever from Ken Garff Honda in Orem where they don't have 2012s yet because of the tsunami that didn't sweep Karen away but did lead to a bunch of still-new 2011s for great deals. We feather our little Orem townhome nest with everything we can pack in there from Babies-R-Us. I negotiate with our landlord every few months to get him to lower our rent. He hires a property manager, and I prepay a few months' rent with my back-end commission check from Houston, and in the shuffle we get a month for free. I am dishonest and don't bring it up.

Karen always has new stuff and we always take trips, but we are always broke. Karen keeps a wishlist of whos-its and whats-its galore without which she might die. I get them all for her. Laser-hair removal, massages, whatever hair makeover she needs again and again, jeans from Nordstrom that don't even fit her. We keep up the "dating" with expensive dinners and a movie at least once a week. She tells other couples who don't go on dates that we go on at least one a week. It's awkward when she does this, because it seems to make other couples feel bad. Karen's grandparents remark how when they were our age, they ate peanut butter sandwiches and stayed home and isn't it nice we are doing so well. I smile to cover up however much of it is on credit cards. It's all part of the Karen show. We are not doing well. We are just as poor as everyone else, but Karen can't admit it.

Karen sets my friend Danny up with one of her friends. Danny served his mission with me in Oregon. He doesn't contact Karen's friend in a manner pleasing to her, and she yells at him next time he comes over. She's just scared Becca won't like her anymore. Becca doesn't care at all. Karen still yells at Danny and calls him a selfish loser and a deadbeat and a bunch of other things. I'm not allowed to talk to Danny after that. He's just as "unhealthy" as my parents. Several years down the road, Karen will call Danny to recruit him "to her side" of our divorce.

Soon after we move to our townhome on 1600 South in Orem, our new church family asks us to speak on Sunday. As long as we are in Utah, we usually go to church because Karen needs the peace of mind that her parents won't find out she is playing hooky. The church leader who invites us to speak asks me how I stay in such great shape. I tell him I couldn't afford not to with all the stress of marriage. He opens up about how he doesn't like his wife or his responsibility of parenting teenage girls. I tell him he can't afford not to exercise either. You just get up at five a.m. and go, dude!

The day we give our talks, while Karen speaks, I don't daydream or mutter to myself as has become my custom. I listen to Karen as she talks about Jesus and the Church, and for the first time it becomes clear to me that she actually doesn't believe any of it. She will never pray with me. When I try to read scriptures with her, she makes fun of me and leaves. Now that we have Rex, I pray with him and read him scripture stories and it really bothers me that Karen never joins us. I hate it. We have no unity in our home. How can any of this be? God wanted me to marry Karen, God wants me to have faith and be close to Him, Karen doesn't believe in God, but I committed to God I would stay with Karen.

In our Church, they often teach a lesson with a triangle where the bottom two points are the husband and the wife and the top of the triangle is Heavenly Father. As you move up the sides of the triangle closer to God, you naturally move closer to each other. I want to call bullshit every time that stupid triangle comes up. The closer I get to Karen, the farther I get from God! I'm not mad at Him anymore and I'm ready to try to hear His voice again.

When we first met, Karen told me how much she loved books and theater and *Les Mis* and Shakespeare and Broadway. But while she was pregnant, she wouldn't let me read to Rex in her tummy. Jean Valjean was still in the convent when she yelled at me about how stupid it was to read this crap and that it wasn't going to do anything for Rex and she just wanted to watch her shows. If it's not *Twilight* or a *People* magazine, she will not read it. She has so many shows now. Every time we move, all she wants is a DVR so she doesn't miss any shows. I am afraid the crappy dialogue from all her shows will rub off on Rex and dumb him down in the womb. Being a first-time parent is hard! Everything scares you. Karen spends eight hours every day watching TV. Reality TV seems like the only thing that helps her relax. Everything runs smoother for Karen while she sits on her couch watching TV.

Karen starts calling Rex "offspring" and goes through postpartum depression. She would rather use a breast pump and have me feed him than nurse him. Especially at night, she sleeps, and I warm a bottle. I am happy to fill in the gap. I love being a dad. It's not hard for me at all. I find it refreshing having a new person to take care of who actually allows my caring. When he's just a few days old, there is a picture of me eating some Panda Express with chopsticks in one hand and holding Rex in the other. This is a really telling photo. First, it's me doing two things at once: this is my life now. Making sales calls on the phone while playing with Rex, paying bills while washing the car, trying to get the bank to reverse one of Karen's late charges while sending work emails. Second, the Panda Express: it shows Karen's mom Julie is there, Julie loves Panda Express. Karen's mom Julie was the angel to me my mom wasn't allowed to be. I don't know how Julie makes it through so many years being the same thing to Brian that I am to Karen. Whatever good is in me is nothing compared to Julie. Julie is the only adult member of the Adams family not on depression medication. Finally, and most importantly: Rex in my arm. He is my life now. When I am working, I am on the phone with one hand and cruising Rex around in his cars with the other. He will spend his toddlerhood on my shoulders, whether we are walking or running or rollerblading.

When he gets older, we play a game of eating with sand and sticks and rocks for breakfast, lunch, and dinner. We play my favorite game when I get him after his naps. He lays there in his crib singing and waiting for me. I peek and hide and peek and hide and peek and hide again. When I finally hop into his room to get him he squeals with delight, flips around in his crib, and buries his face in his bedding, squirming and ready to be tickled.

Karen, meanwhile, can't stand it. She says our games are stupid and wants him to watch more "Baby Einstein." She wants to go back to school for another degree . . . even though she doesn't have a job . . . or career prospects. Her dad has a PhD, and she wants one too. And all of a sudden, three months after Rex is born, she decides we are going to move from our townhome in Orem to one right next to her parents in Twin Peaks. And we have to move now, so she can get out of here and go back to school now, and it all has to be now, and I need to make it happen.

Yes, Karen.

Apartment 2005

Our home is flooding. I don't care. I hope it will all wash away. Karen's brother Mark borrowed my flip flops, and the flood took one of them. Might as well take everything else too. What good is a twenty-pound sandbag going to do against a trillion gallons of water? The levee on the dam broke, all the highways are full of water, why not one more little townhome? I am a sandbag, and Karen's family the Adams are a flood of water. They have drowned me the past year we have been their neighbors, suffocated me and pulled me under their laziness and drama and fake superiority over my family. Now I just want this flood to wash them away.

We have been living only an hour away from my parents' house in Kanab for a year now, and I have only seen them once.

Brian, his sweet and aging dad, and I go pheasant hunting. During the drive, we listen to this Jewish comedian who talked about sex with Jews vs. Mormons. The guy said Jews have a concept of duty. Husbands do their job and wives do their job. When it's time for church, they go to church. When it's time for meals, they eat. When it's time for intimacy, they go into the bedroom. Not Mormons. With Mormons it all depends how they "feel." If they "don't feel like it," they don't go to church; if they "don't feel like it," they skip family meals, and if "they don't feel like it," the wives turn down sex. I laugh out loud hard, but laugh even harder on the inside. This is the story of my life. Karen has absolutely no obligation or duty to me, just a lot of "feelings." Her only obligations are to her parents. Which is less and less fair, because I have all but cut my parents off, but we do whatever her parents want us to do. Attend events, visit grandparents, watch kids. We are in, no question.

She starts her schooling to get her Master's degree down the road in Cedar City like she wanted to, and I rent her an apartment because she's worried about commuting when she may be tired or busy at school. She's long since stopped nursing. I feed Rex formula bottles and lots of eggs. I make the money and take care of the home and Rex, Karen leaves and go to school. She has delusions of greatness to be a lawyer or professor, but I know it won't happen. Not soon, anyway. Not like this. She hates work. She hates being a wife, hates being a mother, she tells me she doesn't feel like any of it is important. She wants other people to think she is important. I need her to distract herself from her misery for my own sanity. Her being gone gives me some space to be alone. I love it. When Karen isn't home, her parents don't come over as often. It's just me and Rex.

The time we do spend with her family, they rain praise on me all day. They start telling Karen's younger sisters "they just need to find a Matt." That's a thing now. I'm not even sure I want to be Matt anymore, but they sure love it. I do want to be a good example to Karen's sisters of how they should be treated. But I don't like being put up on that pedestal. And maybe they can't tell, but we have a terrible relationship. I'm just good at making it all look like it works. Karen's next younger sister actually will marry a boy named Matt in a few years.

My sister Kelly hasn't found a university program she wants to stick with, so she moves in with us. Kelly, like my brother Kyle, swallows her tongue enough to never piss Karen off enough to get herself booted from my life. We find a way to make it Karen's idea for my sister to move in so Karen can be the hero, and she's not home often anyway, so it works relatively easily. Now that my sister lives with us, she opens up to Karen in the evening about some personal and intimate difficulties in her life. My sister has been going back-and-forth with same-sex attraction, and some drug use, and family dynamics, and hasn't found the right balance. Four years later, Karen will twist up all these personal details about my sister in front of a divorce judge in an empty courtroom. A week after that divorce proceeding, my sister will drive her car off a cliff and be lucky to walk away.

Before I left on my mission, Kelly made me a bet. She said, "I bet fifty bucks you get married within a year of coming home." It's just the norm within our church, frankly, especially with the kids who try to do things right while growing up. No doubt a lot of it comes from wanting to finally have sex. You go on your mission, you come back, you get married to a beautiful girl as a reward. She knew I was a sucker, and I suppose deep down I did too. I knew enough to know that I would be nowhere near ready for marriage at twenty-one, but suckers will be suckers. I would much rather finish my Bachelor's at BYU, and maybe my Master's too, and save up a lot of money before I ever got married. When I got home and started dating, I purposely only dated girls who I was sure were not marriage material. That's what dating is all about, right? Dating. Stick to the plan. I would write the reasons I couldn't marry them in my journal. One girl had glasses and I didn't want wimpy vision genes in my bloodline. Another girl had red hair, and I was not willing to go down that road either. No matter what, I was not getting married when I was young and dumb. I also knew I didn't need to start a family before I had a credit card.

When Kelly moves in, I wonder, why did I get married so fast? I did it to make other people happy. I tried to make God happy (at a time I wasn't even talking to Him). Tried to make Karen happy. Tried to make her dad happy. I didn't try to make me happy because I was still sad and lonely and angry that my mission was over. My sister Kelly is always right about me!

Before all this, I didn't want to end up like my dad. I didn't want to be working at Red Lobster as a young, poor, married college student like he was in 1990 with two-year-old Matt in his arms at his graduation. I have the picture in my baby book and love to look at it but didn't want to reenact it.

Kelly knows me, the good and the bad, better than anyone. The night I graduated high school, I took off my cap and wrote her a poem on the flat top-part because I could see she had a rough road ahead with some of the choices she was making. She looked at me with big grateful puppy eyes that night, as she had her entire childhood. She stole my basketball shoes when I wasn't looking to wear them after everyone was asleep. Stole my socks, read my journals, ate my snacks. Moving to Utah from Canada when we were young was hard on us, and Mom bought us a basketball hoop our first Christmas to give us something we could do at home together. The first time Kelly picked up a basketball, it was game over, she found her one true love. We played basketball together for countless hours on that little court with that big hoop. She had rhythm, coordination, poise, and a killer instinct. When she would beat me, I would get so mad. She, like me, was always looking for other people's approval, my approval most of all. As we became teenagers, we didn't spend so much time together, and she found other teenagers who were less busy to spend time with. But we always played basketball.

She's the one person who knows me well enough that when she recommends I do something, which is rare, she is always right, and (now) I always do it. When my wife screams at me and everyone in my life and everyone else leaves, Kelly finds a way to stay by my side. She always stays within reach.

Except when I got home from my mission. She was lost. I saw it when I got off the plane. We all get lost from time to time. But when I met Karen, my sister Kelly was gone. If we had a strong relationship at that point, she would have told me not to marry Karen.

Even though it would have cost her fifty bucks! Girls can pick up on things from other girls that guys may miss. Even from her distant position in my life, Kelly could see I didn't really like Karen and I had some weird duty I was trying to fill, just like she knew I would.

She was just into her senior year of high school, and they made the playoffs in basketball. They were going up against a team they had never beaten. I found the game broadcast from my RA dorm room in Felt Hall and tuned in on the radio. She was on fire! Three-pointer after three-pointer after three-pointer. She scored so many points I couldn't believe what I was hearing. They barely lost, but everyone watching or listening heard one name above all the others: Kelly Livingston. Even though she was off in her headspace acting a little wild, I knew she would be back, and in the meantime she had hoops to center her when the chaos in her head became too loud and red for her to bear. The important thing is that soon we were there for each other again. After the divorce, Kelly will frame a fifty-dollar bill for me and present it to me during one of her trips to Atlanta. Around President Grant's big head she had written: "From the best bet of 2007, in case she does take your every last dollar."

That August, 2012, we bring Kelly along as our resident Rexsitter for our annual La Jolla beach trip to San Diego. I am a loyalty points aficionado. While I am working from home and traveling around a little bit, I rack up points with hotels, restaurants, department stores, even gas stations so I don't have to put our trips on credit cards. I am all over discount deal websites wherever we go. I hate living in debt like we do and do all I can to minimize it.

We go to a tide pool, and I have little six-month-old Rex strapped on my chest in a Baby Bjorn. While we rummage among the starfish, we smell something terrible. I almost puke at first and then again a few minutes later. We look around for the dead seal carcass that must be rolling in the tide. No carcass. The smell is overwhelming. We get back to the car and I unstrap Rex. My entire torso is brown with his excrement. No wonder he kept so calm while we dashed around the surf! I am so proud of him for pooping I throw our clothes away in the parking lot dumpster, wipe us off with his wipes, and drive us off to dinner. Anything he breaks or messes or spills only lasts a moment. I love his messes so much. They are the sort of messes that I can handle. He doesn't judge me or blame me or hate me or hold grudges afterward or say it's all my fault. A lot of my true self comes back out when I get to be Rex's dad. Some dads may not like having an absentee baby's momma, but I love it. It's much easier to focus on him than his mom.

As much as I love him, he loves Auntie Kelly more. He always wants his Auntie Kelly, especially on ocean adventures like in San Diego. That's another reason my relationship with Kelly matters so much. We spent a few years apart, but now Rex brings us closer together more than anything before, even basketball.

Later we are in a little family gathering wherein a helium balloon sticks to the nine-foot living room ceiling. Normally Rex would just sit there and ask someone to get it, but Auntie Kelly knows he can do more. She says, "You can do it, Rex!" so he stands up on the armchair and goes through a couple hip swing motions to prepare to leap. He says, "I can do it. I can do it!" and launches his thirty-inch body toward that hundred-inch high balloon and nearly grabs it. If Auntie Kelly thinks he can do it, Rex thinks so too.

After Rex turns three, they start skateboarding together. From Utah to New York, Atlanta to Miami, Kelly skateboards with Rex. He sits on the board between her legs, clutching her front leg in both his little arms and smiling like the moon as she weaves through traffic. I do the same thing with him on my shoulders while I rollerblade. When we ride down the big West hill in the Central Park loop in New York, Kelly and Rex pick up too much speed and get violent speed wobbles. I routinely go twenty-miles-per-hour on my rollerblades, and while I can't tell exactly how fast they are going, I know it's faster than twenty. They hit a stick more than an inch in diameter and split it in half, and one half hits a guy on a bike, the other flies past my head. This is going to be a bad, bad crash. Except Kelly regains control and they don't crash. Her face is pale and her hands are shaking, but they ride it out. "Again!" shouts Rex.

Most of the time I work from home, but a few times a month I fly away for a few days. When I am gone, Karen cannot handle being alone with Rex. She texts me complaints like, "I have better things to do than be here with your offspring. Come home early!" Even though her family only lives a few minutes away, they are usually busy. That opens the door for Gramalisa to come spend time with Rex! I'm not there so I don't get to see my mom, but Karen hates parenting so she starts asking my mom to come take Rex on outings. My mom is working full time and juggling a few kids still at home too, and we aren't in regular communication, so I don't know the extent of it, but Karen starts setting up playdates for Rex and Gramalisa. It doesn't matter what she's doing or where she's working, Gramalisa finds a way to be there in a hurry. She loves him. Sometimes she sends me pictures of them at the grocery store, at Barnes and Noble, at the park. Not often because she doesn't want to impose or bother me, but every once in awhile. I know I can't celebrate these times with Mom because I'm not allowed to, but I am so happy she gets to see Rex. Until my time-bomb wife explodes again.

Our live-in nanny, my sister Kelly, misses a shift at work while I am out of town. She doesn't get fired or anything, just misses a shift. Mom hears about it and calls Kelly and parents her a little bit. Tells her she needs to not miss work! My wife overhears their conversation and pits Kelly against Mom for getting after her for missing work. Karen loves creating drama like this, it's a situation that doesn't concern her one bit, yet she inserts herself to try and cause drama. She gets it from Brian. They love creating drama. After she talks to my sister, Karen assumes the authority to call my mom on

Kelly's behalf so she knows she is not allowed to yell at her daughter for missing work. Karen calls my Mom right away and calls her a terrible parent, how dare she reprimand her daughter who is eighteen now, she lives with me and that means I am in charge! Then Karen rattles off a bunch of dastardly things my mom did with Rex too, like let him walk on the dinner table and give him an oatmeal bath when he had a skin rash. Karen never forgets anything she hates. And she hates everything about my mom. And she lets it all out now.

Gramalisa is completely shocked and surprised by the phone call, the insults, the tone. With Karen continuing her list of grievances, Mom hands the phone to my dad. Now he gets to defend his wife from the same kind of verbal beatdown Karen gave him last Christmas. He tells Karen it's time to end the phone call because she cannot talk to his wife like this. Kelly's mom. Rex's grandma. Matt's mom.

That's all it takes. Game over for Gramalisa once again.

Karen starts to cry when my dad hangs up and is still crying when I get home later that night. I meet her at her parents' house, where she tells me and her parents and her siblings how loud my dad yelled at her and how evil he and my mom are. We take their daughter under our wing and all they do is yell at us, right, Matt? The whole situation is so ridiculous. I just nod my head like yeah. I will never be able to reason with any of these people. I want to go work out or walk with Rex or do anything other than sit in this room full of whiners. But as they say: happy wife, happy life. She's going to die one day and this will all be over, but it just doesn't look like that's going to be soon. She doesn't even have any cavities. Her teeth have so much enamel! I saw her x-rays, the enamel around her teeth is white and fluffy like big white pillows. She has never broken a bone. She has babies like it's nothing. This woman who is supposed to die seems pretty indestructible to me.

Karen concludes that once again, my evil parents are not allowed to see Rex anymore. Evil Gramalisa and PJ (his new grandpa name, short for Papa John) are immature and unhealthy and irresponsible, and they lose Rex privileges. Just when things had finally gotten better, here we are again worse than ever before.

I don't know at the time, but Karen also has my mom keep Rex in Kanab overnight several times when I am out of town for work. He doesn't sleep many nights as a toddler. We stay up all night and watch *Animal Planet* and eat snacks all the time. He wants to play all night one time in Kanab with my parents. Mom wakes up around two and hears noises coming from the garage. There she finds Rex and PJ, playing with a tape measure and giggling at each other. Toddlers love tape measures, they are tactile and noisy and unpredictable. Like a cat. Not long after this little episode, Karen tells Gramalisa and PJ she trusts them more with Rex than she does her own parents.

In the fallout, Kelly moves to a basement bedroom for rent across Twin Peaks in a home she soon discovers is a drug house. She's only been there a month when they party too hard one night. Kelly gets home and a guy runs up to her and says, "I just have to tell you there's cocaine in this house and I just took a lot of it!" Someone calls the cops and several people leave in handcuffs. The next day I help Kelly move into an apartment with old friends and she falls back into old habits, but at least they don't rave like the other house.

I take Karen to Vegas for Rex's second New Year's Eve at the end of 2013, and Rex stays with her parents. He stays up all night like usual and we don't hear the end of it for weeks. "We can't believe he didn't sleep, why would you leave us with a toddler and keep us up all night, worst night of our lives." Just like Brian when he couldn't pee in our Irvine apartment.

Vegas is a bust. Karen makes me promise to take her, but I hate it. I work in Vegas a lot and prefer to stay in Summerlin to keep away from the casinos. The strip, the shows, the creatures, they are all too loud and too nasty for me. Karen has been thinking and talking more and more about the big tattoo she wants to get that is banned in our church. She takes me into a tattoo parlor and tries to actually get a tattoo on the spot. I stand my ground, and that completely ruins what's left of the night. We go back to the hotel, and she eats a mountain of French fries with miniature glass bottle Heinz ketchups and watches reality TV.

Early Sunday morning, I come home from a church meeting and see Gramalisa sitting there on the sidewalk. She clearly hasn't slept. She awoke at three a.m. and drove over because she couldn't sleep and needs to see Rex. She asks me when she can see him again. I tell her that as far as I know, we have decided she probably doesn't get to see Rex again. I am the most loyal of husbands. Still I walk inside and wake Karen up to petition her to let Rex see his Gramalisa just for a minute. Just this one last time. Please. She's been up all night and sitting outside for an hour, can she just hold him for a little bit?

Karen concedes this one last time. Gramalisa comes in and dresses Rex for church, hurriedly, and then we part ways. She waves to us and cries as we drive away to church. On her drive home she will keep crying, and she will cry and cry and cry. I can feel her sadness all day, but I am not allowed to care.

Mom is a full-time Master's degree student at the same school as Karen at the same time as Karen. Mom is also working full-time in Kanab and has two kids at home. For more than six months, she goes way out of her way to be at Karen's disposal to watch Rex, only to have Rex taken away instantly at Karen's pleasure. Gramalisa calls her mom to get help too, my GramaRee. GramaRee lives in a little trailer off Bluff Street in Twin Peaks. She meets Karen a few times. GramaRee tells her daughter the second-best compliment of her life. GramaRee says, "Well, it's obvious she is just jealous of your beautiful family, Lisa."

My mom and GramaRee have a difficult relationship. I won't learn the details until years after my divorce, when Mom and I bond over the truth in the hardship and heartbreak in our lives. GramaRee was hard on Mom all through her youth. She was hard on her for marrying Dad. Mom didn't often turn to GramaRee for help. But she did with the Rex situation. That's how impossible it was. When GramaRee told Mom of Karen's jealousy, it helped Mom realize it wasn't her fault. She only gave my mom one greater compliment, after a few of us had been born and we were still living in Canada: "You are a lovely mother."

With the Adams, it's like the whole world is part of a caste system, but only Brian knows everyone's spots. So if any citizens of the world want to know where they fit, they have to ask him. Doctor Adams and his family are royalty, John Livingston and his family are beggars. I am lucky Karen stooped down to marry me. During Thanksgiving, King Brian sends the proclamation to the beggars of the kingdom they get to be like him for a day, and he asks me to invite my Dad to go shoot shotguns with us. The usual shotgun crew is Brian, his dad, his son Mark, one or two of Karen's cousins, and myself. But this time, my dad is coming along too.

My earliest years were spent on my paternal grandpa's ranch in Alberta, Canada. My dad dropped out of flight school to trade his student loan for a personal loan to save the ranch for his dad. We grew up shooting gophers, badgers, ducks, and any other game or pest that crossed our crosshairs. When I was two, my dad took me to a duck-filled swamp to scare the ducks into the air so he could knock 'em down with his twelve-gauge shotgun. He shot a duck and it landed right at my feet. There was nothing Dad couldn't shoot. He's what they call a dead eye. If he sees you with his shooting eye, you're dead.

My parents finally gave up after five rough years on the ranch, and we moved to British Columbia for my dad to go back to school. It was already deep into the school year, so I homeschooled with my mom. Dad didn't take his guns with us. We had to get creative when varmints crossed us in British Columbia. A skunk made the mistake of repeatedly knocking over our trash bin at night. It sprayed our van, too, and Dad suspected it started sneaking in through the cat door. Since Dad didn't have his guns, he stayed up late crouched by the cat door with a tennis racket in his hand. Right on cue, the skunk crawled through the cat door and into the target zone. My dad whacked the skunk so hard with the tennis racket he sent it back out the cat door and against a wooden pillar in the garage, where it slumped dead. The next morning, I lifted the garbage bin lid and saw the dead skunk.

The day we all go shooting during Thanksgiving break, Brian is throwing the clay pigeons to the shooters. Left-handed and cross-eyed though he may be, he knows how to throw clay pigeons perfectly. Just like the Native American spirit who threw the stars into the night sky where they stuck forever, Brian throws clay pigeons just right so they hang in the air for what seems like forever, making for easy targets and perfect shots. Except for now that my dad is shooting. He's throwing really fast and nasty ones. They are roaring fast, switching directions, curving left and right, and Brian calls them roosters. Clay pigeons are meant to simulate real game, like a rooster pheasant. The fun comes from throwing clays that can be shot, not out-throwing the shooter.

"Ready for another rooster, John?" taunts Brian. "Oh, ya missed him, here's another one for you!"

My dad hits some of the clay pigeons, but not many. He plays a good sport and keeps trying. I say nothing.

We take Rex to Oahu for his first Christmas. He eats more sand than food. Karen wants to go to the luau at the Ko Olina Marriott, but it costs three hundred dollars per couple. Rather than pay, we willingly walk into the time-share pitch presentation like all couples do at some point for some requisite opportunity-cost trade-off, only to say how much they regret doing it afterward and how deceptive the programs are. It's still worth three hundred dollars in luau tickets. I paid for the entire vacation with loyalty points I accumulated while traveling for work. I hate my job because it pays so little. But working from home ninety percent of the time makes it worth it.

I travel about eight days a month. I do the math and find that with all the accumulated hotel, credit card, and airline points I earn in those eight days, I actually make more from the monetary value of my travel rewards than I earn in salary dollars. Karen and Rex often join me on Seattle or Denver trips. Anything to not be left alone with Rex. Work is easy, my schedule is easy, the pay is meager, but I have a big travel budget. So I use it wisely and rack up the points to pay for lavish vacations.

During the timeshare presentation, Karen gets our presenter fired. She decides to pretend to be deaf so we can get out of it sooner. Our sales guy Octavio hates his job and tells us as much early on in his pitch. Strange way to try to sell dream vacations. He jokes about getting fired and hating his job and ripping us off. Then he says we are wasting his time. This makes Karen feel poor, which we are, and she can't take another instant of this abuse. Deaf Karen turns on the waterworks and a supervisor comes in and cusses out poor Octavio and sends him home on the spot. While we wait for the supervisor to return, we decide what to say to him. Karen decides the supervisor doesn't know she was playing deaf, so now she isn't deaf anymore and the fact that Octavio told him she was makes the supervisor more sympathetic, and he gives Karen whatever she wants. We get Luau tickets, hundreds of dollars in resort credit, vouchers for equipment rentals, and a room upgrade.

I accidentally let the story slip at a Rook night with Karen's parents, and they start dying with laughter. Karen yells and cries at me for telling them and puts me in the "dog house" for weeks. The dog house means basically I am not allowed in our bedroom and she gives me dirty looks and won't talk to me and I have to tell her extra sweet things I love about her. I am in the dog house a lot, somewhere around once a month.

Another asset I have from work is tradeshow giveaways. I go to a lot of conferences and trade shows, and many of our vendors will give me all sorts of stuff for free to show at the conferences. I am really good at getting in with the conference organizers and securing a short speech in front of the whole group of attendees, so I use that face time to secure the free items. All the vendors want me to get up in front of the entire conference and demo their item for them. After the conference, I keep the item and sell it on Amazon or eBay. I am really good at this. I make hundreds or thousands of extra dollars a month doing this. I also email random companies from my work email address asking for free samples. Usually they send me a few dozen, straight to my home address, no questions asked.

I sell braces and duffel bags for hundreds of dollars. I sell educational tools for hundreds of dollars. I even sell a lightning detector for three or four hundred bucks. Anything I can get my hands on. We have racked up several thousand dollars on interest-free credit cards I am always opening up, but I need to keep it to a minimum. This is the first time I have ever lived beyond my means, and I hate it but will make it work. I hustle and hustle some more. I need all the money I can get because we spend so much on her car payment, rent, all the TV and Internet and cell phone and movie subscriptions, eating out, Karen's other apartment, Karen's Master's tuition, and lots and lots of movies.

While I hate being poor, I love the flexibility of my job. I also love the owner of the company, Susan Rogers. Everyone loves Susie! When she first hired me, she and her husband Rob took me out for sushi and seaweed salad, and that little gesture meant a lot to me. Every year she takes me, only me, to a conference at Big Sky ski resort in Montana during Super Bowl weekend. We work all morning and ski all afternoon for three straight days. My first time on this trip, in my efforts to impress her, I did a front flip on my snowboard. In the video our friend Ben took, which is still on YouTube, she says, "Oh wow! Would workers comp cover this?"

2012 rolls into 2013, and Brian decides I need to go back to school so we don't have to be poor forever. I've been backpedaling with Karen since we met and haven't really had time to set professional goals or make professional plans of any sort. It's frustrating, I'm not writing at all anymore, which I used to do for work and loved it. My initial reaction to going back to school is "No way!" I will barely have enough to pay for Karen's tuition this year to finish her Master's. Who will pay for Karen's online shopping if I am in school, and who will pay for my school? Julie often brags about working as an RN to put Brian through his Master's and PhD, staying up all night working long hours in the NICU. That's because Julie is made of gold. She has every right to brag. Karen just won't do this. I know that if I go back to school, I will have to find a way to pay for it, which means I will need a student loan. And how will we take care of Rex? I have him seventy-five percent of the time as it is, Karen only survives her couple days a week with free babysitting from relatives. Wherever we move for my Master's, we won't have family nearby.

I am stuck. It is impossible for me to progress in my career and take care of my family. I don't want to think or talk about going back to school. It just doesn't add up. But Brian insists.

Brian wants me to get a law degree. We run his three-mile loop together most mornings, which means he has all the time he wants to tell me things. He tells me about which credit card he used yesterday, how much he has left on his mortgage, the cash balance in his safe, how many rounds of shotgun ammunition are in his stockpile, which BYU football games he will go to that year. He talks and he talks and he talks. He praises me on how smart I am and tells me how well I will do in law school. I want to want to go to law school. I really do. My best friend Dan is getting ready for BYU law school in the next few years. But I just can't do it. All growing up I read John Grisham books, and Mom always told me she thought I would be a lawyer. The fact is, I know I will not survive four years of a full-time

JD while taking care of Karen and Rex. It's too long, too expensive, too hard. So I decide to get my MBA. I find the fastest and cheapest MBA within one day's drive; Utah State University. Done. As soon as Karen finishes her Master's this summer, we will move to Logan and buy a house and I will get my MBA.

Karen's Master's is just a distraction. It's in the vague discipline of "communications," and she has no real emphasis, no real direction, and no job prospects upon graduation. She wants a Master's so she can tell all the other wives she has a Master's so they will know she is an expert on anything she says, they cannot argue with her, and she is better than them. I know this but I don't care because it keeps her busy from thinking about how miserable she is. And it keeps her out of the house.

During the morning runs with Brian, I keep waiting for him to say to me, just one time: "I know Karen is crazy and it must be hard on you like it was on me." Just please acknowledge that she is bat shit crazy. I will feel so much better. Nope. He never hints at it. Never even a smidge in that direction. I want to tell him, "You know that love of sports you gave her on these runs when she was in high school didn't work? She actually hates sports. And she hates running." But I never do.

Brian tells me about the one other psychologist on the earth he respects besides himself. Only her, she is the only one in the whole world. He has read everyone else's research and they are all idiots and perverts except for her. They are all just in it for fame or money, and they all just want to get a book deal or sell you prescription pills. He says his level of proficiency as a psychologist came straight from God, and when he tells someone to do something, it's because he gets it straight from God. He gives me handouts to use in the lessons I teach at church. He also has Karen and I meet with him privately so he can give us lessons.

The lesson he gives us most often is "two halves of the brain." Matt is one side; Karen is the other side. Both our brains are half Matt and half Karen. Matt doesn't do anything Karen wouldn't approve of; Karen doesn't do anything Matt wouldn't approve of. This makes it easier to reconcile things like not talking to or spending time with my parents: Karen wouldn't approve of it! Karen doesn't seem as concerned whether I approve of her decisions.

He has me proofread his therapy manual that he says soon will be adopted globally as the new addiction recovery guide for our church. If only someone would read it, he says, they would know it's inspired by God. He says he knows so-and-so, who will hand it off to so-and-so. He asks Karen to help him make it into YouTube videos so he can share God's teachings with the world and get the attention they deserve. He is just God's instrument to help make people better.

These delusions help me realize Brian suffers a lot too. Just like Karen. His father's health is waning, which makes Brian the glue that holds his difficult family together. Brian has two sisters who married men he doesn't approve of and both of them have struggling teenage boys without decent father figures. Brian feels like it's his responsibility to insert himself and be the father figure for the cousins. He stretches himself into his immediate family and tries to save them with his teachings. His sister who lives across town married a "bum" Native American named Ronnie, and they always need money. Brian takes care of them. He often refers to guys he doesn't like as "bums."

As the oldest boy, Brian is also the executor of his parents' estate. He talks about his inheritance a lot and knows there will be family squabbles when his parents pass away. He tells me often part of it will come to Karen and me. Lots of guns and money are in my future. After the talk of our inheritance, Brian often says how he just wants to retire and stock shelves at a grocery store. He craves the repetitive work of not having to think about anything or fix anything. He just wants to grab the cans of green beans and stick them on the shelf. He turns into a simple man when he talks openly about his dream to stock shelves. I kind of want to go stock shelves sometimes, too.

When Brian talks about stocking shelves, it reminds me of my favorite job in high school. The same kind of hard, mindless, repetitive, liberating work. I worked at Kanab Furniture where the owner, Phil Baird, owned a moving company too. Delivery, assembly, disposal, and relocation of large, heavy objects. I loved it. One time Phil sent me out of town to pick up a new sixty-foot moving trailer for him. He sent me to Las Vegas to pick up carpet. Phil's fabulous wife, Gay, let me borrow her convertible for my senior year Homecoming dance. "Just don't leave the top down in case it rains. It always seems to rain when the top is down overnight, even if it's not on the forecast." I got home late and left the top down. It rained cats and dogs all night. The upholstery was completely soaked through. Gay just laughed.

Working for The Movers was my favorite job ever because it was so hard and monotonous and rewarding. No thinking, just moving. One time we moved over thirty thousand pounds in one day. On the truck, to the destination, off the truck. We started at six a.m. and finished well after dark. I have never worked a harder day in my life. I loved it.

Brian often takes jabs at Karen for going back to school to get her Master's degree. Playing cards at night, she will say something about a project or an assignment, and he looks her in the eye, completely ignores what she said, and changes the subject as if she said nothing at all. I look around and wonder, is anyone else in the same room as me? How can anyone be that rude? Karen is closing the gap on him and his untouchable PhD, and he knows it. She starts mentioning that she wants to go on to get her PhD too. Things get tense around Brian when Karen says she wants a PhD too. He deflects and subject changes and redirects her the best he can. It's Matt's turn now to start applying for his MBA. Karen's turn is almost over. My turn. I don't want to do it, I can already feel the burden of student loan debt and a wife who is going to do anything to get out of being home with Rex, but I am going to do it. I hate my job and hate living in Twin Peaks, and it will be easy to get into Utah State, which is in the exact opposite corner of Utah from where we live now. Change sounds good.

Brian and little baby Karen watched a lot of violent R-rated movies while Julie was working RN hours and Brian was doing his PhD. She tells me that's where her love for violent and profane action movies comes from. I hadn't seen many R-rated movies at all before I met Karen. R-movies are a regular part of our routine now. Sex, violence, profanity, all things I stayed far away from before I met her. In our church we don't watch Rs unless maybe it's *Saving Private Ryan* or *Passion of the Christ.* Those are R for a reason. Because I didn't grow up watching R-movies, I don't feel good about watching movies with nudity and swearing. But I do it anyway. I am getting comfortable with feeling uncomfortable all the time.

After three years of marriage, I finally see Karen's baby book for the first time. She's seen mine many times. When I see hers, she is mortified. She leaves the room and won't even look at it, so her sister Rachel, who gave me her phone number, gives me the commentary. The book is short and Karen isn't pictured extensively, but it's still cute! Her hair is cut short and she dresses like a tomboy. I gather that she hadn't been a tomboy by choice and that her dad had been expecting a boy and was not happy that his oldest child was a girl.

When Brian was really young, his only brother passed away from leukemia. Brian's parents bring this up from time to time, usually during reunions or holidays, always with a really somber tone and often with tears. He battled the cancer and they all watched him slowly die. After I learn about Brian losing his brother, I stay up late more often crying with gratitude that by the grace of God I have been allowed to keep my one brother. I pray that he won't get kicked out of my life like my parents.

For all the things Karen hates, she loves Halloween. Our first Halloween together in 2009, we dressed up in skin-colored tights as Adam and Eve, and I put real grape vines on my loincloth. Her friend

Heather ate one of the grapes. Now in 2012, we have a baby to use as a prop, so we go for a cowboys and Indians theme. We meet people all the time who ask Karen if she is part Native American, or aboriginal Australian, or Middle Eastern. Some of her cousins are, Patrice's bum husband Barry has Native American blood, but not Karen. Sometimes she is strikingly beautiful, like a Disney princess. When I first saw her teaching my Comms 101 class, I liked her nose and drew a picture of it. So our one Halloween living in Twin Peaks in 2012, we dress up as Native Americans and dress little Rex up as a cowboy and strap him up on my chest where he made the dead seal smell poop a couple months ago. Hands down our best costumes ever. We both get spray tans and Karen wears traditional moccasins and a beaded leather dress. I am in a loincloth with wolf skins draped over either shoulder, hair shaved into a Mohawk, full face and body war paint, moccasins too. I would wear it every day if I could! Rex has his button shirt and jeans, a horse, sidearm in a holster, and boots.

Karen doesn't have a lot of stamina for walking or exercise, but on Halloween she goes all night with no complaints. We host a huge couples game night at our apartment and then trick-or-treat until after ten p.m. Rex falls asleep on my chest and I feel so needed, my sense of adventure is satiated too, and I am so liberated not having to wear clothing all night long. We get home late, which is great because it means I don't have to find a babysitter and take Karen on another date that night.

Karen hates being home in the evenings. She always wants to be somewhere else. If we stay at our place in the evenings, it means we are losers. And if we are home, she grunts and hmphs and watches reality TV and eats ice cream. She wants dates and shopping. When she comes home on an evening or for a weekend after she has finished a school assignment or taken a quiz or passed a test, she wants me to give her a reward. Like a new pair of shoes or jeans or a trip. I think it's the stupidest thing I've ever heard. You're in school, I want to say, this is your job! But when I fail to reward her with shopping or a getaway, she cries and says I must not love her and eats more ice cream.

I never really learn much more about Karen as a kid. She watched violent movies and dressed like a boy. When Brian and Julie talk about Karen's brother Mark, they say he always wanted to sleep rather than be around anyone. Most rational thing I've ever heard about dealing with the Adams. Had they been my parents, I would go back to bed too! In the home where I grew up, we hiked and explored and cooked and camped and worked together. The Adams do a little bit of this but mainly just eat snacks and watch movies. Those are the rewards, the things they live for, the things they love.

Brian and Julie talk about their kids' childhoods strangely. We have Karen the tomboy and Mark the Eeyore from *Winnie the Pooh*. How mean! The memories are not nice or pleasant. The only other childhood memory Brian shares about Karen came when she bit him so he spanked her so hard he broke his thumb on her bum. When I hear this story, I think someone should have called the cops, but her family thinks it's the funniest thing ever, and they laugh on command just like when Brian calls them beached whales. Karen has bitten me a handful of times when she's mad and it doesn't hurt that bad. And now she's an adult!

During the 2012–2013 year in Twin Peaks, I figure out a disturbing truth. I am the son Brian wished he had. The surrogate for his brother who passed away when they were kids. Karen is a girl, and Mark is a bum. Brian wants me to be his chosen one. I need to get away from him, and we need to move, and maybe me going back to school isn't a bad idea after all. But we can't live in St. George anymore. It's just too weird for me. Karen's family stresses me out.

Then the flood comes just a few months before we move in Spring 2013. It sounds like freedom. Just like the tsunami that massacred Japan when we were in Bali on Tim and Shawna's honeymoon. Wash me away, wash them away, wash everything away. Please! While I sit on the flooding stairs and daydream, the Adams squabble about carrying our sofa and recliner upstairs. I get up and carry each heavy piece of furniture up the stairs by myself while they quarrel. Karen yells at me because she has gotten really upset and wants me to be just as upset too. I am not upset about the flood at all. What's there to be upset about? It is what it is. My disappointment sets in as I realize the flood isn't big enough to take any of them away. Is Karen really even going to die? Now she has survived a near tsunami strike, a childbirth, a flood, two semesters of commuting herself to Cedar City for her Master's, what on this earth is going to kill this woman?

I'm not naturally stressed out. Now I've been stressed out for over three years straight. I hate my job. I hate being poor. I hate hanging out with miserable Karen and her miserable family. We just need to go. So we will. We decide to use what little savings we have to buy a house on the opposite end of the state so I can go back to school. It will only be a year and only cost around thirty thousand dollars in student loans. However much Karen hates it, it will be progress, and it will be better than this. I need us to buy a house so Karen doesn't feel poor living in an apartment. She is on Zillow all day, and at least a home is a good investment. Better than her online shopping all day.

We take several trips to Logan to find a home. I can work wherever I want in the Western USA, so I drum up a lot of business in Logan. My brother Kyle attends Utah State University in Logan, and he's the secret reason I am 100% committed to moving there and going to school and buying a house there.

While I am taking work trips to Logan and visiting Kyle at Utah State, our church lowers the mission age for young men from nineteen to eighteen. Kyle just turned eighteen and he can't wait to go. I do the math and see that when he gets home, we will be in school together at Utah State. This is all going to work out! Just like Kennedy had given me a deadline to get me through my first year of married life, Kyle gave me a deadline to get through my MBA. When

Kyle gets home, we will get at the very least several months together as brothers at Utah State University. Yes!

That Christmas, 2012, Karen and I make a rare trip to Kanab for Kyle's mission farewell talk at church. He speaks about the faith of David in the face of his battle with Goliath. Kyle turns white with conviction and spiritual power as he talks. Kyle is David. Not because of his strength, not because of his leadership, but because of his faith. All David has are five stones and a leather sling to fight the greatest combatant the world has ever known. David believed the Lord would deliver him. Kyle believes. And I believe, too.

I want to be there for him when he returns from his mission mainly because of how badly I hurt when I returned from mine. Being there for him doesn't mean telling him what to do or how to live his life or who to marry or what to study. I want to be there for him to tell him I love him and that even though it sucks, he will feel better soon. I think about how sad and lonely I was when I got home, and I want to make sure he doesn't have to go through the same thing. Two years later when he returns from his mission, I will be there in Logan waiting for him.

But it won't be Kyle who will need me. I will need him more. I need him now even before he leaves, but it's not my turn yet. I do the math and figure he will come home Christmas 2014, when I will be halfway done with my MBA. That gives me a solid five months of Kyle before I know we will have to move to get Karen her PhD.

I'm learning how things go with Karen. She has been talking about a PhD the entire time she has been doing her Master's. She needs her Master's so she can apply for her PhD, and she needs her PhD so she can be level with Brian. I need her to get her PhD too. As long as she feels like she is achieving greatness, she stays distracted from herself. I see her cruelty toward me and Rex as simply an outward expression of her inward depression. I have issues with myself too, obviously. I have been trampling all over myself for three years by staying in a relationship where I am made fun of and bitten. It will be several more years before I finally admit that I can't do it anymore. I know that in two years I will need my brother more than ever. I can do anything for two years if it means I get to spend time with my brother at the end. 2013 to buy and fix up a house, 2014 to start my MBA, then in 2015 I get to spend some time with Kyle.

When I first got home from my mission in Oregon, I spent a month in Kanab with Kyle before I went back to BYU. It was one of the best months of my life. The shock of getting home and all my anger and pain hadn't set in yet. My real life hadn't started, and we had a month of summer to do whatever we pleased.

During that month, we did everything together. I took him with me to work at my old job at Kanab Furniture. We rode our little 50cc motorcycle into the red mountains for picnics with a little propane BBQ and a cooler strapped to the back. We went to the high school weight room every day, where we could lift a metric ton together.

We went spearfishing on Cedar Mountain. Even in summer, you are at an elevation of seven thousand feet, and the water is really cold. I may be the only spearfisher ever to shoot for rainbow trout at Duck Creek Lake. Certainly the only one without a wet suit. When we got there, he felt the water and was like, "No way, bro." Smart decision. He's always been the more rational of the two of us. I dove off into the freezing lake for about twenty minutes with my speargun and snorkel. When you are in cold long enough, it starts to feel warm. It tricked me. When I came out of the water, I was purple. Hypothermic. Shaking uncontrollably. I wasn't in any shape to drive. Kyle just barely turned fifteen, so I had to drive home. He tried warming me up with some weird little dog they rescued while I was in Oregon. He laid the dog on me like a blanket, then tried rubbing the little dog onto my skin to keep me alive. We survived.

For his birthday, we went camping near Tropic Reservoir and ate steaks marinated in Barq's root beer. We hunted snakes and lizards with our .22s and slept under the stars. Kyle loved nights like that as much as I did.

When Kyle was ten, we drove to Lake Powell several weekends in a row to get SCUBA certified together with our sister Kelly. During the hour drives each way, we listened to an album called *The Rising Tied* by Fort Minor. After marrying Karen, the chorus from the single on the *Rising Tied* album goes through my head as I think about my family. It's about leaving, being lost, being missed, and not coming back. It reminds me of myself, it reminds me of my dad, it reminds me of my mom, it reminds me of all of us. I remember that we all need healing, we all need to come back home. But I'm still gone. And I have no choice but to stay gone.

I have moments of intense sadness, but I bury my feelings quickly. I made my bed and I am sleeping in it. Figuratively only. Literally I am usually sleeping on the couch, in "the doghouse." I am her "dirty dog" husband who belongs in "the doghouse" most of the time.

In the Spring of 2013, we find our house, right on schedule.

One of Karen's best friends from high school lives in Logan now too. Mindy and her husband Kyson recently married and spend a lot of time with us on our house hunting trips to Logan. Kyson and I go ice fishing, and in four freezing hours we catch one minnow the size of a gummy worm. That's why I spearfish, you can swim right up to the ichthyoids and shoot them! No waiting around for them to bite your worm. Kennedy and I went deep-sea fishing once too and I didn't catch anything then either.

Kyson works for Mindy's Dad, Bill, a tall quiet farmer who owns a ton of student housing in Logan. He lives off the grid in his own house he built on his own land and eats his own livestock and his own produce. I love Bill. After I hang out with Bill a few times, I want to tell Brian, "You talk too much."

Bill reminds me of how my dad could be if his life on the ranch worked out the way he wanted it to. The ranch in Alberta did not work out, so Dad went back to school and became a teacher and we moved to Utah. I won a poetry contest in middle school for a poem I wrote about my dad. Several publishers picked it up. It's called "Capitulation":

> Dreamer Johnny feared how he would look
> If his pathway his heart laid he took.
> He conformed to the norm,
> And performed with the swarm
> Of like people, likewise dreams forsook.

I love being around Bill. He shoots skunks and digs ditches, and I get to help out because Bill has Kyson invite me. Bill has a pond in his backyard where baby Rex catches his first fish.

As we get ready to move to Logan, Mindy starts getting terrible headaches and gets diagnosed with Multiple Sclerosis. She and Karen haven't spent much time together in over ten years, but now Karen gets even more excited to live in Logan because she wants to be there for Mindy. When we move, Karen starts doing things to try to impress Mindy. She asks Mindy what kind of cowgirl boots she has and has me buy her a couple of pairs. She asks Mindy's mom where she gets her hair done and then goes there and gets her hair crimped the exact same way. It's not a good look for Karen. Mindy catches on and asks me, "Why is Karen trying to be like me and my mom?"

Mindy's sickness puts me back into check about my own little problems. Yes, I have a mean wife, but Mindy has Multiple Sclerosis. She hurts so badly she can't walk sometimes and has random bouts of blindness where she can't see. I am so pissed that of all Karen's friends, Mindy comes down with MS. She works hard and really believes in the teachings of the Church and actually listens to her husband. She doesn't need things to make her happy. She and Kyson manage student housing apartment buildings for Bill, and they live in this teeny little trailer next to one of the buildings. Mindy loves it because they live for free and it meets their basic needs while Kyson works through school. Karen makes fun of them every time we visit, and I wish Karen would stop and become more sensible like Mindy.

Before we move to Logan that summer of 2013, I get permission for my family to join me at the trampoline park down the street for my birthday. It is the most awkward party. None of Karen's family come except for her, and she just sits by the cake and watches us jump around with a frown on her face the whole time. She tries to keep Rex over by her but he keeps running to PJ and Gramalisa, and she glares at me and I don't care. Eventually she leaves. I'll deal with it later. Kyle and Kelly and I have a blast, and my parents and other two sisters kind of join in, but it's awkward. My mom and dad are being supportive even though they were supposedly never going to see me again. We can't talk openly or honestly because Karen is in charge, and she will be back soon to tell us our time is up.

One of the obstacles has us run against a bungee cord like runners do in strength training. If you run all the way to the end, you grab the handle and secure yourself to unstrap the bungee cord. But if you don't make it to the end, you get ripped backward and land on your bum or your head or both. It's hard to do! After I reach the handle a couple times, my sister, Kelly, goes for it. She gets close but reaches her failure point just a few feet shy of the handle. As she loses her footing, I leap onto the obstacle and grab her hand and pull her those last few feet to the handle. Her smile makes it a perfect birthday. She is going through her stuff and I am going through my stuff, but for one moment we are just siblings again and I am pulling her through a difficult obstacle like big brothers are supposed to.

Our apartment lease in Twin Peaks is up in July, but our home loan still hasn't closed. I take all our stuff to Logan and move it into storage with one of Karen's cousins, then move into the Adams's basement for three weeks. I can't handle another day, but the loan still hasn't closed. So we move to Logan anyway. I use some of my myriad hotel points to stay at the Springhill Suites in Logan, but our loan has another delay. Karen hates the hotel and needs her house, so I convince the seller to let us move in anyway. I can't believe he agrees to it. His house was on the market for a long time, and I guess he is as desperate on his side as we are on ours. It works. A week or two after we move in, we sign the papers and I buy my first house for $172,000.

I gut the house and paint the house and install new carpet before we even own it. We need this home purchase to happen! As soon as we own it, the burden of living in Twin Peaks next to Karen's parents falls from my shoulders, and a heavy weight goes with it. I feel free. We have twenty-five hundred square feet inside, a quarter acre outside, a shed, a tree, a fence, and I love it! I don't know it yet, but we also have a vole invasion and fertilizing poop spray all spring from the cornfield across the street. But I don't care because they are mine.

739 East 600 South

"MATT, THIS IS BULLSHIT!"

We have been in Logan about a year when I call my mom and she tells me that. She can't take the games anymore. Karen needed help after we had our second son in March 2014, so Gramalisa came to the rescue for a couple of weeks. While my mom was there watching the boys, Karen went off to get her hair and nails done and take friends to lunch. I'm getting ready to start my MBA in August and traveling a little more for work so I can soon shift my focus to school. Mom just got back to Kanab after her visit, and now Karen just hung up on her after telling her all the things she did wrong this time, and now she can't see either of the boys again. The baby ban is back, and now there are two handsome grandsons who will be kept from my mom.

Everything about pregnancy and childbirth that was new and novel for Karen with Rex becomes inconvenient and annoying with Rhett. I read about it. It's not uncommon for women to have much harder pregnancies the second time around. After Rhett arrives, Karen's postpartum depression hits far worse than it did last time.

I take two-year-old Rex with me on most work trips so Karen only has one baby at home. I drive with Rex to meetings in Boise, Salt Lake City, and Las Vegas. We are halfway to Reno when Karen calls and says she can't be alone with baby Rhett. She's frantic. She doesn't think he's her baby, and she doesn't know what to do with him. She thinks she needs to leave the house and let his real mother come back to take care of him. I am always in a high-stress state, but my stress kicks up even higher and I feel sick to my stomach as we turn around. I keep Karen on the phone for most of the drive and calm her down. I know she's all talk, she won't actually leave or do anything, she just wants attention and can't have me doing anything but giving it to her. Secretly I am relieved I don't have to get through more work days with Rex. I love it, but he's a rambunctious toddler, always running away from me, and it's getting hard to keep him in eyesight and track him down when he runs off. This way I can play with him all day tomorrow and just work on the phone. I'm thinking all of that while Karen tells me she hates nursing Rhett, she hates holding Rhett, she feels trapped in the house, and she really thinks she needs to leave. Even though we just finished using Gramalisa again and then kicking her out again, I sure wish she would come back. I don't know how to handle this.

"I just wish she would die!" I want to say to my mom.

Things happened so fast the past year, I forgot about waiting for Karen to die. Mom finally yells some sense at me and my nonsense delusion comes roaring back. I want to say, "Just wait awhile and she will be dead and then we can go back to normal! Promise! God loves us enough to let her die and be happy and let me live and be happy." I want to break down and be honest and apologize for everything, but I can't. Instead of saying anything honest, I tell my mom, "Too bad, this is just the way things are, there is nothing I can do. The Great One is in charge and Whiny Boy Matchu can't do anything about it." I don't know what I want my Mom to say to me in response. I want to cry and tell her I'm taking the boys and coming home to Kanab. I want to tell her I am so sorry my wife uses Rex and Rhett like bargaining chips to get out of being a mom. I'm so glad my mom calls "bullshit" this time. She never swears and hardly ever stands up for herself. She gets my attention. She's always been good at that.

When I was in the second grade, I was a hellion. Worse than I should admit. Some kids got detention, I got suspended. One night at dinner I was being a punk, and Mom went Bruce Lee on me. She raised her right arm in a karate chop and came down on my thigh with an audible, "Hi-yah!" The world stood still for a moment, and then we burst into laughter. I have never laughed so hard in my life, and she laughed with me. I didn't act as much of a fool much after that. It was like when my dad said bitch, we turned that corner and I thought he was cool. My mom became really cool to me with the karate chop.

When we moved to Utah in 1999, Mom started working in the school system to help us all get into university and get scholarships. She wanted to have college savings for us, but we were too poor. She did what she could and got a job as the liaison between the high schools and several universities in Utah. All five of her kids will go on to get Bachelor's degrees, and two of us have Master's.

When we first moved to Utah, the seven of us lived in a four-bedroom house with a small yard of red sand. Every day after school before I walked inside, I would take the laundry down from the clothes line and go inside and fold it. Mom knew I didn't want to be praised for it. I knew things were hard. My Dad made twelve thousand dollars that year. I don't know how they did it. I wanted to be a contributor and I wanted to do it because it needed to be done. Mom never had to ask me to do it and never made a big deal out of it. But I could *feel* that my mom appreciated it, and I loved that.

After the first school year in Kanab in the summer of 2000, I wanted to go to basketball camp with Tanner. We played all the time, and starting in 2001 in middle school, basketball got pretty competitive. A guy named Fred House brought to town a week-long camp where we could learn to dribble between our legs and make half-court shots sitting in a chair like he could. I knew we didn't have the money, but I asked mom anyway. She gave me a check for the full amount and got me into that camp. One day before Tanner and I left, she gave me five dollars to buy lunch too. I was overwhelmed. I told her thanks and gave her a hug and put the money back in her wallet. In movies and in the hallways at school, kids would talk about stealing from their parents. My mom gave me all she had. I started working that summer in 2000 pulling weeds and mowing lawns and would slip a little money into her wallet when I could. I knew she would just spend it on us anyway. My sense of duty and industry comes from my mom.

My most vivid memory of Mom comes from all the way back at age two. Kamikaze Matt was playing by the bonfire at the Livingston family reunion. Then I dove right into that fire. I almost burned both my arms off. My grandpa yanked me out and I could see over his shoulder my mom screaming bloody murder. That image is forever singed into my memory, and it surfaces when I think Mom is in trouble. While we live in Logan, I see that image a lot.

Rex turned two on February twentieth before Rhett was born a few weeks later on March eleventh. The stress and sleeplessness of having two babies and an increasingly disinterested wife takes its toll on me. Rex doesn't like sharing the attention, so he acts out more often. Breaking things, talking back at us, biting me, normal kid stuff. Karen wants me to start spanking Rex, so I do. He has a very strong will. Karen wants me to spank him often, and Brian wants me to scare him. His tells me the best kind of parenting scares your kids. While I believe Karen is scared of him, I don't agree this is good advice. He says to pick them up fast and suddenly, don't shake them, just pick them up fast and that will scare them and get their attention. I don't do this. But I do start spanking Rex. Not like Brian spanked Karen, I will never hit him hard enough to break my thumb. At night I have a nightmare that I kick Rex in the face over and over and watch his face crumple in like a tin can. Then I stop and everything is still for a moment. Then he blinks his big blue eyes. And then I see Mom's screaming face as I look back over Grandpa's shoulder after he pulls me from the bonfire. And then I wake up and run to Rex's room in the basement and just sit next to his crib. I don't spank him for long, just a few weeks. But I keep having the nightmare for the next two years.

Rex gets a tummy ache one afternoon and falls asleep while I am patting his back. I don't want to leave him, so I just slump down on the floor and lay on my back with him on me tummy to tummy, and we both take a nap. I wake up because my arms are numb, but I don't dare move, so I lay there with slumbering Rex for three more hours before he wakes up and his tummy feels better. I don't love disciplining Rex, but I love being his dad.

I tell him stories every night because my Mom did that with me. For about four years, we do "The orange lizard and the green lizard." Orange lizard is Rex, green lizard is Dad, and red lizard is Rhett. Auntie Kelly has many guest appearances as pink lizard. The lizards save the universe from aliens, fly in their spaceship, transform into dragonflies, drill to the center of the earth. My mom did the same thing with us when we were babies with the story of Felice and her flock of baby birds. We all had a baby bird name and Mom was Felice. I always had such sweet dreams after Mom told us stories of Felice and her little flock. That's why I tell the lizard stories every night. They are the highlight of my day.

Karen doesn't join us for bedtime routines. Ever. Brushing teeth, reading scriptures, telling stories, saying prayers. She has too many shows on her DVR to catch up on. I string out bedtime as long as I can to stay in Rex's room and not have to go rub Karen's feet and watch Kardashians. Karen gets pissed and comes in to tell us to be quiet and that Daddy needs to come rub her feet.

Before I start my MBA, Karen decides she now wants to become a certified and court-appointed mediator. Not to actually work, of course. This is just another thing she can do to elevate her status and sound smart. She wants to be the final authority on every argument, so everyone has to listen to her. We will be having some discussion with neighbors or friends, and she will issue the final judgment "because I'm a court-appointed mediator." The course only lasts a week and costs a few thousand bucks I don't have, but I know she will do it whether I agree or not. She will never work a single case. But she loves telling people all about it. "Hi, guys, I'm a mediator." Her qualifications are her identity, just like Doctor Adams. Soon there will be another Dr. Adams. Before I start my MBA, Karen already has her list of PhD programs to apply for. As soon as I graduate, we will move so she can get her PhD. That's what we do, we take turns. She knows she's not happy with things now, but once she has her PhD, she will be happy with herself and her education, and then she will get a job, because she hates staying home with the "offspring." She despises motherhood. She thinks she wants the praise of the workplace.

There are actually already two PhDs in Karen's family, Karen will be the third. The second PhD is Karen's Aunt on her mom's side, Aunt Brooke. They vilify her because she ran away in high school and left the Church. She works for the government, and I only meet her a few times. She ran away when she was a teenager, had a baby out of wedlock, and turned into a Democrat. The first two are crimes against the family, but her political views are far worse. Karen reaches out to her often while writing entrance essays and filling out applications for her PhD, and Brooke answers. She relies on Brook because when Karen asks the other PhD for advice, her dad, he pretends he doesn't hear her. He has mentioned many times that PhDs are hard, a lot of politics slow the process, and most people wash out. Brian doesn't approve of Karen trying to achieve his status. Karen doesn't care. She will get her PhD and gain equal footing with her dad no matter what.

Karen shadows a real mediator in Logan for part of mediator training. A lot of the mediations Karen sits in on are for couples seeking divorce. Utah requires mediation before a divorce hearing. After mediation, the couple often has to see a therapist alone or together or both. This reminds Karen of the therapy she didn't finish before we met, so she decides to go back and see the same therapist a few hours south of us. I don't mind because it gets Karen out of the house all afternoon and evening a few nights a month. The first two or three sessions are great. Karen wants to start to see things from other people's point of view, she wants to forgive my parents because they are who they are, she wants to spend more time cooking and helping at home. She's actually talking sense for once! I begin to hope she will change after all. Maybe she won't have to die, if she can just get some of this sense to stick long term.

She calls my parents as part of therapy homework and has one or two pleasant conversations with them. Then she snaps.

Karen wants all of us to go to group therapy, her and me and my parents. Karen's therapist's idea. We will all be teachable and loving, and by we I mean Karen, and we can finally stop threatening each other, and again, I mean Karen.

Karen starts to realize she's going to need to change and calls everything off. During her fourth visit with the therapist, she leaves early and says she will never go back. She tells me it's to the point where she's talking about herself and growing up and her relationship with her dad, and she won't do it anymore. "What does any of that have to do with your parents?" she asks me. I know she has issues with her dad, but she won't talk about it. She still wants to do group therapy so she can rail on my parents in a group setting. She's pretty shaken up by the last therapy session. She sees a doctor and starts taking a second medication on top of her Elavil. It helps, but makes her lows even lower when she forgets to take both medications.

Kyle has been on his mission for a year now, and I am waiting for him to come back to Utah State in Logan and save me. But I am starting to struggle. Karen dislikes staying home so much she signs the boys up for full-time daycare while I am working so she can get her hair and nails done and go shopping. I absolutely hate this. Kids need love and kids need parents. Now she's spending a hundred bucks a day on daycare so she can go spend another hundred bucks getting her nails done and her hair crimped like Mindy's mom, then bribing Mindy, who doesn't even like her, to let her buy lunch. Rhett is barely six months old and she won't nurse him anymore and now he's going to be around a bunch of sick toddlers all day. He ends up spending a lot of my MBA days sick with the flu and the cold.

I need something to focus on or I'm going to snap. I fixate on our unfinished bathroom basement. If I can finish it and make it beautiful, then Kyle can move into the basement next year and be right there with me. And it will be easier to sell our home and move to Chicago or wherever for Karen's PhD next year. And we can install a huge tub and a TV so Karen has a place she can go hang out and stay in the house more without feeling trapped.

I go overboard on the bathroom. In 2013 I lead my company in sales and have a big enough bonus coming in January to pay for the whole bathroom. I want black and white marble and chrome fixtures and a separate room just for the toilet. I can't control much in my life, but I will have the bathroom I want. If I do it right, Kyle will love it too so he will live down there. And the house will sell super quick when we need to move. The contractor has never put an electrical outlet up high where I want it for the TV, but he gets it done.

Karen can't believe it when Wii spend my entire bonus on finishing the bathroom. I love it. I put all that money to good use, and she can't waste any of it. She tells me after that she wants to go on a vacation to Bora Bora instead. Too late now! I am okay with spending a few thousand bucks on a vacation she won't like, like all the other ones we take, but Bora Bora would cost ten grand. Too much. Not going to waste ten thousand dollars on a vacation she will hate. The bathroom needs to be done. On Mother's Day, I give her some black

Tahitian pearl earrings instead, and she throws them in my face. I just laugh. I probably deserved that.

Most everything else she wants, she gets right away from her Honey Matchu. I am Whiny Boy Matchu when she's mad and Honey Matchu when she wants something. Once we finish the bathroom, she tells me out of the blue that her childhood dream was to have a Newfoundland dog like Nana in Peter Pan. I've never heard this before. I google it and find there is some debate among Disney scholars as to whether Nana was indeed a Newfoundland. She looks more like a Saint Bernard. Karen is a court-appointed mediator with a Master's degree, and she says Nana is a Newfie, so there is no point in me arguing. We pay a thousand bucks and get her a Newfie. She won't even play with it.

Newfoundlands are members of the largest breed of dogs, and even the puppies are huge. We get it papered under the name "Alaska Astra Livingston," and Karen tells all her friends that Alaska Astra the Newfie has papers. She doesn't want a dog; she wants to have the biggest and most expensive dog so she can brag about it. I feed the dog, I scoop the poop, I walk the dog, brush her fur, build her a huge fenced enclosure with an igloo house. It may not sound like a lot, but it feels like a full-time job. These dogs are a lot of work. Alaska won't stop crying and barking, so I go back and buy her brother, another thousand bucks. Alaska Astra and her brother, Chief Spotted Eagle. Then Karen buys a Persian cat, too. We name him Moose. She plays with Moose all the time. Moose is zero work compared to the dogs.

All our neighbors are members of the LDS Church too, and we only live one block away from the church building, so Karen comes on Sundays. She doesn't want anyone thinking she's not up on church. At church, we participate in a lesson about compromise. A schoolteacher named Nathan shares an example of when his wife wanted a dog. He didn't want a dog. So they did a lengthy compromise where they got her a fish and then he got a basketball hoop outside. I have never heard anything more ridiculous. I know I need to say "no" to Karen more often but I don't dare.

Doctor Brian Adams is still the ultimate authority on relationships. You remember the "two halves of the brain" lesson. He tells us all the time he "speaks Julie" for his spouse perfectly. By this I know he means he brainwashed her into thinking she wants whatever he says she wants. He and Karen are doing the same to me. As long as you both do this, you will never go to bed angry. That's the rule for the lesson, never go to bed angry. I know he knows Karen will never think of me when she makes decisions. Even if she does, I have never been honest with her, so how could she know what I want? I just tell her what she wants to hear and take it one day at a time. It's just not how she works. She does what she wants and then says, "Matchu, I need it, I might die." And then she finds a reason to get mad at me anyway and lock me out of our bedroom.

He names his second lesson for us "always give a ten." This is the same as the Boy Scout Kool-Aid I grew up on: Always do your best. You either do or you don't. Simple. Another thing Brian knows Karen just will not do. She gets depressed about almost everything and gives a meager effort and then blames it on someone else. No problem, I'll make up the slack. Her ten and my ten are just different.

Several years ago, my buddy Dan from BYU got banned from eBay for selling TVs the wrong way. eBay has a lot of rules about pricing and things you can and cannot sell, and they didn't like how much money Dan made, so he can't do it anymore. Dan is bored getting ready for law school stuck at home with a wife who has mental health problems, and I am bored getting ready for my MBA stuck with a wife who has mental problems, so he comes to visit more often. In summer 2014 before my MBA begins, he convinces me to open an eBay store with him so we can make some cash. Dan knows eBay inside and out. He sets up templates and automates our selling process, and we start humming in the orders. We sell phones, sports jerseys, and women's leggings. Anything that's hot. The leggings sales are amazing. Yoga pants are on the rise, and we ride the gravy train. We open leggings stores on Etsy and in the UK and in Australia and drop ship everything from China. We sell eleven grand worth of leggings in one month. Karen gets free samples, so she doesn't bother us about what we are up to in the basement.

We sell so much by knocking everyone off and undercutting their pricing. Our first few weeks, we sell so much we get cease and desist letters from eBay and all the angry companies we are knocking off, and we have to shut down. But we pocket a couple grand each and make a lot of fun memories. The month we spend together will go a long way to build our friendship so we can support each other during nasty divorces we don't yet realize are looming on our horizons.

Dan and I convince ourselves and each other: "Happy wife, happy life." He sounds like Squidward from *SpongeBob SquarePants* when he says it. And he says it a lot. We both know we married wives who will never be happy. We will never be able to make them happy. This was the silent conversation our souls have while our voices mumble hopefully, "Happy wife, happy life."

Dan is sleeping over and Bill and Kyson text me that they found a skunk squadron and we better get over there and grab a shotgun. We pile on the back of Bill's Gator with our shotguns, and Bill holds one loosely across his arms while he drives. Bill gets headlights on the first one and shoots it without even stopping. Just casually lifts his shotgun onto the steering wheel and blows the animal away. We watch it tumble through the air and roll into the ditch. Dan whoops and hollers, having the time of his life. In Kanab, we did stuff like this in high school. When we talk about "clubbing" late at night, we don't mean dancing. We mean taking golf clubs, piling in a vehicle, driving through a field, and whacking varmints as if we were a caveman holding a club. We get back to Bill's pond, and he spots the muskrat who's been messing with his pipes, so he holds the light on it while I blast the muskrat beneath the night sky.

Dan leaves, and I get a text message from my old boss Matt Kennedy. "We started a new company called Simple. I think it is going to be big." I look at his new company website and can't make heads or tails of it. I send a short text back and he doesn't respond again. Nice of him to think of me. I want to call him and ask more about it but know I can't. When I think of Kennedy, I wonder what could have been.

One night we stay with friends in Park City. Long after Karen and the boys are asleep, I feel a familiar stirring in my soul for the first time in a long time. I want to hear God's voice in my life again. I want to feel his Spirit guide me like I used to years ago. I am wearing myself out toeing the chaotic line of what Karen wants. We have two boys now, and I am trying to read scriptures with them and pray with them and teach them the importance of paying tithing and fasting and serving others, but Karen wants none of it. To her, church is just that thing you do for a few hours on Sunday. I get up out of bed and go walk around the neighborhood. I look up and loudly utter a prayer that I feel lost. Marriage isn't what it's supposed to be. I want to do the right thing but keep getting more and more frustrated. What should I do? The scripture comes to my mind: "With God all things are possible."

March tenth, 2014. The most badass night of all of Karen's badass nights. We are up watching BYU basketball, and she has a contraction around ten p.m. She turns on the timer on her watch and marks the time of the next contraction. A few minutes of this, and she looks at me and says, "See you in a while. I'm going to drive to the hospital to have this baby now." We both know she's kind of joking but kind of serious. A couple hours later, she sends me this text: "Oh shit I'm six centimeters! Get here!" This means she is nearly there. It took all night to get to six centimeters with Rex; now she's there in less than two hours. At around ten centimeters the baby has enough of a hole to start coming out. I call a neighbor to come over and sleep on the couch in case Rex needs a buddy, and I take our baby bag to the hospital. Soon she's ready. Half an hour before Rhett comes out, Karen asks for a hair tie from the baby bag, I hand it to her, she buns up her hair, and says, "Let's go." Two rounds of pushing and here comes Rhett, whooshing out like he's coming down a waterslide. Karen is not going to die in this pregnancy. She is the healthiest of all women. Look at how she just had this baby. She will never die. She is lady Rambo. She just put on her headband and fired out a small human torpedo through a hole no bigger than a water balloon. When she winces a little with the birth pains, I am the one who almost passes out. Karen holds it together. "Suck it up and hold my hand!" She survived dengue fever and two childbirths. She's invincible.

It will be two years before her death delusion comes back to me. Nights like this one give me a lot of hope. I am so proud to be in the same room as a woman who can bear children like this.

A few months later, lady Rambo will put her hairband back on and use oversized Ace bandages to wrap her breasts up tight until the milk dries up so she can move on from breastfeeding and Rhett can go to day care. She nursed Rex for an entire year. Rhett gets less than half of that. I read a lot of books and know that to the extent breastfeeding is possible, it ought to happen for at least a year. I don't say anything. It's her body, her choice. At least Rhett got what he got. Plenty of infants aren't able to breastfeed at all. It's critical not only to their nutrition and physical development, but also for their emotional and psychological and cognitive development. My brother Kyle breastfed until he was like three, and he's the smartest guy I have ever met.

Car seats are humongous. We are up watching Kardashians talking about Rex and Rhett and their huge car seats and our little midsize CRV. Karen decides right then she needs a bigger car. She goes on her phone and tells me she just bought it. Six hours and eight thousand dollars later, she has a brand new 2014 Honda Pilot we can't afford. But we buy it anyway. That's how it works. I cut my losses and get excited that we have all the extra space for our San Diego trip. My sister Kelly comes with us just like last year, and we play for five days in the sand. On a drive to the beach, Kelly points to ships far out at sea and says, "Look Rex, a ship!" And little one-year-old Rex replies in perfect English, "No, Auntie Kelly, that's an ocean liner." The annual leopard shark migration moves through right when we are there the second week of August 2014. Leopard sharks have really small teeth, so I jump through the shore break and play with the sharks, grabbing them and petting them. Rex gets scared when he sees one suck my hand into its mouth, and he never gets scared, especially with Auntie Kelly there. But I stop messing with the sharks when Rex jumps up and down in disapproval, shaking his finger at me and telling me I will get eaten by a shark if I don't stop. I love when he does that. He will do the same thing at Christmas that year. We are all making a music video and I try to turn the dining table into a slip-and-slide but the table goes end-over-end instead. Rex stands over me (on top of the table that's now over me too) and shakes his finger and says, "You were doing a bad, bad idea, Daddy!"

My sister Morgan and her husband Jon have their first baby the same Spring we have Rhett. On our way back to Logan from San Diego, we pass through Las Vegas where Morgan and Jon live. We time it up to be there on Morgan's birthday so we can stop and get her some new running shoes.

When Jon gets off work, we take their little guy, Travis, with us to dinner so Jon can take Morgan on a birthday dinner date. They aren't big date people but we think this is a nice gesture. We go to PF Chang's with the babies, and Jon tells us he will take Morgan to Fazzoli's. Karen hates this idea. After Morgan and Jon leave and we sit at our table, Karen throws a fit. Now we have three tired kids throwing fits because kids always do this at nice restaurants, and Karen's fit is even worse. How dare he take her on such a cheap date when we took all this time and energy and came way out of our way to watch their baby? Doesn't he know a birthday is a special occasion? She makes me step away from our table right then to call Jon during his birthday date with Morgan and ream him for his wrongs. I tell him he should take her somewhere else. Jon says sorry and he sure will.

Only Jon and Morgan aren't at Fazzoli's. They aren't anywhere else either. On their way to dinner, their car died. When I call Jon, he's sitting with Morgan at a mechanic shop getting it fixed while I tell him his birthday plans for my sister aren't good enough. They don't even eat dinner. They fix the car and then come back for Travis and we all part ways. They don't complain or say anything at all.

We get home and it's time to get to the Utah State campus and start my eight-month sprint to get my MBA. My boss Susie wants me to keep my job while I go to school full-time over the next year. Basically, she will pay me to do nothing. It's not a lot of pay, but my salary is up to a whopping $45,000 from the $36,400 where I started, and it lets me keep funding Karen's lifestyle while I get a student loan to cover my MBA tuition. For some reason I decide I want to move to Atlanta and work for Delta Air Lines after I graduate. I will do sales or business strategy for them. I fix my gaze on that end goal, another distraction to pass the time. Georgia State University in Atlanta is one of the best prospects for Karen's PhD because they need white females and they have a high acceptance rate. PhD programs love diversity and are often required to diversify their cohorts. I know that an inner-city Atlanta school will not have a lot of Caucasian applicants.

We travel to Atlanta together so I can meet some people at Delta and Karen can meet some people at Georgia State. I want to live in Atlanta. When I think of Atlanta, I can breathe. Of all the cities we look at that have lots of jobs and a PhD in Communications, it's the farthest away from her family. I need space. In Logan I still don't have enough space. Her family doesn't visit often, but they are still around. I explain to all my MBA friends I need to get a job in a city where Karen can get into a PhD, and everyone looks at me like it is impossible. You take the job you get, no questions. One of my classmates asks me, "Yeah, but dude, if you get a great job somewhere, you're going to take it, right?" Nope. I will take her PhD opportunity over my job. Happy wife, happy life. If I like my job too much, she will either get me fired or make me quit anyway. Putting myself first will only happen after she goes away. I made my peace with this when we were first married in Irvine. Tick tock.

I commit so hard to the idea of moving to Atlanta and working at Delta that I lose the rest of my identity. In one of my HR classes we do an exercise where we list out the pieces of our identity through the roles we play in life. Then we rank in order of importance and take them away, one by one, until our main identity role is left. Father, husband, brother, dad, this hobby, that hobby. The teacher wants to show us who we are. Our primary role. My *sine qua non*: "Job applicant at Delta Air Lines."

One memory from the NPR internship where I hated working with Elaine the carrot-haired carrot eater when I first met Karen stays with me. We had this guy on the show who was so strange. He was some sort of public figure. During his interview, he described the one thing he took the most flack for. He said that during one of his shows, he got all existential and said, "I'm so *baroque.*" Even then when he told the story, he said those words with all the command and texture of an artistic masterpiece. Like he was calling himself the Mona Lisa. I got chills. The arts community railed him because he elevated himself to the status of the post-Renaissance masters by calling himself *baroque.* But I could hear when he said it, he was truly describing himself. I could feel it. He was describing the way he felt, the way he thought, the way he was. This man had self-awareness. He knew exactly who he was, and people were mad because it was the truth. At the time I wanted to chime in and say, "Your hair is baroque." He had self-awareness and I had none. Zero. No identity. Gave it all up to please an unhappy wife.

The week before Thanksgiving 2014, Karen gets a disturbing phone call late one night. Her sister just flipped an ATV. Karen packs the boys immediately and drives them to Twin Peaks to be with her family. On the drive, Rex poops in his car seat all the way from his head to his kneecaps. Worst poop since the tide pool eruption on my chest. Karen handles it and doesn't even complain. Doesn't blame it on me or call me a lousy husband for staying home to go to classes.

Karen's sister Whitney was driving the ATV, and her date and passenger ends up paralyzed. He nearly dies. The repercussions of this will last for years. People blame her and make fun of her at school and won't be her friend. The Adams family gets weird looks at the grocery store, and they answer nasty phone calls and have things thrown at their front door. Whitney stays with us for awhile and tries to keep her head up when everyone wants her to feel guilty.

During the same week, Karen's brother Mark calls off his upcoming Christmas wedding. It's a disaster of a fall for the Adams. Mark's fiancé, Adrienne, reminds me of Karen. When we all get together, Karen and Adrienne trade blows back and forth, making fun of each other and everyone else. Adrienne asks Karen to make her bridal shower invites. Karen ignores her instructions and sends the improper invites to all of Adrienne's friends without Adrienne's approval. Adrienne sees them, hates them, then sends her own invites afterward. Karen finds out. She won't be disrespected like that, so she starts talking about Adrienne behind her back. Especially to Mark. Mark starts looking at Adrienne differently. Adrienne tells him to stop talking to his family, tells him to come stay at her house and not to visit Twin Peaks until after the wedding. Everything sounds so familiar. When Mark bails, I feel happy for him, but I let his failure feed my ego. Only really tough and secure guys like me are marriage material. All women are bipolar. Some guys can deal with it, some can't. Weak Mark.

A month after they break up over Christmas break, we sit around the card table with Karen's parents. They claim they had no idea Adrienne might be manipulative and bipolar, but we all agree her behavior proves it. How could they not know their oldest daughter did the exact same thing to me? It happened right here under this roof.

The Adams are such a mess that we invite the Livingstons to come to our place for Thanksgiving. I can't believe Karen wants this. I love it. Karen is so worn out by all the drama in her own family that she actually decides my family can come visit. When she got to Twin Peaks with both boys, she couldn't handle both of them and her family. She asked Gramalisa to come take Rex. No matter how many times we ban her, she always comes to get Rex when we need her to. Now it's Thanksgiving week, and my family might as well drive Rex all the eight hours back home to Logan and stay for turkey when they come. Rex still doesn't like sharing the spotlight with his little brother and has hated going to daycare for several months now, so having all the Livingston adults to himself is a nice break for him too.

Rex can be awfully cute. One night he walks over to his baby brother crying loudly on the couch. Rex stands firmly next to him and places his little doctor hands on Rhett's little chest. Then he lifts his hands high in the air and rubs them together, yelling "clear!" while smacking them back down on Rhett's chest like a defibrillator. This makes Rhett only cry louder.

"He's not clearing, Daddy."

Another time I walk up to Rhett's bedroom and find Rex straddling the crib with one foot and the bookshelf with the other. Thus suspended in the air, I watch him lift the lid off Rhett's humidifier and release a wider spray of steamy air in the room. Next he unscrews the dropper from the top of Rhett's bottle of teething medicine. I stand out of sight in the hall watching Rex lean to his right to fill the dropper with humidifier water, then lean to the left and drop it down onto Rhett's face and into his mouth. Rhett loves it. He coos and giggles, madly in love with his brother.

"Look! Brother's teething, Daddy!"

Before my MBA, Rex has me around most of the time. I am gone eight days of the month traveling for work, but while I work from home the rest of the time, he can always find me. With our own house, there are so many more adventures to have. We hunt spiders in the garage and in the basement. We hunt voles in the yard and in the shed. We walk the dogs. We plant a garden. Now that I am in school, and gone several hours every day, Rex isn't impressed.

During Thanksgiving when my family hops in the Pilot with Karen to get famous Utah State Aggie ice cream, they pass me heading the other way. They stop for a minute to say hi. Rex is pissed. He looks at me and points to the tall clock tower on campus behind me and says, "No, Daddy, go back to your tower!" I think to myself, he must feel like I have abandoned him.

Rex already knows Karen doesn't like being home, she says so all the time. She sends him and his brother to our next-door neighbor's day care just so she doesn't have to parent them. Now he thinks I don't like being home either. I walk around campus and cry instead of going to class. I don't even want to be doing this stupid MBA. I am piling on debt, wasting my time, and leaving Rex at home where he feels abandoned and unimportant during his most formative years.

I miss long mornings making dinosaur pancakes with Rex. The two of us help Mommy and Rhett cool down by giving them hugs and helping them take a deep breath and count to ten. He sits on my shoulders while I mow the lawn. I let him pull the trigger on the BB gun when we shoot the voles that dig the holes up and down our yard. I miss him.

He's good at self-soothing, too. I opened the front door at the Logan pool and cut his toe open. It bled a lot. He got reasonably upset and cried like any toddler would. No outrageous cries, just the tears of a kid with a big ouch. Karen kept telling him to be quiet, getting angry with him. He breathed slowly for a minute and said, "Be niiiiiiiice, Mommy."

In the dead of winter, we go sledding until Rex freezes into a little human ice cube. We get in the Pilot and he says through his sobs, "N-n-need t-to t-t-take a picture, Daddy." I hand him my phone so he can take a picture with his frozen little fingers, and then he stops crying.

At Rex's birth, the doctor messed up on his circumcision. We get it redone after I see Rhett's circumcision and realize something is definitely wrong with what they did on Rex. He doesn't complain at all on surgery day. We medicate his groin with cream three times a day for weeks after, and he still doesn't complain. When I take him on work trips, we always get rooms with two queen beds so we can jump back and forth between them all night. We eat Thai food and Vietnamese soup and all sorts of pasta together, and he refines his palate.

We live across the street from a giant cornfield. Poop is the best fertilizer. Everyone knows that. I have just never seen it sprayed out of a giant sprinkler before now. Well, our corn farmers figure it out, and when the wind blows, the poop mist hits us in the face and covers our cars and our windows and our yard. The poop makes the ground so soft and fertile their corn grows like crazy and they get several harvests. After the last harvest, the corn still completely covers the ground. In come the voles.

They are everywhere. Thousands of them, maybe tens of thousands. Our front yard looks like a worm farm turned on its side. During Thanksgiving, we hunt voles for hours. We have two pellet guns and thousands of rounds of BBs. One shooter gives the whistle, everyone stops, passes the gun to the one who gave the whistle, and then pop! We confirm seventeen vole kills in one afternoon. Auntie Kelly is the great videographer of the family. She holds up her phone and takes a five-second video of our lethal line of vole killers while whistling the haunting theme song from the cartoon "Peter and the Wolf." We made our own little movie scene. We have a perfect day.

As the school year picks up speed, I spend more time on campus. Karen gets even more bored. She starts working for tips at the lone restaurant in Smithfield where we live. It usually costs more to have a babysitter for the boys than she makes selling food and drinks. She loves working at the bar and pouring drinks for people. It reminds her of being at the bars in Florida.

Kyle Returns to Logan

"If you don't start kissing girls you're going to go to hell."

I want to welcome Kyle home with a place to stay and endless brother workouts, but Karen would rather condemn him to hell. The court-appointed mediator has the final say on every topic, including Kyle's new dating life. She tells him to kiss girls or burn in hell while we all sit together in a Wendy's in Beaver, Utah, waiting for our food on our way down south. Ten years earlier we had spanked the Beaver Beavers in a football game, and the same Wendy's refused to feed us. A bunch of coaches and teachers whined and complained, but most of us loved it. We beat them so bad they refused us service.

Kyle only got home from his mission a month ago, but Karen wants him to get out on some dates and kiss some girls. Privately I tell him this is absolute crap and that he will know when he is ready. But neither of us dare to argue with Karen.

She talks the same to Kyle as she does with me. She just wants to control us. She wants Kyle to practice dating on her, to take her on a date, as soon as we get back to Logan.

Karen and I go to the movies every week, and now sometimes Kyle comes with us. I love it when he does. He takes a lot of pressure off me. Karen always wants to impress him and look desirable so he will listen to her. She knows most of the Livingstons hate her but she wants to keep my closest siblings, Kyle and Kelly, on her side.

So she tells a lot of jokes around Kyle and saves the meltdowns for later when he's not around. She keeps asking and asking him to take her on a date, which he doesn't want to do, but when we get back to Logan he finally says yes.

They go to Café Rio. Kyle asks her if he can get a burrito and Karen replies, "I don't care what you get, I'm not paying for it. You're buying." Kyle has no money, just like I had no money when I got home from my mission. This makes Kyle as mad as he can get. He let her rope him into a date and now she wants him to pay. Kyle has no tolerance for this kind of thing. So he asks her why she thinks he should buy, since she's the one who asked him on the date.

All my siblings get their food paid for when they are with me. That's how it works. Even when I don't really have any money, I still pay. When we met Kyle in the Las Vegas airport after his flight home from his mission, I paid for the hotel rooms and made the travel plans. It's just my role in the family. When Karen asks him to buy their food on the date she asked him on, she's breaking all the rules.

In the evening after they get home and Kyle leaves, Karen cries and tells me Kyle made her feel uncomfortable. She makes me give him what he later calls a "disappointed father talk." I take him aside the next day all serious and tell him he has to make it up to her. He can see I am under some strange spell and there's no sense reasoning with me about Karen, so he plays along. He buys her four gallons of famous Utah State Aggie ice cream and she squeals, overjoyed at the sight of all the treats. Apology accepted.

Karen lets us go to Kanab for Christmas, 2014, because Kyle has just gotten home from his mission. She supports me in spending time with him. Every Christmas growing up, we went snowboarding, and we decide to bring back the tradition. Gramalisa offers to watch the kids, but Karen still won't come. I know it's a bad idea to leave the two of them in the same house, but I do it anyway! I made my two-year deadline, and now I want to be with my brother every chance I can get! The base of snowfall is so deep that Kyle and I ride over and off someone's roof. We are brothers reunited, just like when I got home from my mission.

In the silent moments riding up the lift, I start getting PTSD, thinking about all the things Karen must be yelling at my poor mom right now and the list of grievances she will have for me when I get home. I check my phone but don't have cell phone service. I let ignorance be bliss, and we keep riding our snowboards.

I see a bunch of missed calls from Karen when we take a break at the lodge. My dad has missed just as many from my mom. We don't have many moments anymore, but we both look at each other after seeing all our missed calls like, "Uh-oh, what have we done?" We walk each other's earshot and call our women back at the same time. Gramalisa is at the store with Rex, and they are afraid to go home. Karen is at the house with Rhett, and she dares my mom to come back. They've had possibly their worst fight ever. Karen starts crying and yelling and spouting off about all the drama, and I want to get back on the ski lift. I want to pretend to lose service and hang up, but I don't.

Karen calms down enough to finally say she caught my mom texting her best friend that she hates Karen. My first thought: of course my mom hates you. You treat her like dirt. What do you expect? Karen says she can't believe I left her in the same house as my mom. Yes, I knew I had that coming. I do such a good job listening that somehow Karen calms down and asks us to come home soon. We will get home when we get home. I don't say that.

When we do get home, our families segregate as usual. Eventually I determine the course of events. They are as follows:

1. Rhett knocked over the TV. Rather than apologizing or helping pick it up, Karen got upset about it and blamed my mom for not having it mounted to a wall. She called my mom irresponsible and stupid.

2. After Karen yelled at Mom for not having her TV mounted, Mom writes a message to her friend saying that Karen is really upset, they are home alone with the kids, Mom would rather be with anyone else in the world than Karen, and she doesn't know what to do.

3. Karen asked my mom, who she has just insulted and yelled at, if she can borrow her laptop. For some reason my mom said okay. Karen snooped through Mom's Facebook messages and found the message.

4. Karen handed the laptop back to Mom with that vindictive Karen-look, and the moment she does, Mom knew Karen has seen the message. But Karen didn't say anything.

5. Mom took Karen and the boys to the public library and read the boys books and played with them for a few hours. Then she bought them lunch at Lotsa Motsa pizza. The whole time Karen was stewing and steaming and getting madder and madder.

6. When they got home, now that she had gotten free food and entertainment from Gramalisa, Karen finally boiled over. She laid into my mom: "How dare you write such a mean message to your friend about me? Don't you know that everyone loves me and you idiots are lucky that I come here at all after the terrible things you have done to me and my family? Haven't you ever seen *Modern Family*? Don't you see how everyone treats Gloria? I am the Gloria in this family, and you need to treat me like they treat her!"

My mom was dumbfounded. After Karen's explosion, she took off with Rex and started calling Dad while Karen started calling me. This is the second-to-last time Karen will ever stay in Kanab.

Soon we are home in Logan again with Kyle, where I want him to live in our basement. But now Karen tells me he's not allowed to live in our basement, after I finished the bathroom and planned on it for a year. Karen tells me under no circumstance can Kyle stay with us, not even for a week. She calls it "inappropriate" because he needs to be on his own and date a lot of girls, and we would be invading his privacy by having him live with us. Even though I listen to her and don't invite him to stay at the house, she talks it over with him again and again to convince him it's his idea not to live with us. He doesn't care that much and easily gets a room with some other guys. We both let it go.

Kyle is a strategist. He tells my mom over Christmas he will never make Karen mad because it's important to him to stay in my life. He sees that making Karen mad is a one-way ticket away from me. He sees what happened to my mom, my dad, my sister Morgan, and all my friends who made Karen mad. They are gone. He will not let that happen. He knows I need him. We make a tradition that every Friday we have our brother time. I skip class, cancel meetings, clear everything from my schedule, and he does the same from seven a.m. to noon every Friday morning. We lift weights and run, eat a big breakfast together, and usually have some sort of life discussion. Karen is not invited to any of it. She doesn't like this. But since Kyle never made her mad without apologizing and she wants him on her side, she allows it. Kyle has her figured out, and he's the only person I ever saw do it.

Ever since she missed out on our Christmas snowboard trip, Karen keeps talking about going snowboarding. She says she's a great snowboarder, and she can show Kyle and me what real snowboarding is all about. I am used to her talking about her greatness in sports. She always says she took second in state tennis her junior year of high school. But she will never teach me tennis or play anything with me or exercise or walk the dogs. She wants Kyle to think she's amazing, so it's time to take the Great One snowboarding. As with most things involving Karen, I'm curious how it will turn out.

Kyle and Karen and I pick a perfect Saturday and go snowboarding. No matter where you are in Utah in January, you're no more than an hour or two from a ski hill. Our first time up the lift, Karen brags to us how she will do "s-curves" all around the mountain and that we better keep up. She is sitting in the middle with Kyle and I on either side of her, smiling subtly but keeping it hidden.

We all stand up to ride off the lift, and Kyle and I give her plenty of space in between us. Instantly she goes down. We see her gloves flying up into the air and we hear her unhelmeted head smack the hard ice surface beneath the lift. We both instinctively reach toward her and we slow to a stop just in time to slide her out of the way so the next party doesn't run her over as they dismount. She immediately starts to cry and the ski crew radios her a snowmobile. They lay her in a pull-behind sled, and we ride next to her for the medical evacuation ride down to the lodge. Usually these are from a skier who went over an icy ledge or a boarder who cracked his neck trying to backflip. Nope, the Great One just fell over trying to get off the lift. They quickly confirm her concussion, so she will need to sit it out for the day. I am under Kyle-immunity just like Friday mornings, so we leave her there and enjoy the day. We drove an hour and a half to get there, and sure it's a bummer she fell down before she could even get one run in, but we paid for the day, and we are going to get at least a few hours in. She's done crying now and tells us she doesn't want to ruin the whole day and that we should go have fun. I speak Karen fluently, just like Brian taught me. This is her way of asking me to say, "Oh, it's not your fault, let's just leave and we can go get lots of ice cream and watch a movie." Nope. I won't say it. I quickly agree with her, and we zip out of there before she can backtrack.

The Livingston brothers are back, and we shred Beaver Mountain the whole day. Not to confuse Beaver Mountain with Beaver, Utah; Beaver Mountain is way up north near Logan, and Beaver, Utah is down south by Kanab and Twin Peaks. We talk about getting rich and living out our dreams on the lift and film each other going off jumps and catching big air. I don't think about Karen at all. We take our shirts off for a few runs because we can. We howl like wolves because we can. We start laughing at my ridiculous wife and we can't stop laughing. I love being able to laugh at her, just for a little while. We check on her after a couple of hours and she's sitting with an EMT named Rhett and playing with his phone. This is her way of trying to make me jealous like I was of her old boyfriends when we were dating. She wants me to step in and say, "Hey, Rhett, sorry there, partner, but this woman isn't big enough for the two of us. So I'm going to have to ask you to leave." I used to do stuff like that all the time. Once in the BYU student center when Karen and I were eating lunch, a guy walked by and winked at her. I puffed my chest at him and calmly said, "Do it again." He literally ran away squealing like a girl.

Brian loves that story. He often asks me to retell it. For the second time in one day, I ignored Karen's subliminal message to me. And Rhett, the EMT, thank you for taking such good care of her for just a few more hours. She punishes me for this by talking about Rhett for a few weeks after. She gets his number and texts him sometimes.

I don't care. I have my brother back. He's struggling with the post-mission blues like I did. But he has good advice all around him, and only Karen wants him to hurry up and date and get married. He doesn't listen. He will take his time and let himself adjust to normal life.

Kyle's middle name is Lewis. We dub him "Uncle Lou" with "Lou" short for "Lewis." I love hearing Rex call him "Uncle Lou." Rex always talks fast and he says his uncle's name like he's hocking something, like spitting something up, which he does often. Reflux still keeps Rex up at night. He often sleeps all night on my chest in a sage green recliner we bought on clearance from my friend Braydon at RC Willey in Provo when we were first married. When Rex says "Uncle Lou," he refluxes it more like "Hakka Lou."

I tell Kyle I want to use our Friday workouts to beef up my quads. I only have to tell him once. I am six feet tall and built like a marathoner, Kyle is five-foot-eight and built like a powerlifter. He won a medal for powerlifting at least once in the Utah Summer Games. By the time I graduate in May, we will both be deadlifting five-hundred pounds. When real weightlifters see me deadlift so much, they hang around and watch. We lift as much or more as anyone in the campus gym. One guy tells us about a competition he's training to go win. He's around thirty pounds heavier than Kyle or me, and we are lifting a lot more than him. He sees us loading ten plates on the bar and watching it bend as we lift and tells me, "You're pretty lean, man! How much you pullin'?" Kyle loves this line. He leans over to me when he feels the itch to chuckle and whispers, "You're pretty lean, man! How much you pullin'?"

We are committed to excellence in everything we do. We run six-minute miles and sprint hundred-yard dashes as hard as we can. We set PRs on the rowing machine every single week because if you aren't getting better, you're getting worse. We get straight As in school and study scriptures and pray together. All we do is win.

After lifting, we always have breakfast, usually at Kneaders. Kneaders is Panera Bread, only better. Kyle and I are cinnamon roll aficionados, and we agree the best cinnamon rolls in the world are at Kneaders. After you burn a thousand calories in a workout, you can eat whatever you want, so we eat a lot. Either cinnamon rolls or bottomless French Toast or both. One morning Karen stops by Kneaders to say hi to us. She took the boys to daycare so she can go to CrossFit. Her latest trend. Like a lot of "CrossFitters," Karen starts going so she can hit on guys and be hit on and pretend to be an athlete. She wants to get a rise out of us and starts to make fun of us because CrossFit is so much cooler than what we do. We shrug it off. Who is she kidding, she can't get us down. I glance at Kyle as she laughs at us and the look in Kyle's eye brings me so much joy. His look says, "We both know all you like to do is eat ice cream and buy clothes that don't fit you and fall off ski lifts." I love it. She leaves. We laugh. When I am with Kyle, I am allowed to laugh at Karen. Four hours every Friday morning, I have my brother back, and we can do whatever we want. No more disappointed father talks, no taking care of the boys, no making Karen happy. Friday mornings are sacred.

On Friday mornings we are back at his tenth birthday watching Tokyo Drift at the movies and then taking turns drifting in my car in the church parking lot. We are back on the trampoline in the front yard watching *The Exorcism of Emily Rose* on my little TV with an extension cord from the living room. We are back on the 50cc motorcycle with the barbecue on the back going to work at Kanab Furniture. We are back in the Tahoe I rented to drive to Grand Junction for a work trip I took Kyle on before he left on his mission. We met one of my customers from Snow College for breakfast at a gas station. Kyle told the guy he was headed to West Virginia for his mission, and my customer replied, "Well, you better eat up, son, because you're not going to be fed anything but roadkill out there!"

I lose my iPhone once, break the screen twice. Don't even care. I have my brother back. Nothing can bother me now.

Karen loses her phone in Spring 2015 too. Rex throws it in the pond at Bill's house where he caught his first fish. We finished fishing, and during our picnic lunch, Kyson and I are trying to snuff out a beaver. I look over at the dock to see three-year-old Rex run up behind Karen at the end of the dock, pinch her phone from her back pocket like Oliver Twist, and chuck it into the water. I look at Kyson and laugh. Karen tries to catch him and spank him, but he's too fast. I run to the dock and try scooping it out with the fishing net, but no luck. The pond is thick with algae, and I don't have Matt Kennedy the Swamp King to retrieve it like he did with the golf disc. Later Rex told me it's not his fault, the fish told him to do it.

Since Kyle and I are both in Logan, the Livingstons come for Easter in 2015 just a few weeks before I graduate. Karen likes hosting as long as everyone thanks her and tells her she is amazing. But three-year-old Rex, bubbling with wonder and personality, is the center of attention. He also unseats Karen and becomes the new king of ice cream. He eats it so fast he gets brain freeze almost every time. He eats his Easter ice cream bowl with his usual Sonic speed, and just as the brain freeze locks him up, he stutters out, like a dying cowboy uttering one last thing, "More . . . brownicecream!" His outburst becomes a running family joke. Brownicecream! He says all three syllables in one and blurts them right through an impending bout of deep brain freeze. And eats the next bowl just as fast.

Karen has a lot of magazines lying around. She loves her magazines. She grabs a *Cosmopolitan* with FLOTUS Michele Obama on the cover and tries doing an Adams family pastime and getting some gossip going. We Livingstons don't do that sort of thing. At all. Ever. Karen holds up the magazine and gives her opinion that FLOTUS has on a "fugly" dress that does not look flattering on her. Karen asks my Mom if she thinks so too and Mom quickly pounces on the opportunity to agree with Karen. Gramalisa doesn't want a fight today. Then Karen asks Kyle what he thinks. The question repulses him, but he stays neutral with his reply, "I. Do. Not. Care." Karen gets the last word on everything, so she responds with an eyebrow raise at the end for effect: "Kyle, I will respect your opinion when you date twos *and* tens."

Kyle has been coming over two or three times a week for almost four months and has about had his fill of Karen. The Michele Obama thing bothers him because he sees all of Karen's miserable insecurities. She knows she has gotten fat and doesn't look great, so she gives labels like "fugly" to other women to make herself feel better. He refuses to give an opinion on Michele Obama so Karen can't pull me aside later and tell me how uncomfortable Kyle made her feel and make me give him another disappointed father talk and then ask him to get her more ice cream so she can get more out of shape and more insecure. No thanks.

With summer approaching, Kyle fades out of my life toward his first summer of sales, and I hope he will find a boss as good as Matt Kennedy. I knew he won't, there will never be a boss as good as Matt Kennedy. And there will never be a brother as good as Kyle.

Poland and Cancun

When we cross the border into Slovakia, we know for sure we took the wrong road. Not only do we not have Visas, but Slovakia doesn't like Americans.

We are on our capstone MBA trip and getting a little lost. My friends Tyson and Isaac agree to come with me for our one day of down time to do some exploring of our own. Our program director makes us promise one thing before we leave: "Don't leave Poland. We are all under extreme risk if you do." Now that we crossed the border anyway, we step out of the car to take a picture by the graffiti-laden cement "Slovakia" sign. We see the remnants of an abandoned brick building behind the sign that looks like it barely survived both World Wars. Next to the building, we see an old car. Next to the car, we hear voices and see two guys behind the popped car trunk. The two guys come out from behind the car, and we peel out of there as fast as we can in our little Volkswagen station wagon and get back into Poland.

They should have never rented us the Volkswagen in the first place. You need a special international permit from the DMV to rent a car in Europe. All the rental car companies are in their own little trailers at the Krakow airport. The first company tells us no because I don't have the permit. Same with the second. We don't get that far with the third company because their prices are outrageous. We look at the fourth trailer, smaller and dingier than the rest, and my friend Tyson looks at me with a twinkle in his eye and says, "Well, this is it, boys, it's this one or back to Warsaw." We both know it will work out.

Isaac our lawyer friend says, "Guys, this is totally pointless, we don't have the form. And even if we get the car, if we get pulled over, we are completely screwed. We will likely be thrown in jail. No MBA class after us will get to go on this trip again. We aren't in Kansas anymore."

I love Isaac for his realistic pessimism. Between the two of us, we see every angle of a situation. He sees all the reasons to say no, I see all the ways to yes. In an HR class, the professor gave us all an impossible problem about an insurance company doomed for bankruptcy. Like the unsolvable Kobayashi Maru in *Star Trek*. We solved it. The professor said no students ever had before.

Tyson has already gone inside to sweet-talk the lady at the desk in the fourth trailer. I ask Isaac to stay outside because I don't want him to talk her out of renting to us. Tyson slips the lady a cash tip in advance, and we have a deal. We finish the paperwork and pay her and she never asks about the special form she knows we don't have. Tyson elbows me in the ribs and smiles just like Squints in *The Sandlot* before he kisses Wendy Peffercorn. We walk out and dangle the keys in front of Isaac, who's shaking his head thinking none of us will ever go home again.

The signs on the road say "Koniek" with a picture of a deer. We yell "Koniek!" every time we see a deer. When we get back to the group, we learn Koniek actually means "warning." Now we understand why when we point our fingers into antlers on our foreheads and ask locals about the "konieks," they don't respond. I drive the little Volkswagen because Isaac and Tyson don't want the liability in case we get pulled over. They are smart. We use a map but still end up in Slovakia. We are trying to make it to the highlight of the South Poland Tatra mountains: Zakopane.

We roll into Zakopane around midnight. The snow has blanketed the landscape like the snow on the ranch in Alberta used to.

Every winter Grandpa Tom pulled us around the ranch in a horse-drawn sleigh. The horses wore bells and red velvet just like reindeer.

At night the snow was so thick in the woods it muffled every sound. All you could hear was silence. That's what Robert Frost is talking about when he writes, "the only other sounds the sweep of easy wind and downy flake." In the morning, the huge ranch windows had beautiful snowflake designs painted all over them like stained glass made in heaven. Grandpa said Jack Frost was the artist. When we looked around the downy woods, I looked for Jack Frost sitting high in the trees. I saw him many times, but he was always gone by the time I tried to show Dad or Grandpa.

I pull out my phone in Zakopane and try booking an Airbnb, but it's past midnight and everything has closed. We start looking for a hotel. It takes us half an hour to drive up one driveway only to find everything locked up. We finally find a resort place with the smallest ski hill in the world attached to it. We pay cash and give a false name and crash hard and fast.

Before we started our illegal little escapade to the mountains, I couldn't get out of Krakow fast enough. We started the day in Auschwitz. I will not visit there again. The evil deeds done there linger in the dirt. It was raining when we went, and the dust from human bone smoke stained the leather upper on my shoes. The whole time we walked around, I imagined burning the whole place to the ground. I determined what would burn, and what wouldn't. All the Jewish luggage still on display would burn. The mountain display of their shorn hair would burn. Clothes, no problem. All the wooden buildings would burn. I didn't know if the brick ones would. The huge cement human furnaces wouldn't burn. Not quickly, anyway. I wanted to burn it all. None of us said a word on the bus ride back to Krakow.

One of the people we stayed with said something about taking their teenagers to Auschwitz to show them how good they had it, and how bad it was for the Jews during the Holocaust. I wanted to slap her for cheapening this crucible of human suffering into a lesson for self-centered teenagers. The evil stuck to me like the powdered bone remnants stuck to my shoes.

When we left Krakow in the Volkswagen Saturday night, we had thirty hours to get back to Krakow and catch our train to Warsaw to join our classmates Monday morning. We Google "things to do in Zakopane" and decide to spend most of our time hiking Morskie Oko. They call it *The Eye of the Sea.* The biggest lake in the Tatras and a favorite vacation spot of the Pope. But first we shake off the long night and short sleep in the sauna. You can find a sauna everywhere you go in Eastern Europe. Most residents even have one. Tyson and I become undefeated sauna champs. Nobody outlasts us in the hot room. We beat Russians, Poles, Estonians, Ukrainians, the only guys who can beat us are the blue-blooded Fins.

The Zakopane resort sauna has the perfect setup right by the indoor lap pool and a few steps from soft snowbanks outside. They even have an ice bath in there. We frolic between the snow, the sauna, the ice bath, and the indoor pool for an hour. We are in paradise and feeling brand new, gearing up for the twenty-mile hike. We finally depart when we heat the sauna so hot it sets off the smoke detector and shuts itself off. In a blissful delirium, we complete our hike and drive back to Krakow.

We return the car before midnight with a few hours to spare before our train. We elect to sit out the wait in a twenty-four-hour McDonalds. We already booked the red-eye train back to Warsaw, which doesn't depart until three a.m. We stumble into McDonalds with six huge trash bags of sheepskins we purchased from a street vendor before leaving Zakopane. They smell terrible. The McDonalds janitor finds this suspicious. He walks tall and muscular and carries himself like he is KGB.

He walks up to me, sticks his finger in my chest, and says, "Open ze bags!"

I refuse. He asks us to leave. We refuse. He goes behind the counter and pulls a phone off the wall, speaking fast into the receiver and giving our description to whoever is on the other side of the conversation. Isaac turns white.

Tyson and I kick into action. We look like smugglers. We are in Poland, and they may have laws about transporting goods. And now we probably have the real KGB hot on our tail. While in Europe, we heard crazy stories about how Russia still taps everyone's conversations and throws citizens in jail for no reason. We can't jeopardize our freedom or our sheepskins! We sneak out the side entrance just as two vans of cops pull up to the front. We run to the nearby train station, heavy smuggle bags bouncing up and down our bodies. The smell gets worse as the hot bags mingle with our sweat.

"Do they see us?" yells Tyson from behind me. "Run, boys!"

Isaac doesn't need encouragement. He's never run so fast in his life. Soon we are inside the station, safe and sweaty and stinky like the sheepskins we are smuggling.

At three a.m., we board the world's stinkiest train with the world's stinkiest cargo. For three hours we choke on the smell of pee-stained train upholstery and sweaty sheepskin vapors in a half-sleeping stupor. Somehow we bumble into the lobby at the Warsaw Westin before any of our classmates are awake around five-thirty a.m. We go to breakfast with sheepskins in tow, easily worth two or three hundred dollars apiece. We only paid fifteen dollars for each of them. I sell two for fifty dollars each to classmates, and keep four. Tyson works some similar deals. I leave my clothes in Poland to make room for skins. I convince our program director to give me her carry-on bag so I can fill it with skins and smuggle them back to Utah.

While I am on my capstone MBA trip, Karen and the boys are in Twin Peaks with her folks. Karen's getting in a fight, as usual. Her dad finally levels with her on getting her PhD. She can't do it. No chance. He tells her he forbids it. She married a "stallion," and she has to stop getting in Matt's way or he will never be able to focus on his career and make the big bucks. Karen calls me crying and upset and tells me how everyone is out to get her again.

"But you support me, right?" she asks.

"Of course I do," I say.

After the conversation with her dad, Karen becomes more determined than ever to get her PhD. She's already gotten into three programs and has scholarship offers from two. Both scholarship offers are from schools in Arizona. I almost have a job lined up in Tucson but I don't want the job. And I don't want to go to Tucson. It's too close to her family. I want Atlanta. I want far, far away. I need to get away from everyone. Karen got accepted by Georgia State in Atlanta, but she doesn't have a scholarship, and we are past the scholarship deadline. This puts me in a pickle. Would I rather pile on more student debt to go to Atlanta, or take the scholarship and stay an easy day's drive away from Brian?

Brian calls me the next night with the same story Karen told me. I tell him we both decided Karen will get her PhD. I appreciate his concern, but it's not up for discussion. Brian says okay but I can hear his anger. I have never disagreed with him before. He doesn't want another Dr. Adams in the family. But I know that without another degree and title to distract herself, Karen will implode. She's nothing without her "expert status." I get the, "Dr. Livingston, I presume?" joke all the time. Now when people presume within earshot of Karen, she chimes in, "*Actually,* that would be me. I start my doctorate this fall."

Karen texts me that she needs me to take her to Cancun when I get home so we can get on the same page. I am thinking, we are on the same page, I already told your dad. In Karen's mind, since I am on a vacation now, she gets a vacation too. I know she will hate it like every other vacation, but she books it on one of my credit cards, and soon I'll be going from frozen Poland to sunny Cancun.

Karen doesn't know what to do with her dad, so she needs to leave. The stallion conversation with her dad peeled back some fraction of the pain he had fractured deep inside her way back when she was little. The same pain she ran away from after the third visit with her therapist. Maybe I'll never understand the extent of it, but I do understand that I am filling the place of the son Brian had hoped

Karen would be and that Markell never will be. Karen doesn't know how to deal with her dad's disapproval except to distract herself by thinking about another vacation. I can't blame her. I just wish she would let me take her up the road to Bear Lake. They have really good shakes there.

Going to Cancun is the easiest thing in the world. You pick from the all-inclusive package, and in one click you have a flight, airport shuttle, and a resort. Everything else is taken care of: food, activities, more food. They lock you in to this filthy little isthmus full of bars and booze and folks and food and sand and sea. We spare no expense and do all of it. Ziplines and dinner shows and ATVs and underground water caves. We are just masses of asses like everyone else, paying for cookie cutter experiences. I have bigger adventures in our garage with Rex every Saturday.

Karen doesn't want to talk about options or PhD or her career goals. She doesn't really have anything to say, and I know that. I knew that before we came. We don't have adult conversations. She tells me what she wants, and I wing it. After our trip to Atlanta together, we both want to go there. We just can't do it without a scholarship. We both know turning down all that scholarship money from ASU or U of A makes no sense. The scholarship deadline has long passed. We both float statements of how great Atlanta will be, but we both know it's not going to happen. But it feels like it needs to happen.

From a really windy beach in the midst of choppy waves, Karen and I barely hear someone yell, "Help!" I look out and see a head bobbing twenty yards out in the sea. In one motion I run over and dive in, as most swimmers are getting out because of the conditions. I get to the teenage girl in no time. She looks really weak and feels really limp and can't talk when I get there. I turn her around onto her back and grab under her arm and chin with my right arm like I learned with my dad for the lifeguard merit badge on Tropic Reservoir when I was a Boy Scout.

The girl and I are caught in a riptide. I'm trying to swim us back to shore, but the waves are crashing over us, and we are going farther and farther out to sea. My heart races, but I resist the urge to thrash in the waves, conserving my energy to tread water and keep us floating as high as possible. I try to swim at an angle and gradually wend our way back to shore, but even this feels futile. We are quickly floating out to sea. I think back to the lifesaving merit badge treading water next to my dad the day when I learned how to rescue someone. Dad breathed long slow breaths and moved his legs slowly. He's really good in the water. He floated in the water that day like a genie floating in the air. So I picture Papa John and keep treading water like he would and hold the girl's head above the water while the tide carries us out. Not long after that, a jet ski zips out and hauls us back into the beach. The girl's parents are hysterical, and they quickly whisk her off the beach.

Just like that, Cancun ends, and Karen and I are in the same predicament we were in before we went. Part of me hopes the money for Karen's school in Atlanta will magically materialize before we get home. I can't face Arizona. I am trapped by her dad and we need to get far, far away. Atlanta needs to happen. I don't know how, but I know it needs to happen. I remember the night in Park City: with God all things are possible.

I call my whole family on Sunday and ask them to fast that we will go where we need to go. My whole identity rests on getting to Atlanta. I just know I need it. When I tell my mom, she says, "Okay, let's do it!" I know when Mom prays, God listens. Every time Gramalisa prays for something for her kids, she gets it.

The day after our family fast, Karen gets an email from Georgia State University: full tuition scholarship. We are headed to Atlanta. It worked.

Fasting is a regular ritual in our church. In the 1840s after the evil Mormons were forced out of America and into the Louisiana

Territory, a huge locust infestation threatened all their crops. The Mormons were forced out, the Mexicans were forced out, the Cherokee, the Catholics. Anyone President Jackson thought was weird, he sent away because he had a growing country to run.

Back to the locusts. Under the direction of Church President Brigham Young, the members fasted together that the crops would survive the locusts. After the fast, a huge flock of seagulls came and ate all the locusts. Fasting works. In Isaiah, it's said to be the key to "break every yoke." Pretty much every spiritual leader in history attained enlightenment through fasting. Jesus, the Buddha, Guru Nanak, and many others.

The first Sunday of every month, every church member in the world is invited to go without food and water for twenty-four hours in a collective spiritual effort. They donate the money they save by fasting to a relief fund to help people in need. These funds are used to house food storage facilities all over the world. The funds are also used to fund natural disaster relief efforts.

When I was little and we lived in Canada, my dad fasted a lot. One time Dad got so skinny and pale, I asked him why he wasn't eating. I thought he was dying. I was maybe four years old. Dad said he was fasting. I thought "fasting" meant he was finding a "fast" way to die. He didn't die, he was petitioning for God's help to get out of a bad situation. Those were hard years for him and my mom. We lived in a mouse- and snake-infested home where Grandpa Tom broke promise after promise to PJ. PJ fasted until he knew where to go and what to do next.

God helped him get out of there.

God helped Karen and me go to Atlanta.

A few days before the scholarship email from Georgia State, Karen texts me when I am on campus. She says she has important news. She loves giving me cliffhangers and making me ask for more. I finally get her to spit it out. "That Marilyn Manson song from *John Wick* came out on iTunes. I bought it." She loves the movie

John Wick. In a month, she will give me a fake leather John Wick jacket I don't want for my birthday.

When Karen watches action movies, she makes hungry noises at the male leads and licks her lips. Kyle doesn't go to movies with us anymore because it's so disgusting. He asks me, "Dude, why do you let her do that?" I let her do whatever she wants. I just don't want her to bite me or start crying. Of all her favorite movies to watch and lick, she likes none of them as much as *The Covenant* with Taylor Kitsch. I watch it with her several times a year and rub her feet while she moans for Taylor Kitsch. Karen has the best-looking husband in the room almost everywhere we go, but she always tries to make me feel inferior. I don't realize yet that five years of this has worn down my self-esteem and filled me with insecurities I never used to have. I know her comparing me to Hollywood guys helps her deal with her own insecurities, but it lowers my self-esteem all the same.

I miss writing so much. I need to vent. I have a lot to process with graduating and moving and changing jobs. There are enough bright spots with Kyle and life at the Logan house that I write a dozen journal entries, more than any other place we lived. I'm hopeful that Karen will finish this PhD and finally feel better.

We plan the remainder of our time in Logan out to perfection. Our home sale will close on May 1. I graduate with my MBA from Utah State on May 1. I call my company owner May 1 and quit my job. Trifecta complete, we pack our furniture in a moving POD to meet it in Atlanta two weeks later.

It may sound hard to quit my job and sell my house and move sight unseen to a city two thousand miles away so my wife can get a PhD she really doesn't want but I hope she does. It's not hard at all. It's easy. I'm not in charge anymore. I'm just riding off into the unknown believing it will work out because it has to. I don't have a job, but I am recession-proof, Kennedy taught me that. I don't want my house, I don't want my MBA, I don't want my job. I just want to be me again, and in Atlanta I will start to do that. It's May 2015 now, and what I've been doing since I met Karen in September 2009 hasn't worked, so let's get rid of it all and start from scratch. I text my friend Dan: "Sometimes you need to lose everything to find out what you have." I know I have more to lose, and I want it all gone. I want to find out who I am down there beneath this mess of a life I've made. Most of my heroes in literature and leadership lost everything at one point: Edgar Allen Poe, Johann von Goethe, Andrew Jackson, Ulysses, Jesus.

Deep down, more than anything, I need my mom. I need some *Star Trek Voyager* nights with Captain Janeway and Twizzlers licorice. I need some Scrabble nights with large fries from McDonalds because they are the only fries in Kanab. I need her forgiveness because I feel like shit for all the bullshit I've given her since I got home from my mission. I know I am hurting her every day, and I hate it. I need to talk to someone who will listen so I can feel known, and since I got rid of my mom, not a single person really knows me anymore. When Mom called "bullshit" last summer, I knew she knows what I am going through. I need more of that, but I know I can't have it. Not while I am married to Karen.

I don't know if Mom leaned on me too much or if I was too much of an emotional support to her in my dad's absence. I don't know if she and my dad have serious marriage problems. I don't know what to say to Mom or how I will even get anything out when I see her. But before we leave Utah for good, I need my mom. I need to be seen and known and loved, and Mom still loves me. I know I don't deserve it, but I know she does.

Every second Saturday in May, Kanab hosts its annual Mother's Day 10K run. PJ loves to make it a family run, and we ran it as a family several times when we were younger. I can't remember the last time I ran. We spend a week in Twin Peaks and then time it to be in Kanab the weekend of the 10K before we drive off to Georgia. I will run with Mom. I can't say much or be much or do much, but I leave my grumpy wife and two perfect little boys at the house asleep and get in the car with my mom and the rest of the family at five-twenty a.m., and we head to the bus pick up, which shuttles us to Tanner's family's Moqui Cave parking lot where the 10K begins every year.

I run step-in-step with Momma, and for the first time ever she runs the entire race. She wants to stop and rest but I don't let her, I tell her she can do it, and we slow down a little but then speed back up again. During the race, I tell her several times I love her and even though I have no right to say it, we both know it's the truth, and I feel so much better. Somehow she finds the strength to keep running and finish the entire 10K in under sixty minutes and win her age group! Someone snaps a picture of us as we cross the finish line side-by-side. After an hour running with my mom, I feel everything I needed to feel. I frame the picture of us finishing the race together and mail it to her for Mother's Day a few days later. First I pay a lady through Etsy with really pretty handwriting to write on really pretty paper that I put in a frame next to the photo of my really pretty Mom something she always says to her kids when things get hard: "We can do hard things."

Section 8

I don't know till we get here that we are moving into an apartment in Section 8 housing. Peachtree City, just south of Atlanta, has a really high cost of living, so we took what we could find online that didn't break the bank. Now it makes sense why these apartments are almost half the cost of all the others in town. We needed to move here since I am going to work at Delta soon, and everyone who works at Delta lives in Peachtree City. The day after we arrive, I put in our notice. When we get there, our apartment isn't ready yet, so they let us sleep in the model apartment. Our POD full of stuff hasn't even arrived. I put in our notice before we ever set foot through the door to our place. We will pay through June and July, and then find somewhere where drug deals and robberies aren't happening every night.

I call PODS to get an update, and ours has been sitting in someone's driveway in Texas. It's springtime, moving season, and as we drive around Peachtree City, I see other people's PODS everywhere and wonder if any of them are even at the right home. Some of them are there in the driveway day after day after day, like another garage, what are people so busy with that they can't load or unload their POD and get it off their property? When ours finally arrives, one guys hops out of the truck, and with some really cool hydraulics technology, drops it in the parking lot all by himself. I can't believe how efficiently he unloads his burden. I want to unload my burdens that easily.

I'm finding a job, living in the ghetto, and getting yelled at more than usual because it's all my fault. I know this means more stress shopping, and we will need babysitters ASAP so I can keep Karen from biting me.

I stuff some things in our patio closet and feel something sticky fall on my arm. I look up and see a stream of barbecue grease pooling beside the grill on the patio above us, fiesta music blazing, and the sound of a hundred matadors skipping around up there. We are in the basement unit. The little matadors above us will skip around all day and all night and never stop skipping. At first, all I can see is the nuisance of their grease and their noise. Soon I will broaden my view and see an opportunity. The energetic little bull runners upstairs will end up getting us out of this two-month minimum commitment in Section 8 housing one month early.

A few nights in, I park and walk from my car to the apartment just as it's getting dark out. I cross paths with a guy thumbing a thick wad of cash between his hands. His drawers are drooping to his knees and when he turns to pull them up, I see a gun tucked in his waistband that somehow hasn't fallen out. I don't change my pace or bat an eye, but I have two little babies just a few steps away, and this can't be happening on my doorstep. I look back over my shoulder as I go inside the apartment, find our rental agreement, and scrutinize every line until I find our way out of here: complaints section.

If residents are unsatisfied with living conditions they can file an official complaint with the office. Complaint must be reasonably settled within one week. If a resident files three unresolved complaints within thirty days, they may break their contract and all monies will be refunded, even the deposit. Game on! Thank you, dancing matador children upstairs with the leaky barbecue! I file three complaints through mail and email spaced exactly eight days after the first, and we are gone after just a few weeks.

For the first complaint, I go up to see the matadors at three a.m. and cannot believe the noise as I knock on the door. It's three o'clock in the morning! One of the kids opens the door for me. They all stop running and they all stare at me. Kids. Lots and lots of Hispanic kids. They are everywhere. On the counters, on the furniture, on the floor. At least a dozen of them, maybe more. Their little grandma sits quietly on the couch just looking at me. Expressionless. I wave and smile and shut the door, and they all go back to running around. What a mess. There's no way the management will mess with these people.

We don't get away before getting haunted. I don't sleep much the entire month we stay, usually from the little matadors upstairs. I shrug off the noise and try to return to sleep but tonight, it's not little feet upstairs, it's a scream down the hallway. As soon as I come to attention, I know I am hearing Rex. He sounds terrified. I run out of my room and into his but can't find him anywhere. Even with the lights on I still can't see him. Then I hear him shudder and see him crouched behind his nightstand behind me. I hold him as he tells me he was trying to hide from the eagle that flew in to poke his eyes out and fly him away. We both hide behind the nightstand until Rex says the eagle has gone. I am so glad we are leaving soon. I have never seen him so terrified. Every night for months he prays and asks me to pray too that the eagle won't come and get him.

Karen knows how to get what she wants from people. While I am driving to Delta for interviews and networking like crazy to make money, she is finding people people to watch our kids so she can relax. All our in-state babysitters are gone. Karen gets on Care.com and finds us a nanny named Hannah. Hannah will be with us until the end. She walks right past the drug dealers and gangsters into our little apartment to watch the boys so I can take Karen to get her weekly fixes of frozen yogurt and R-rated movies. Hannah comes almost every day, at least for a few hours. She will dress the boys up like cows to go to Chick-fil-a and take them shopping at Target and walk Rhett in his stroller so Rex can splash in puddles. We are one step closer to Karen's dream of being a professor and working in an office where she will never have to worry about motherhood, but why should she sit at home and wait for school to start in three months when she can have me pay a nanny for that? Karen finds a few backup babysitters for the evenings when Hannah isn't available.

Our first few weeks at church, Karen finds a backup nanny and I find an interim boss. I don't know if she likes her backup nanny more for watching the boys or for the fact that her husband starts crushing on Karen right away, and she loves the attention. He will text her a shirtless selfie in a few days. I just shake my head. He's a firefighter and EMT. Karen joins the boys and I on a short walk in the Georgia humidity on the golf cart paths behind our ghetto apartment, and she passes out after just a few minutes. Pete the shirtless selfie firefighter comes to the rescue in no time and strings her an IV from a floor lamp to bring her back to life.

One day the boys are with Pete's wife at their home out in the woods, and Rex goes exploring and finds a bunch of ground hornets. Rex loves bees. He used to play with them at our home in Logan. He would hold them until they stung him and then he'd cry for a little while and then do it again. Ground hornets have a much higher level of venom. He gets stung by about fifteen of them all at once. Even if you aren't allergic, this is a near-lethal dose for a toddler. I hop in my car and speed away from work, and Karen leaves her nail salon or wherever she has gone, and we meet at Pete's house to find a drowsy Rex full of Benadryl and hornet stings. I leave my car there and hold Rex while Karen drives us to dinner with my new boss. Rex soon falls asleep on me in the car, sleeps all through dinner, and keeps sleeping until the next morning when my prayers are answered and he feels much better.

The dinner sleeping-Rex didn't get to enjoy is with Dave Taylor who owns The Blind Guyz. He hires me on the spot, and we divide the area just like when I sold pest control, and we set off on a killer summer. I sell the blinds, he installs them and sells them more blinds, and we split the profit fifty/fifty. I can't believe he is willing to pay me so much. We don't have much competition, and the area is booming with new homes, and every new home needs window coverings. Dave doesn't know what he has gotten into. I sell everyone. I get to know all the real estate agents so well some of the homeowners think they have to buy from us, like it's part of their HOA. We play it up and let the customer believe whatever they like, Dave and I are both like that, we just keep talking until they order our blinds. We have killer sample displays, we use special color words like "ecru" and phraseology like "double hung" and "blackout" and "energy efficient," and people sign on whatever line we ask them to when we tell them how beautiful their home will look. It's such a relief that I can pay for all the boys' caretakers again.

Karen really, really, really wants to buy a house. Her eyes are glued to Zillow when they aren't on the Kardashians. I have the income history to buy a house, like we did in Logan, but since my current job is commission only, we can't get a loan. Karen tells me we need a house so she doesn't have to be the only mom in Peachtree City who doesn't have a house. I do all I can think of and try to convince Dave to commit mortgage fraud. I ask him, look at these commission checks, Dave, they are insane. You're paying me two or three grand a week most of the time. Just put me on salary so I can get a mortgage and then put me back on commission afterwards. Yeah, well, that's mortgage fraud. Dave calls a friend and finds out as much before going forward with my desperate plan to please a desperate wife. Karen decides she hates Dave and it's all his fault and I need to quit.

I am interviewing like crazy at Delta. I network with current Delta employees I find at church, BYU alumni on LinkedIn and Utah State alumni on LinkedIn. My dad has an old pilot friend from FIT before Dad left his dreams of becoming a pilot to go save the ranch in Alberta. If you get an employee referral for a job posting, your chances are ten times better to get the job, so I get referred for all the positions I can. Delta calls me in for interview after interview, but they keep promoting from within instead of hiring me. I kill it in the interviews, and I know I am a great fit for many of the positions, but it's just not working. Later in the summer, Delta will announce the biggest round of layoffs in company history. Almost ten thousand employees lose their jobs, including several of the guys who were lining up interviews for me.

Finally, I've had enough. I make the third and final round for another position and respond to an early question. "I'm so tired of this, let's just part ways now instead of you pretending to listen and me trying to make you like me, okay? I showed up, so you can check your box there that you interviewed enough external candidates to get permission to promote someone from within. Thank you." They let me leave. From May to October 2015, I will apply for over seventy positions and interview for forty-three of them. Ultimately, I will apply for an entry-level position working in the airport so I myself can get promoted from within. I will finally get the offer in October but won't take it. By October, an old friend will come to town and make me a job offer I can't refuse.

The White House

God reminds me He Himself moved us to Georgia when He sends Matt Kennedy to town with news that his new company is ready to hire their first salesperson. If Karen wants a house, then she is just going to have to deal with it.

He and his business partner make me an offer over dinner a few days before Halloween 2015. I finally have an offer from Delta, but I know before Matt and his partner Aaron make me the offer that I will take it, regardless of salary. Kennedy told me about this Aaron guy before. When he calls me, he says, "Livingston, we need you. I told Aaron if I ever got a chance to do business with you again, I would."

Kennedy and Aaron are in Utah, but the company runs online, and I can sell the technology anywhere in Georgia. Aaron chimes in. "Anybody who can sell worth crap will be making three-hundred-k within two years." Then Aaron tells me that working at Delta sounds stupid, and he leaves. I can't say I disagree. I fixated on Delta to make sure I got far away from Utah and Doctor Adams more than anything else.

Before Aaron leaves dinner, he and Kennedy gave me a quick rundown of their tech. They write quick consumer loans based on a customer's recent activity in their bank accounts, no credit check, no paperwork, no manual underwriting. My wife has every store credit card she can get, and I know if you can make it fast and easy for consumers to borrow money, they will do it.

"We think we can get to a hundred million," says Matt.

"This will be a billion, easy," I reply.

Then I ask for an equity/salary combo.

"It's a little late for that," says Aaron. No dice. I should counter: "What if I sell five million my first year?" The entire company will do thirty million in 2015, so this would sound almost impossible. He would probably reply, "Sure, dude, good luck doing that!" But I will sell that much for him in 2016. A few months later, Aaron will send a company email that Kennedy has secured his spot in heaven for recruiting Matt Livingston. It will make me feel a kind of good that I haven't felt in a long time. Reading his email will make me feel valued. It will make me realize that my wife does not value me. It will make me want to leave her.

The company we will later call Imaca brings my Self back from the dead. I become unstoppable. Kennedy and Aaron and other guys who are really smart believe in me, and I crush it. The rift between how Karen treats me and the treatment I get at work starts to widen. She scoffs at me and tells me how poor we are and how lucky I am she puts up with me. Aaron says I am securing people's spots in heaven. I realize for the first time I am not a worthless adult, and I'm starting to let myself get pretty fed up with my angry wife. The boys and I are more than "the absent-minded professor" and "the offspring."

I decide not to get her a second bowl of ice cream for her nightly Kardashians binge, and she calls me a "fucking pussy" with an ice-cold glare. I say nothing, but for the first time feel my skin get hot with anger. I am not okay with this anymore. Whether she is going to die or not, this has to stop. I am not an idiot, and I am not a pussy. I am the best sales employee in a hundred-million-dollar company. I'm not up for being put down anymore. She doesn't hate Matt Kennedy because he said something she didn't like years ago. She hates Matt Kennedy because he loves me. She hates everyone who loves me.

I go to the Lucky Brand Outlets in Savannah, and for the first time in my adult life buy my own pants to wear for my new job.

Karen finds out and starts crying and tells me I can't do that. She's not mad that I get to wear jeans at work, which is a dream come true, she's mad that I acted independently and she didn't pick them out. In her mind, I am her property. She picks out my clothes. She wants me to apologize and tell her I am wrong and being selfish, she wants me to feel bad for leaving her out of my shopping spree. For the first time I see clearly she really just wants to control me. I wonder, "What have I gotten myself into?"

Time in Atlanta away from Doctor Adams has already brought clarity to my mind, and I am finally thinking for myself for the first time in my adult life. They're just pants! Of course I can buy my own pants! I am sitting here looking at a pathetic wife who wants me to apologize to her for buying my own pants and then take her on a date afterward to make it up to her. I don't want to have these kinds of conversations anymore. But I still apologize to her just like I apologize to her thirty times a day every day for everything I do and sixty times on Sundays. I still prefer to take the blame and protect her fractured feelings rather than deal with her screaming and crying and kicking me out of the bedroom. But I've almost reached my breaking point.

After Karen struggles to park her Honda Pilot in the parking garage at Georgia State, she needs another new car. We agree a late-model Honda Accord will work, since she just needs a reliable commuter car to get her through school. We already spent all the money from selling our home in Logan on me taking her to Six Flags and paying for our new nanny and now a full-time daycare too. Karen's PhD fees add up, we pay expensive health insurance premiums before I start at Imaca, and I begin repaying my $35,000 MBA loan. We can free up a few thousand dollars trading in the Pilot for an older sedan. Cool.

Why do I let myself believe Karen will follow through with our plan? She leaves the lot with the newest sport model Accord. Instead of saving us money, the Accord payment costs a hundred dollars a month more than the Pilot did. We go from $312 a month for the

Pilot to $431.88 for the Accord. We started at $253 with the new 2011 CRV we bought in January 2012 for Rex. How much will her next car payment be? I am so mad after I buy her another new car. She's immediately singing my praises and posting pictures about her amazing husband, so instead of saying anything to her, I mutter myself through how I will afford the higher payment. Every time I drive down a hill in our 2003 Corolla with the check engine light on, I will slide it into Neutral. That should save at least five bucks a week in gas money. Also, the cat. Shaving the cat costs fifty bucks a month. I open my Amazon app and buy some used cat clippers for six bucks. I need to cut out a hundred and twenty a month, I get fifty for shaving the cat plus twenty-ish for hopefully not breaking the Corolla transmission which puts me at seventy. Close enough.

For Christmas Karen wants a five-hundred dollar plastic ring that lights up when you get a text message. If she doesn't get it, she might die. She won't stop talking about it. I tell her no. She says fine, she will get a boob job instead. I say no again. She buys herself the five-hundred dollar "Ringly" for Christmas anyway. I return it. Time to start setting some boundaries. She wants a boob job to fix her self-esteem just like she wants a Ringly to fix her self-esteem just like she wants new pants every week to fix her self-esteem just like she wanted a PhD to fix her self-esteem. None of these things will make her happy. Enough is enough.

My sister Kelly moves out to Georgia and moves back in with us for a couple months in October 2015 to finish out the year with us and her nephews. This is where Rex begins riding between her legs on her skateboard. He can't get enough of it. They will leave around lunchtime and not come back until after dark. They travel ten, even twenty miles in a day together. Peachtree City doesn't have sidewalks; it has a hundred miles of golf cart paths. They are perfect for skateboards too. We use Kelly for free babysitting to give our Nanny Hannah a break.

Kelly gets some sort of weird rash, but we still ask her to do an overnight with the boys so I can take Karen to Savannah for her birthday. She doesn't complain, so I have no idea her rash turns into hives and her whole body is red and puffy. But in the midst of her body freaking out and taking care of two little boys, Kelly doesn't answer her phone fast enough one of the times Karen is trying to get an update. When she does check in with us, she still says nothing about the hives.

When we get home the next day, my angry wife has me sit Kelly down to watch me give her a disappointed father talk. She doesn't care about Kelly's condition at all. We sit in the living room and I yell at Kelly with her face big and puffy from the hives. Then Karen even has her apologize for eating some of the pizza we left money for them to buy. What? I step out of my body and see myself talking, watching someone else in my body saying these words. Why am I yelling at my own sister for doing me a favor and watching two very rambunctious children so I can take my wife on another stupid date? How long will I yell at everyone I love on behalf of someone I just wish would die?

Kelly finally apologizes to the Great One's satisfaction and we let her go to Instacare. I feel so filthy. That was not right.

Now Karen won't let Kelly be alone with both boys from then on. Whenever we are gone and Kelly is there with the boys, Nanny Hannah has to be there too. They do not get along at all.

My faith quickly comes back to me in Georgia. I finally don't hide from God. I start to tell him I am dying here in this marriage and I feel Him listening. The pains from returning from my mission and feeling abandoned are gone. I still mutter a lot to myself but I start replacing some of my destructive self-talk with prayers. I pray with gratitude for my boys and that I don't have to listen to Brian Adams anymore. And I pray that somehow my marriage will get better.

Karen tells our new church bishop if he doesn't make her happy she won't come to church. She says it just like that, in the main hallway, in front of a bunch of people. She wants power and recognition, so he gives her some. He asks us to teach the new Marriage and Family Relationships class. We will get a group of couples, graduate them in a few months, and get a new group. We will end up teaching two groups. Teaching this class will finally open my eyes about my marriage.

The lessons are complete disasters. We are supposed to teach from the lesson manual provided. Instead, Karen gets Brian on the phone to give us the real scoop on the weekly lessons. She quotes him and trumps the lesson manual every week. Nobody can challenge her since her dad has a PhD and now she almost does too, so she's the authority. Our first lesson is about communication. A wife in the class says sometimes when she gets angry she sends her husband an email because it's hard for her to talk about her feelings. I am about to tell her how great of her to find a way to communicate her feelings and that there's no one right way to communicate but the key is to keep your heart open and keep communicating, but Karen cuts me off.

"That's never acceptable and that's passive-aggressive behavior. You should stop sending emails." Karen says this. Author of the most passive-aggressive email of all time, to Gramalisa, about how she folds the laundry wrong. Karen keeps going and lets this poor gal have it. She continues, "If all you do is write emails, then you and your husband are living like roommates with no meaningful communication."

When Karen says that, I realize I've been living with a roommate my entire marriage. I've not once been completely honest with her. Then the gal starts to cry and runs out of the room. Karen has a smug look on her face like "serves her right." On the drive home after church, Karen tells me she will never go back to church and that she will never teach that stupid class again.

Then we teach "Unity and Equality." I read through the lesson and realize I am in real trouble. Karen does next to nothing. I do almost everything. I earn all the income, pay all the bills, do the cleaning and the yardwork, and do the parenting. Karen looks at me and the boys and hocks her throat in disgust at us and goes back to watching the Kardashians because she is better than us. I even shave her stupid cat just like I groomed her stupid Newfies in Logan. Even though they were a lot of work, I kind of miss those Newfies. They were almost as big as horses when we moved from Logan. We left them with an older lady whose two Newfies had recently passed away. Chief and Alaska were her answers to prayer.

We keep moving forward in the lesson manual through an increasingly hostile class environment. The next lesson is "Controlling Behavior." More eye openers. I read through the chapter and realize that Karen uses every single one of the harmful tactics listed in the chapter to control me. I'm nervous going into the lesson and Karen is running late.

I say in my normal self-deprecating way, "In just a minute, the brains of my marriage will be here and we can start."

One of the husbands responds, "What are you talking about? I have all the brains in my marriage. I say what goes." His wife nods fiercely and supportively, and in the middle of all this, Karen walks in and looks at us like we are guilty of a crime.

Karen launches into her ultimate brag, that I take her on at least one date a week every week, and that we are still boyfriend and girlfriend falling in love. I feel sick when she says this. For the first time ever, someone responds to her with a challenge.

One of the guys in the class says, "What a waste of money, eating out that much!"

It gets better.

In the middle of the lesson, Karen teaches the group how to give criticism to your partner. She calls it a compliment-sandwich. Compliment-criticism-compliment. She gives an example: "You are really good at *this,* but could you just do *this one little thing* better, oh and also you're really good at *this,* too." You give one big compliment, and then a little criticism, and then follow it up with another big compliment. The compliments are the pieces of bread and the criticism is the middle part.

The class hates this idea.

One husband says, "That is the stupidest thing I have ever heard! If you have criticism, you give it straight and say what you mean! Otherwise you'll never understand each other!" I love it. Then he and his wife start going after each other. They are a power couple who run marathons and triathlons together and I love them.

The husband says, "Yeah I'll tell you something, it pissed me off last Saturday at our son's soccer game when you forgot the cooler at home."

And then she fires right back, "Well, I only did that because you forgot to get the Gatorades like you said you would!" They apologize to each other and kiss. I love it. It's so real. No walking on eggshells. Real honest love.

Karen gets up and leaves. I don't have to say anything. Guys who have good marriages say it for me.

Now I know for sure: Karen and Brian are full of crap. Why didn't I see this earlier?

When we move out of Section 8 to rent the little white house Karen found for us, we cross an invisible boundary into a different church family. Karen doesn't want to switch churches at first, but after this lesson we switch right away. We can never return to the old church after what they said to her. Our new bishop's wife has a boob job, and now Karen says she really needs new boobs. I tell her I am not buying her boobs. She decides instead that she's getting a tattoo, for real.

I am exhausted from staving off her boob job requests and I am exhausted from five years of her telling me she's getting a tattoo that I know she never will because if her parents find out they will disown her. So I say, "Fine, go get a tattoo!" She's gone for less than thirty minutes and comes back with a "tattoo." Her eyes are as big as grapefruits when she lifts her shirt over her ribs and shows it to me. It's clearly fake. The fake tattoo says "Fortis Fortuna Adiuvat" or "fortune favors the bold" in Latin in big black cursive letters. The same tattoo John Wick has. I shake my head and laugh out loud. She tells me it's real, but I know you can't get a tattoo that fast.

Karen leaves and goes to a CrossFit party where they all drink and play poker and the owner of the gym hooks up with all the girls. She wants to show her ink to people who will appreciate it. I don't even care. When she gets back, I see her skin peeling off around the fake tattoo she got. Her skin is red and irritated. It's real! She starts to cry and pours her soul out about how meaningful those words are to her ever since she watched John Wick kill a hundred people. She says this tattoo will give her strength to do her PhD.

Her depression no longer represents how I feel inside like it did when we first met at BYU. I'm feeling pretty good these days and I can't even take Karen's antics seriously anymore. I still feel bad for her, but she's getting out of control. It's time to grow up. In 2016, we will do more loans for Imaca in the state of Georgia than in any other state, even California or New York where they have six times the population. One of my guys sends me that bar chart, and I feel great about the achievement. I am a stallion, just like Brian said. The one thing he got right. Things are rolling for me, but Karen seems far worse than ever before. And she was pretty bad before.

When I finally wake up in my marriage, I wake up all at once, all in the same day. Some of our new church friends invite us to go wakeboarding with them. Four-year-old Rex gets to go first. He gets up on his first attempt, and I can't believe my eyes. He's riding for several minutes, so I get out my phone and snap some pictures of him while holding two-year-old Rhett. Karen doesn't approve of my recklessness. The boat is going maybe three miles an hour on a glass-flat lake. I routinely walk across fallen-log bridges with both boys on my shoulders. This is not reckless. She snaps at me across the boat, loud enough for everyone to hear, "Stop taking pictures, you're going to drop Rhett, you idiot!" and she glares at me in front of the entire boat of people. I let myself get mad at her for the first time. I look back at her with anger I've never let her see before. I sting her good and hold my gaze until she's the one who looks away. I don't ever let my feelings out, even if only in a look, and it feels good. I stare right into her pathetic miserable glaring eyes with the anger of a slave looking back at an abusive master.

After a few other riders, it's my turn. I strap in, but when the boat starts pulling me, I can't remember how to get up on the water. It's been a couple years since I've been wakeboarding. I am forgetting to bend my knees. When Devin, the boat driver, starts picking up speed, I am still on my back with my board parallel to the boat. I must be displacing hundreds or even thousands of gallons of water while I hold on but still I don't stand up. I'm like the parachute a small plane releases to stop quickly after landing. Usually it doesn't get this far. Usually one of two things happens: either the boat pulls you up, or you let go of the rope. Not this time. We remain in this weird stalemate far too long while Devin keeps revving the engine and I stay down in the water. My arms hurt and I wonder if the rope will snap off the boat, but I just hold on. Eventually I'm displacing what feels like the entire lake and Devin stops and circles the boat back around to remind me to bend my knees. "Holy cow, Matt, you are strong!" he says. I laugh and he continues, "You were pushing so much water I couldn't even get the boat to go! Bend your knees a little, and you'll get right up."

I bend my knees and crush wakeboarding the rest of the day.

Devin's words stick with me while we drive home, "Holy cow, Matt, you are strong!" We get home and put the boys down to bed, and I decide Karen needs to apologize to me, so I sit her down on the couch. I've never gotten her to apologize for anything, not once, but she needs to apologize for calling me an idiot and glaring at me on the boat. She tries turning it back on me and making me apologize, but I don't let her. I want to think it's not a big deal and let it go like I always do, but I don't let myself.

"Stop! I am not an idiot, and you don't get to treat me like an idiot anymore," I say. "Now, apologize."

She's stunned. I'm doing to her what she does to me all the time: demanding an apology. Only she actually hurt me. This isn't some imaginary grievance like the ones she's always bringing to me.

Karen starts to cry and tells me it's the depression's fault. She tells me at her last doctor's visit he told her she needs another medication because her depression is worsening. He told her she is the worst case he has ever seen. She has two medications already, and this will be her third. And then I see it. All in an instant her face changes, and she turns into a little old lady, looking at me, a little old man, and she's still just as miserable and I'm still just as stuck. I'm never going to make her happy, a PhD will never make her happy, a new house will never make her happy. I can stay here for fifty years if I want to, but nothing will change. It's all the Acutane's fault and my fault and her depression's fault. Her life is everyone's fault except her own. She is miserable and always will be. And then I hear Devin's words again. "Holy cow, Matt, you are strong!," but I don't want to be strong anymore. I am not strong enough for this. I finally admit it to myself. I can't do this. I can't kick my mom and my dad and my sisters and my friends out of my life anymore because Karen hates that they love me. I can't look into my sad little boys' eyes one more time asking me to stay and play while I stick them with one more babysitter or daycare so I can leave them anyway and take their mom on one more date so she can go on one more shopping spree and brag about it to one more person who doesn't care. I don't want to be strong and tall and handsome anymore. I don't want to be Bradley Cooper or Tom Hardy or Keanu Reeves anymore.

I just want to be me.

The vision fades but I sit on the couch and let it resonate. For the first time in my adult life, I feel *aware*. I can't wait for Karen to die anymore. My life needs to change, and it needs to change now. I felt anger for the first time today, and now I feel stress and fear and anxiety and a bunch of other feelings. I feel them all over inside of me. I wonder if I have heart disease, because I finally feel all the anxiety I have kept bottled up inside, and it scares me. I wonder if I have cancer from all the stress I feel in my heart. I close my eyes and try to feel my mind, my brain. I picture my brain and see it tearing in two halves like a piece of string cheese. I wonder if I am insane, if I am in real trouble, if it's too late for me. Have I lost my mind? I feel like I am lucky to be alive. I should have had a nervous breakdown by now. And now that I am paying attention, I know I'm not far from that. No more. I don't need to be strong anymore. I need to get away. I need to be me. But how?

We are approaching Kyle's wedding in August 2016. He and his wife will get married in the Salt Lake City LDS Temple. The namesake of the school where Karen and I met, Brigham Young, broke ground for the temple in the 1850s. Right near that temple are the headquarters for my company.

I start spreading the word that *the* Matt Livingston will be coming into the office for a visit. I have always sent lots of goodies to the folks working hard at the home office to thank them. I start getting lots of notes and emails from people who want to see me. I start making appointments and am feeling good about finally meeting all my work friends. Among them are many females. Among the females are many single females. Among the many single females there's one a few people have warned me about. Kennedy warned me about her. She's a homewrecker. She pursues married men and has gone after lots of the higher-level guys at Imaca. Now I need her to go after me. This is my way out. If I can get her to make Karen mad enough, I am sure I can get away.

The homewrecker and I work together a lot. Her department sends all the money to our stores, and I need them to get their money fast, so we talk several times per day. Before I head to Utah, I make sure she knows we will be seeing each other. This could not be more perfect.

I need to meet Nikki, fall in love with her, and damage Karen past the point of no return. This is my shot, and I'm going to take it. I reached my breaking point, and now I have a way out. But it's a huge gamble, and I'll need to execute it perfectly. I can't tell anyone, or the whole thing will fall apart. I need to do this alone, and I need to take it as far as I can. Karen will get so angry that it will work. If Karen suspects I am playing a game, it won't work, she will tell Brian and we will be stuck in his stupid lessons the rest of my life. I can't take it too far, either. If I go too far, everyone will turn against me, and my kids will hate me and disown me because I will be an adulterer. I just need to convince Karen that I have fallen in love with someone else. And to do that, I need Nikki to fall in love with me. That part will be easy. She probably already has. But what about Kyle? How can I go faking an affair and ruining my marriage the same week of his wedding?

I am Kyle's big brother and I am his example. For Kyle's sake, I should not do this. Kyle needs to know that eternal marriage like they teach in the LDS church isn't just a dream. Maybe I am strong enough to just stay married. I cannot risk losing Kyle. I've made it six years already, what's another sixty? Nope, I can't. I can't take one more day. My kids are young, they won't remember anything, everyone else seems not too fond of Karen, but what will Kyle think? My only hangup is Kyle. I cannot do this because I cannot lose my brother. It's not worth it to play this risky move the week of his wedding. I can't do it. But I have to do it. My most important duty as his big brother is to do the best I can. I'm finally going to do that, even though he may hate me and call me a pussy just like my wife.

I'm going to do it. Kyle, please forgive me. This is my best chance. I love you. Forgive me. I will always love you. I've only ever wanted to be a good example to you. I screwed up. I am so sorry. I can't fulfill my commitment on this one, the biggest commitment I ever made, the same one you are about to make. You are doing it the right way with the right woman. I did it the wrong way with the wrong woman. You believed in yourself after your mission and trusted God and gave yourself time. I didn't believe in myself and tried to make the wrong people happy and now nobody is happy. All I have are my kids, and my wife won't even let me see them most of the time. She would rather have them with daycares and nannies, and I hate it. I cry every time I drop Rhett off at daycare, and I know he will be damaged his whole life because he has a mom who will not love him. She doesn't love me and Rex either. Rhett bawls his eyes out every time I leave him at daycare, and as soon as I drive off to work, I do the same thing. My marriage broke me, Kyle, and I don't know what I'm doing, but I'm going to break free. I'm going to make her so mad that it will all just go away.

Kyle's Wedding

She's not as cute as I hoped, but she will do just fine. I can already tell she's in love with me. One of the Imaca owners announces loudly as I walk in the office, "Well, look at that, it's the great Matt Livingston!" as he hands me a Fresca from a mini fridge. I am nervous and anxious for my secret evil deed I am there to commit. I only have enough time for a quick hello with Nikki, and then it's on to the next department. I'm not going to have enough time today to let Nikki set her hooks into me. I'll have to come back tomorrow.

I have met very few of my coworkers before today, and now I get to meet everyone. They are so happy to see me. My work friend Jade and I have been teaming up to send them See's Candy all year. We pick it out together, I Venmo him, he picks it up and drops it off. Imaca is filled with people who respect me and treat me well. I am the king of the afternoon. But clearly I am not going to fall in love in the middle of all the rigamaroo of today.

Today is Thursday, and Nikki comes in at six a.m. on Fridays. After I leave, I text her that I will come in tomorrow at six a.m. so we can talk some more. She asks me what she can bring me? Water, please.

Karen has been texting me nonstop to hurry up and bring food for everyone. I meet up with Kyle and we go to Café Rio and buy a boatload of food for everyone and to spare. We and the boys are there, my three sisters and their kids, my parents, some of my dad's family from Canada came down too. We are in a seven-bedroom Airbnb packed to the seams. There are enough bodies that I have plenty of space from Karen. She's trying to impress them all with her expert opinions about everything. Rex got super tan at our stopover in Vegas at the Golden Nugget where we swam in the shark pool for two days. We met the Adams there before driving to Salt Lake City for the wedding.

My sister Kelly and Rex are inseparable and always have been, but even more so now after their months of skateboarding in Peachtree City last fall. None of us can keep up with them. Kelly met us in Vegas for the two days so she could spend that time with Rex. She tells everyone at dinner she's buying a bullet bike and my Eeyore brother-in-law, Mark, says, "Just make sure you watch out for object fixation." None of them, not one of them at the table, not nobody in this world, knows about the object I am fixated on. Fall in love with a stranger to irreparably damage the large wife who walked in front of all of us on the way to eat pizza somewhere on the Strip and thereby gain separation from her forevermore.

Tomorrow morning, at six a.m. sharp.

But right now we are all sitting at the table eating Café Rio while Kelly makes videos of Rex, who just gave her the sweetest compliment. She wants him to say it again for the camera, but he's a little zoned out just eating his food, and somehow he ends up blurting, "You look horrible!" Mid-laugh, Kelly corrects him. "No, the prettiest girl ever, remember!" and he quickly mimics her correction before she has finished, and repeats the correct statement he gave just moments earlier: "The prettiest girl ever!" We laugh for days at Rex videos. When he introduces us to strangers, he says, "Hi, this is my dad Matt from Imaca and I'm Rex, I'm a genius."

At five-thirty a.m. with not a creature stirring at the Airbnb, I smash some pushups and shower so I can meet Nikki in a more private setting. We meet on the parking deck and walk inside together.

She hands me a huge bottle of Smartwater. I can't believe I am really doing this! We take the stairs instead of the elevator, and her heels clank loudly, echoing against the stairwell walls. I want to say, "Sssh, someone might hear us!" but I know nobody is listening. A few souls enter and exit the office, but nobody is looking. We sit together on the couches in the break area and talk for half an hour, and I ask her a bunch of questions. I need enough ammo to get her to fall in love with me on the double. She's an open book. She tells me about her jellyfish tattoo and her friend dating the married guy, and I can see the hunger in her eyes.

I text her a few minutes after leaving the office, "I can't stop thinking about you."

She texts back almost instantly. "I was about to tell you the same thing."

Game on.

My heart rate is through the roof, so I put all that cortisol to use at the nearest Anytime Fitness and then head back to the Airbnb. Everyone is still asleep or in their rooms, and nobody knows I was gone or asks where I went. I wait for someone to say something, but nobody does. I have an alibi and a time-stamped key fob swipe at Anytime to prove where I went, just in case. I need time.

Nikki and I text constantly for the next two weeks. We talk like we always have about work, but the calls last for hours. We share songs back and forth, one of them is the theme song from the *Suicide Squad* movie, a remake of "You Don't Own Me." It helps me describe to Nikki perfectly how I feel about my marriage. I am not owned anymore. She's very sympathetic.

I give a killer toast at Kyle's wedding luncheon. I am a good public speaker. When I can add some real feeling into what I am saying, I move people. I say some moving words for him and Bailey that day. The emotion I bring comes from a good place, but it's full of conflict. I don't think anyone else can sense the conflict or feel the inner turmoil I am experiencing as I pour all the hope in my soul out for my brother and his wife. I think they only feel the love I have for Kyle, the strongest of all my loves, the brotherly love that kept me going when otherwise by now I would have quit and found a different way out of my marriage.

I don't know it yet, but I will never have to see my father-in-law again, the one who followed up on his daughter's prediction and really turned me into a liar. Luckily, he has found another Matt already. For years he has told Karen's younger sisters they need to find a Matt just like me. Karen's next sister in line has done just that and brings her fiancé named Matt over to the Airbnb to play games with us Friday night. I stare at him and think, good luck, they're calling you "Rachel's Matt" for now, but soon they will stop, and you will be the only Matt. You've got a rough road ahead of you, Matt.

At Kyle and Bailey's open house, Karen will not stop talking. We are all at Bailey's parent's house, and at the dinner table, it's all about Karen. In the living room, it's all about Karen. Now that I am officially not her Honey Matchu anymore, I leave to go play with the kids. One of them screams "snake" and while all the other kids run away, I see Rex freeze and poise like a hound dog and then tear off into the grass. I take off right behind him. Rex takes off like a Tesla, no lag, his acceleration astounding for a four-year-old. He can go from full stop to full speed in an instant. He catches the snake, and I catch him just on the edge of the lawn near a ravine, and then we all drop each other and fall to the grass. His eyes are wild with excitement. This is so much better than sitting inside at the table listening to my wife talk and talk and talk about how she's an expert at everything. I'm so embarrassed at the way she interjects and overpowers people like this. Karen can talk all she wants for now. I won't be here much longer.

At the reception, I start talking business with my cousin Neal, who I haven't seen in years. We talk about customer data and fraud prevention and third parties like Clarity and DataX and FactorTrust. I tell him with the volume we are doing at Imaca, we will get to $100 million by the end of the year, and soon we will have enough data to underwrite our own loans without having to use third parties. I'm just getting started and want to go into predictive analytics and collections tactics, but Neal's over it, he doesn't really care. I shut up and smile and realize I am high on work because work provided Nikki, who is about to get me out of my marriage.

Before we moved to Canada, I grew up around Neal in the Salt Lake Valley. Neal taught me how to play Mario Kart and throw a baseball and dig under the cushions on a couch to find spare change for my piggy bank. He and his brother, Scott, played catch with me all the time. They went on to play college baseball. Scott got injured lifting weights and spiraled down a path of painkillers and prescription drug abuse because a coach told him to lift too much. Scott's sad drug story reminds me of Tim's sad drug story. They needed love, not drugs. Just like I need love.

So many people go down and out forever from one bad choice. I made one bad choice, but I will not let it drag me down any longer. When all these people see me again, they will get to have the real me back. Especially Kyle. If he will still have me. I really don't know if he will. It's pretty messed up to use someone else's wedding reception to plan the destruction of your marriage.

The boys and I go home to Peachtree City sans Karen. She stays to do something with her family for an extra day. As we walked through the terminal to the shuttle, I have Rhett in my arms like a hammock, Rex sitting up on my shoulders, and our two bags slung around my back. I remind myself, *I am still as strong as ever.* Only now I am going to be my kind of strong. Rhett got upset on the plane and scratched Rex in the face so hard I had to use three Band-Aids to stop the blood from streaming down Rex's face. Rhett acts out a lot. Poor little guy did not get enough love his first two years. I am going to a place where I can hold him and snuggle him and read to him every day. No more leaving him behind with nannies and daycares so he can wonder where Mommy and Daddy are. Mommy can keep staying out all day doing her nails and going to lunch. I will stay with you, Rhett.

I keep texting Nikki to make sure we are falling for each other. But my emotions really start messing with me. The thing about Nikki, she has been here before, and she thinks it's real, and she's making plans and talking long-term. She is good at what she does. At the same time, I'm second-guessing my every move, and she's the only one I have to talk to about it. Let's say I do fall in love with her, and Karen finds out, then what? She'll be mad, but what do I expect will happen? I still don't know. So I revert back to my old lie, and I convince myself: Karen will die in an accident on her way back to Georgia. That's God's reason for her going home separate from us. I am here in the little white house with my little white boys and my little white lie and Karen will die in a plane crash and never come home.

I stay up all night texting Nikki and waiting for the news that Karen has died. I usually leave my phone home when I go to church so I can focus on Jesus, but I take it so I can receive the death news in a timely manner when it comes. She boards her plane safely. While the boys and I are at church, I use the Delta Flight Tracker in the app to watch as it crashes somewhere in the Midwest. But the solid red line with an airplane at the end just keeps getting closer and closer to Hartsfield-Jackson Atlanta International Airport. Now she is about to land, so we hop in the car and head to Domestic Arrivals to pick her up.

Karen isn't going to die. Right. I've been waiting six years for that to happen. I need to fall in love with someone else so she just goes away. Right.

Time to call Nikki.

"Nikki, I'm a pretty happy guy, I would say I'm ninety-nine percent happy, but something crazy has happened and I need you to know."

"Oh yeah, what's that?"

I told you, she's a good listener.

"I love you," I say.

"I love you too," she replies.

And then I pick up Karen.

Divorce Court

"You know every single family that lives here has been divorced at least once? That's why we don't even call it Braelinn Court like it says on the sign. We call it Divorce Court."

I throw what few belongings I decided to keep into the back of a U-Haul as my neighbor walks up with his dog to officially welcome me to the neighborhood now that I am on my way out. Karen has long since left. I look at him with empty eyes and gaze past him to that teeny sad excuse for a boat he just bought off Craigslist sitting next to his driveway and think, *No way that thing has the buoyancy to float with him on board. He must weigh two-sixty.* But then I remember how much water I displaced with just a wakeboard and believe it can be done after all.

"We got divorced once, almost twice, but here we are, back together again." His wife approaches and chimes in with some kind of sigh, a half-happy one, I guess.

I will not be getting back together with Karen. No half-happy regretful sighs for me! Sayonara, Divorce Court.

I don't eat a full meal the entire week after we get back from Kyle's wedding. Falling in love sucks. After a few conversations with Nikki, I realize I have never had a real conversation with Karen. I had never been honest with her, not once. Karen personified all the sadness and confusion going through me when we met. Her dad convinced me to get rid of my parents and spank my kids, which kept me sad and confused awhile longer. Now I am trying to fall enough in love with another woman to get away from all these permanently sad and confusing Adams, but it's making me sadder and more confused than ever.

Nikki said she loves me back nearly sight-unseen, and I pour out my life story to her every day now. I feel dirty and sick. Can't eat or sleep. As we keep talking, Nikki teaches me to stop apologizing for everything. I apologize to Karen around fifty times per day. Nikki has me keep track in my journal, and one day I apologize to her over eighty times. I communicate with Karen by listening, saying what she wants to hear, and apologizing for anything I didn't guess right. Compliment sandwich buffet. Yuck! I want my money back.

Now I talk to Nikki six hours a day. I try to eat a slice of leftover pizza while Karen is watching Kardashians. I walk straight past her out the front door and puke on the porch, and she doesn't blink. I am down fifteen pounds just this week, and still Karen doesn't bat an eye. I don't have a plan other than to destroy her. My plan ends there. "Destroy" means I want her to know I love someone else. She will not survive. Does she not see something is wrong with me? How can I get her attention?

I start emailing Nikki from Karen's laptop. I email Nikki every night last thing before I go to sleep and first thing when I wake up. Usually I am sitting right next to Karen while I email Nikki, but she's so infatuated with her phone she doesn't notice anything. I even hand her the laptop with a love email to Nikki right on the screen and she still doesn't notice anything. She will soon enough.

I start driving a friend to cancer treatments. I drop him off at a hospital right next to a big store I've been trying to sell on Imaca for over a year. They finally sign up while we pop in before the chemo visits because they see they should do business with me since I'm the kind of guy who takes friends to chemo. Whatever it takes! Then we are driving home after a treatment and Karen calls.

"We need to talk," she says.

"Okay. I'll be right there." I did it! She found the emails. It's only been ten freaking days now, about time you finally notice my love affair. What a relief. I drop my friend off at his home and hurry home a different way than I normally drive.

I'm not sure what Karen will do when I get home. I half expect her to just take off like she used to all the time when we first got married. I don't think she can take the rejection of seeing that I love someone else, and she hates being a mom, so she might leave me and the boys and just go. I don't have any next steps in mind. I am in full survival mode.

I walk in and Karen says she just got off the phone with her dad. Under his direction she printed my emails with Nikki, read them all, and asks me for an explanation. She keeps her cool like Brian no doubt told her to for about ten minutes. Then she starts re-reading me the emails I wrote Nikki. I love it. They sound retarded, but Karen falls for it just like Nikki fell for it. Pure emotional reaction.

"You said you love her!"

I nod eagerly like Dobby the house elf when Harry Potter gets one of his dumb little riddles right. Yep, exactly. Pretty bad, huh? I watch her face contort like the evil queen watched Snow White bite the poison apple. Now, die! You paid no attention to me for seven years and now you pay the price. Die die die!

"I can't believe you fucking said that! Those words are for me! Did you really tell her those words? Did you tell her 'I love you?'"

I am stupefied. *Those words are for me?* That's all that bothers her? What do you mean, *words*? *I* love her, not *my words* love her. She's not getting it.

I reply back, "I really do love her."

"Those words are for me!!!" Karen screams back at me once again. She grabs the stack of printed emails, storms up to our room, and slams the door.

Not the reaction I anticipated. I am sitting in the green recliner where I spent so many sleepless nights with toddler Rex sleeping on my chest because of his reflux. First I am confused. But then I am sad. I tuck my knees into my chest and break down crying.

Karen doesn't care about me *at all.* She doesn't care who I am or what I feel or what I need or want or who I love. She just wants her words. I am so mad that I ever married this woman. She hurt me. A lot. I'm just property to her like the MacBook she spiked on the floor or the dishes she smashed on the kitchen floor.

I didn't make her mad the way I wanted to. I made her mad in a different way that will work just as well or even better.

I know Brian will try to talk her down, and I know he won't be able to because she never forgives or forgets anything. Sit up there and read those emails, Karen. They are addressed to Nikki, but I wrote them just for you. Read all those words of yours I sent to someone else. I am not your property.

When Karen says she only cares about owning my words "I love you," I pull my knees into my chest in the recliner just like I finally did on the wakeboard, and I am not strong anymore. I let a few sobs out, and they keep coming. I haven't eaten in so long it hurts to cry. I haven't let myself feel in so long it hurts to cry. I feel everything now, I feel six years of emotions I kept buried. I feel all the names I called my parents, all the friends I left behind, all the times Karen called me stupid and forgetful and poor and weak and all those guttural depressed scoffs she threw at me day after day after day. I thought I brushed them off, but they are here. I don't hold on to them, I let them go, and I am shaking and sobbing and weak, but I don't care.

When Karen comes back downstairs she wants to talk about my words some more, but I stop her.

"You hurt me, all the time!" I say. "Everything you say and do since we met hurts me and now I'm all nicked up inside. I only love someone else because I need to get away from you!"

Karen is speechless. I have never done this before. I feel more pain surfacing. I can't hold it in. I am being honest with Karen for the first time in my life.

I say, "I . . . am . . . broken." And when I do, my body shudders even more violently, and I repeat that phrase over and over, crying and crying, sitting in the fetal position in my living room. I can't stop crying and I can't stop shaking, and Karen just paces up the stairs and across the living room, glancing at me while she makes the rounds.

My hands are numb. My feet are numb. My limbs are numb, even my face is numb. I am covered in tears and sweat, am I going into shock? I still can't stop crying. The afternoon sunlight darkens into dusk, and I am still sitting in the fetal position when my tear wells finally run dry. Karen calls her dad again and then tells me she emailed our new bishop whose wife had the boob job and told him we need to meet with him tonight. The boys are with one of her nannies. Bishop emails back, and we are headed straight to see him.

We are only a two-minute drive from the church building. I am completely physically numb, what little electrolytes I had left just streamed out through my eyes, and I still can't feel my hands or feet or lips. Walking down the hallway to see our bishop, Karen asks me about the D word. This is the first time I have ever heard the D word in the context of my own life. I have never once considered it. It never crossed my mind. It is not in the realm of possibility. Until she says it. Then I know it must be. This is the end of the route I embarked on when we left for Kyle's wedding.

"Do you want a *divorce*? Are you done with me?"

As soon as she says it, I know I need it. It feels good to finally know what I am doing. But hearing "divorce" is like hearing "murder" or "cocaine" or "fat." These are things I just don't do. I decided long ago to never do any of these things. These are untouchables, I decided not to do them as soon as I can remember making decisions.

Our church president when I grew up told us what things to avoid and I listened to everything he said. No pornography, okay except for those two times, no poker, no sex, no drugs. I never had to decide against divorce because I decided I would be married for forever, which precludes divorce. But I see that my marriage isn't the forever kind. My wife doesn't even believe in God. I agree with Karen silently, absolutely, one hundred percent, we are getting a divorce. It's a huge decision, but I make it in a millisecond. I don't answer her, but I know it and I know she sees it in my eyes. She stops, but the bishop has left the door to his office open, and I go right in and she follows.

I waste no time. I turn to Karen and say, "Karen, this is going to sting," then I turn back to the bishop and share my feelings. "I hate her! She is manipulative and depressed and bipolar and narcissistic and absolutely crazy!" I am already a mess but waste no time. I have never said any of these words before, and they feel so true coming out. I'm finally telling the truth. Bishop says nothing, his eyes are as big and white as golf balls, but he just sits and listens. My bishop and I are pretty cool with each other. He knows me a lot better than he knows Karen. He knows I'm not crazy. He put me in a leadership position, and we work together to help out some of the people in the ward, including the friend I take to cancer treatments.

Karen is crying by now too. She tries to laugh and repeats my words through her tears, "Manipulative?" as if we are going to laugh it off and make up and say that Matt was just kidding. Nope. Hell, yeah, you are manipulative! You spent our whole life convincing me to do things I didn't want to do. Manipulative.

When neither of us respond, she really starts to cry and wails in despair, "He's right, I am terrible. I know I am." She cries her pathetic hopeless cry, and I cry my honest hopeful cry, and the bishop finally says, "Well, it looks like we have a problem here."

Bishop tells me to go to counseling, and I agree and we leave. I'm prepared for this. Still getting a divorce. Brian Adams will try to convince me to do counseling, and Karen will try to convince me to do counseling, and they will all try to make me live the life that ends with me as a miserable old man still married to her. I do need counseling, lots of it, but not marriage counseling. I need a divorce and to get as far away from these people as possible, and then I need all the counseling I can get. But for now I will play along.

We get home and the babysitter has put the boys to bed. I email the local church-approved psychologist, and Karen says she might as well go cut her wrists. She goes up to our room and locks herself inside.

Before she tells me about her cutting idea, she reminds me several times she just started another semester at school and really doesn't need to deal with this right now. She hates school and she hates me, but now I hate her back and she doesn't want to deal with it. I see again so clearly that she will never be happy.

I think back on the doctor's assessment that she shouldn't even be able to get out of bed in the morning. What does that even mean? I didn't ever see anything in writing. Has she been considering suicide? Has she cut her wrists before? I still want to feel bad for her and I still want God to just take her home. But I don't let myself believe she's going to die like I used to. I need to end this the way rational people end bad marriages: in divorce.

I need to be selfish now. I need to survive. I think to myself: Buckle up, sweetheart, you get just a little bit more of me this semester, and then I'm out for all future semesters. I promise. I don't know how long the D-word has been in your mind, but I am going to make sure we get it.

I don't think she will cut her wrists. But I didn't think she would get a tattoo either.

Karen comes down in the morning, and after she takes the boys to daycare, we go on the back porch and she has me "break up with Nikki" on speakerphone. Nikki has done her part, so I play along and tear Nikki apart. "You know I am married, what about my kids, shame on you." Blah blah blah.

Karen gets on her laptop and orders Nikki a bouquet of black flowers using my PayPal account. I call the Imaca secretary and nix the delivery. Karen's depression gets really bad, she just sulks around. She starts talking openly to our friends about my "work girlfriend," and I just smile. She's making herself madder and madder. It's going to boil over soon. I know she keeps reading all those emails I wrote Nikki. She's a ticking time bomb.

A few days before Karen found the Nikki emails, Kyle and Bailey came home from their honeymoon in Jamaica, and we picked them up from the airport for lunch during their layover. We went to one of my favorites in South Atlanta, Carroll Street Café in Cabbagetown. Kyle ate a lot. Bailey kept quiet. Karen took over. She starts giving them newlywed sex advice and calls herself a "sex queen." I stifle my laughter, and Kyle and I share a moment. She looks at Bailey and says, "Have you tried to stab your husband yet? I came after Matt with a butcher knife when we were first married." I can't believe what I am hearing. Karen admits that actually happened? And now brings it up in casual and conversation with my brother and his new wife?

The mood stays tense as we drive them back to the airport. Bailey will never see Karen again. Kyle and Bailey head straight back to Utah and move back to Logan, where they rent an apartment from Mindy and Kyson next to the trailer where Mindy and Kyson live that Karen likes to make fun of so much.

After our talk with Bishop, Karen goes straight back to her miserable life as if nothing changed. We don't have a relationship. We were roommates to begin with, we are roommates now. I am sleeping on the couch like usual. She wants me to talk to her dad and follow his instructions like usual. I am going to see a therapist and I am excited to have someone to talk to now that I don't have Nikki. How do we get the ball rolling here? Where is my divorce? My plan backfired. I am all alone again, and Doctor Adams will fix me and soon we will be back to normal. How can this be?

Karen says she needs time and doesn't know if she will ever forgive me. I think inside, of course you can't forgive me! You never forgive anyone! You've had it out for me since the day we met, now be your mad self and leave! You're supposed to be shattered and gone by now! How are you already at the forgiveness stage? You better not forgive me! Stop that right now!

I see her with her stack of Nikki emails at the dinner table, filing through them like she's preparing for a court case, getting more and more pissed as she does. How much more does she need? I am so mad she hasn't just left and gone back to Utah to hide at her parents' house. I don't know what else I can do.

Brian keeps calling me and I don't answer. Nikki keeps calling me and I don't answer. I need to think. What do I do next? I can still escape. I'm close. I can work with this. What's my next move? What do I do? Again, Karen will decide for me.

We are on an outing with the boys when she says, "Just give me two more years and then go." This is all just a game to her. I finally call her dad back.

We are all still planning to meet up in Washington, D.C., in a few weeks for a BYU football game. Brian and Julie and Karen and I. Most of the time I am with Karen now, she's on the phone with her dad, so she tells me the new plan. Brian will give us his best lesson of all and then everything will be hunky-dory. I have the seven-year itch like all married men get at seven years, including Brian, and he will get me through it. I think to her in my head, You think your dad is going to trick me into giving you two more years? What a joke. I'm reduced to the servant who will pay her bills while she tries to catch her dad's PhD status. My turn to call Brian.

"How did you get that *low,* fella?" Brian begins our talk with a question and proceeds to answer it for me. I still have a mountain of guilt on my shoulders just like I knew I would when I decided to get out this way, and Brian knows it too. I am a mess. He tells me I need to stop worrying about Karen so much, to start taking care of myself more, and doing what I want to do for a change. I should heal some of my friend and family relationships and start back with basketball like I played when he came to visit me at BYU. I am stunned. He talks and talks and talks. For forty-five minutes I listen to Doctor Adams try to undo all the wrong he did to me for seven years in one really, really long conversation. It's the best advice he's ever given me. He gives me homework and says, "See you in a few weeks for the BYU game, you'll be okay, bud." Okay, Brian. The best part is, Brian, you get to go out on a high note! I'll always remember this great advice you've given me. The problem is, Brian, for me to follow through on your advice, I have to end our relationship forever. I must never ever see you or hear from you again. You see, I'm not under your spell anymore, and you just proved it. Bye-bye.

I open my Airbnb app and cancel our D.C. reservation. The host has a "strict" cancellation policy, I always try to stay away from the strict ones for the same reason I have a fake credit card in my Marriott app even though I have Titanium status: plans change. I'll never be happier to pay a cancellation fee.

I also have tickets to take Karen to Orlando to Mickey's Halloween party with the Hallowishes Dessert Party add-on for her birthday next month. We always have another couple trips on the books. The Mickey tickets are non-refundable. I am so glad I won't have to take her on one more miserable expensive vacation.

It's the third Monday in September 2016. Rex feels sick, so I stay home and Karen goes to school. We drop Rhett off at daycare in our new golf cart I bought last week with the money I saved by not eating since August. Rex stays with me. He has a fever but isn't too sick to have fun. We cruise around all day in our golf cart and play Pokémon Go all across Peachtree City. We eat lunch at Chick-fil-A and buy a toy at Barnes & Noble. We pick up Rhett early, and strap his car seat on the back of the golf cart. On the drive home, Rex falls asleep on me with his head in my lap. I stroke his hair, wondering how this divorce will happen, wondering how much Rex will hate me. I wonder how badly little Rhett behind us has been damaged by not having me there his first two years like I was for Rex. I am so grateful for all of the time I got to spend with Rex. Time I didn't get with Rhett. Rex is exactly like me: witty and funny and fearless and athletic and caring and kind and ruthless and impulsive and reckless and creative and otherwise utterly inexhaustible. I rollerblade with him on my shoulders and we eat sushi at midnight. We walk around on weekends in our Speedos and he climbs on my back for pull-ups and squats. When it rains, we roll in the flooded street and when the sun is out, we burn things with magnifying glasses. He drinks my weird vitamin drinks and we spend twenty bucks on chocolate bars just to smell them and feel our salivary glands tingle. On days like today, I am nothing more than his dad. He's all I need.

While we drive home in the golf cart, I prepare to drive home the nail in the coffin where my marriage needs to die. I have been to the library and checked out Sun Tzu to make sure I will be victorious this time. *The Art of War* helped me put my emotions aside and look at the situation strategically. The enemy is weak. I need to stop going easy on her and I need to crush her like a samurai.

When I met Karen, she had set the password on her MacBook she spiked on the ground when she stubbed her toe to "tPadme." She was embarrassed about her closet obsession with Star Wars and told me not to tell anyone. Most things I learned about her came with the caveat "don't tell anyone" or "don't tell my parents." Now it's my turn to like Star Wars. Just like storm troopers are based on traditional Japanese samurai, I am Sun Tzu on the inside, and I am heading into a battle for my life tonight, and just like Sun Tzu says, I have already won because I will do whatever needs to be done.

I am utterly unprepared for divorce, but I am equally ready for separation. I don't know the difference yet, but I will find out soon enough. I am Mel Gibson with blue paint on my face just like the old Livingstons fighting with William Wallace at Falkirk near Levins Town where my family name comes from. I need my freedom back at all costs.

Since I talked to Brian last week, Karen keeps telling me she forgives me and asking me to move back into our bedroom. I politely decline. She doesn't know the trips to Disney and D.C. are off yet. She doesn't know it's over. Tonight she will find out. She eats and sits down with her TV remote and her ice cream, and I break the routine with a very serious voice.

"We need to talk," I say, surprised at my stern tone.

Karen, for the first time in her adult life, turns her attention away from the Kardashians. She pauses the TV and puts on the most sheepish, girly, capitulative voice she can muster. It makes me sick. I am over it. This will be easy.

"This isn't working for me," I say. Warrior strong!

"It's her again, isn't it!" Karen quickly snaps while she leaps up from the couch and grabs the laptop. "If I find one email on here, that's it, we are done!" She runs up the stairs and locks the bedroom door.

I walk barefoot out the front door and call Nikki. Karen will find something, she must, there has to be at least one email. Nikki answers on the first ring. She knows I didn't mean the break up, and now I am getting divorced for real, and of course she will have me back. I tell Nikki about the loaded gun we keep in our bedroom since Brian Adams says all smart people keep loaded guns in their bedrooms. I think about the two little boys asleep in their beds after a long adventurous day. I am scared of what Karen might to do me, to herself, or to the boys. I don't walk back home for almost two hours, until around midnight. Karen locked every door, so I use my hidden key to get inside, thinking she will be asleep. A few of my clothes are piled neatly by the front door.

Karen walks downstairs with my MacBook and meets me at the door. She found one email. I emailed Nikki a link to a Justin Bieber song a week ago, "Cold Water." Karen turns the laptop screen toward me and shows me the email. Then she sets the laptop on the kitchen table, and we stand there under the doorjamb to the kitchen. Not a great place for us to be. Standing is dangerous and kitchens have knives, which is dangerous, and hard two-by-four door frames are dangerous, but my warrior spirit stands serenely comfortable there in the kitchen doorjamb.

"Get out," she says.

"You get out," I say back.

"You're bipolar and you had a repressed childhood," she says. "Tomorrow I'm taking the boys to Utah."

I did it! If she really tries to take the boys away from me, this thing will be over. Now she believes I am having an affair with Nikki, and she will mess up and I will get away.

"No, you're not," I reply. "The boys and I are better off without you. Now go. And don't come back." I am still speaking the truth. I'm not telling her what she wants to hear. I point at the door. My voice startles me still. It's because the words are true.

Karen looks scared. The strangest look falls over her face as she sees I am no longer under her spell. She has owned me for a long time. Owning me makes up a huge part of her identity. But she sees it: I am gone. She comes undone right here under the doorjamb in front of me. I have never seen anything like it. She can't talk. She goes completely frozen and just stands there, speechless.

I say I will sleep on the porch, grab a blanket, and step out to the backyard. I can't be in here with her like this. I have no idea what she will do next. I just broke free and defeated her. We are over. I know she and Brian will still try to wrap me up in feelings of guilt and plans for therapy, but she knows it's over and I know it's over. I will never spend another night pretending to be hers.

I curl my six-foot body into our five-foot porch swing and distract myself from my sad situation by sending flirty texts to Nikki. I really need someone right now, and she's all I've got. My reality starts to set in, and I hate it. I have tried to do everything right my entire life and here I am about to destroy my family. It feels like a bad dream. Then a bunch of fire ants get up into my blanket and bite my toes. They remind me I am not dreaming.

I wake up dripping in dew at five a.m. and head to the gym and then start tracking Karen's phone. She takes the boys to daycare and heads to Georgia State. I call Nikki and talk for a couple hours and then go home. Karen's car is in the driveway. I walk inside anyway.

"I'm picking up the boys now and we are going to Utah," she says.

She looks different. Disjointed. Scared. This is good. I think.

"No, you're not," I said.

Then different Karen looks at me with different Karen face and I see a few things clearly. If I stay here one more moment, there is a good chance one of us might get hurt. If I stop her from going to Utah, then what? I have no plan. What if I let her go? Does that mean we are finally divorced? I turn around and walk out of the house. I track her over the next few hours. She drives to the preschool and then to the airport. She probably decided it would be too hard to take both boys with her and ended up leaving them at preschool. I call and ask, but she really did pick them up. She will take them back any minute, and then go back to the airport by herself. Her phone keeps on going into the airport. She's probably yelling at them for climbing on things and ready to give them back now. If I head to Arrivals, she'll give them back and go to Utah by herself. But her tracker dot keeps going, deep into the airport. She and the boys are gone.

I just sit in our driveway in my 2003 Corolla and stare at her dot. I try not to think. I walk into the house and through the doorjamb to the kitchen where we argued last night, and I collapse in a heap on the ground and sob loud and hard. I punch the wall where I know I won't make a hole, and the pain helps me keep it together. In the Church we wear protective underwear we call garments as a reminder of our covenants with God. I take mine to the garbage can on the curb and throw them all away. I can't handle this. My boys are gone. She doesn't even like them! They are just property to her. Just like me. She only took them to make me mad. I have a little more rage in store for her.

I walk back through the doorjamb and stop again. I hear a voice. It's the voice of Gordon B. Hinckley, the President of the LDS Church all through my adolescent years. He says, "Things will work out." Well, damn. I can work with that. Things will work out. I threw my little fit and now I feel much better. I get on my phone and order new garments. Then I book a flight to Utah to go to Nikki's house Friday night after work. I can do it. Things will work out.

I work until nine p.m. the next two days and head out early on Friday to see Nikki alone for the first time ever. We need to go on a date. This will be the final act in my charade to get a divorce.

I am so sad. I sit and close my eyes and imagine Rex's hot little head sleeping in my lap while I drive the golf cart with Rhett strapped in the back under the hot Georgia September sun. God knows I need that memory to make it through the week. I am so sad I married a woman who won't mother them and calls them "offspring" and would rather do anything than be at home. I am so sad that all they are to her right now is a way she can hurt me. I am so sad not knowing when I will see them again, when we will get to go to the park, when they will get a prayer and a story to help them fall asleep. I let myself cry and just keep on crying.

No woman who takes those boys away from me can be part of my life. She knows how to hurt me, and it hurts really bad. She doesn't just take the boys. She empties our checking account, takes our box of precious metals and cash, takes my two or three precious little heirlooms too. But these are the last things on my mind right now. First things on hers. She knows the boys are my number one. I know they are confused right now and they need their dad. I need them too. I need to be me. We are almost there. I board the plane to Salt Lake City, where I will make my final maneuvers to get away from their mom for good.

The End

I GET HIGH FOR THE FIRST TIME, DRINK WINE FOR THE first time, and buy a ring on a first date for the first time with Nikki in Salt Lake City on my mom's birthday. Friday, September twenty-third, 2016. All of these firsts will also be lasts. A night like tonight calls for a few last firsts. I would much rather go home to Kanab and start my divorce from there. But I don't know my family anymore. In Salt Lake City, my fake girlfriend waits with open arms to play her part and get me to the end of this. As long as I keep Nikki around, I don't have to face divorce alone. I can pin it on her for now and Karen can pin it on her forever.

Meanwhile, I know Brian has Karen in his office getting all his best stuff about how taking the boys and the money will give me a wake-up call and I will come to my senses. I still haven't logged into our bank account and seen it's been emptied. Brian will do everything he can to keep Karen boarded up with the stallion he recruited for her. He knows she will never get another one like me.

Brian doesn't think I will go through with a divorce. He thinks I will feel too guilty and come back. But I know Karen knows it's over. I am going to shoot one more arrow in her Achilles heel: narcissism. I shouldn't mix my Greek references like that, but nobody has been this vain since Narcissus himself. I am so mad at her for taking the boys. I want her to think I am giving Nikki more of me, the property

Karen says belongs to her. I smile when I think of how mad I am about to make Karen.

I need a divorce.

The rush of breaking so many of my rules to meet Nikki and go on a date distracts me from how much I miss my boys. There are still so many variables that could botch my plan. I am entering uncharted territory with no map, but my inner warrior guides me past baggage claim to Nikki's Civic. I walk right up to her and she steps out of her car and I kiss her. I am all in on this. This will be easy. And it's actually kind of nice. Karen hasn't kissed me in years.

We hold hands and she drives us directly to dinner. Nikki can't eat meat or gluten, so we go to one of the many vegan places on her short list. Neither of us have eaten much the past month and we don't eat much at dinner, but we both laugh a lot.

I have never seen anyone so nervous. She drinks four total glasses of two different types of wine. She's on the verge of a nervous breakdown regarding our situation too. I've already broke up with her twice, and she keeps asking if this is real or if I am just playing games. I don't really answer because, well, it's both. I am playing a real game for my life here.

After dinner we go to City Creek mall and buy some cards and Scrabble. She loves buying cards and sending them to people. She sent me some great cards. I am not the only guy at Imaca getting cards and kisses from Nikki, I know that. I won't feel as bad when this all ends because of it. She kisses all the boys. It's what she does.

Then I remember . . . we are around the corner from a Tiffany's store.

I knew my final act would present itself. Now it has.

Tiffany's. Where Karen made me spend a bunch of money I didn't have to buy her a ring she never wore to make up for something I didn't do wrong on our vacation in Seattle in 2010. I need the poetic justice of spiting Karen by buying a ring from Tiffany's for Nikki. Nothing I can do right now will get Karen more pissed. I need to use our debit card to make sure Karen sees the charge. I finally log in to Wells Fargo and see she emptied our savings account. I just laugh. Take it! I got paid today and have a few grand in our checking account to buy a ring for Nikki.

We go straight to Tiffany's, and Nikki picks out a ring. She doesn't want to and tries to leave, but I insist. She doesn't fight very hard. Adrenaline rushes through me as a ring lady walks over to let her try it on. Nikki knows her. Of course the Tiffany's worker and Nikki are besties. Her friend tells us she is so happy for us and wraps the ring in a Tiffany blue box. I hand her my debit card but my arm weighs a hundred pounds. I don't do things like this. But I need to. Karen loves jumping to conclusions and she will know in her little Karen brain when she sees our "recent transactions," she's looking at an engagement ring purchase.

Up until now, using Nikki to get out of my marriage hasn't really worked. It's made Karen mad, and Monday was better, but I can do better still. This will be enough. I know once I'm gone, Nikki obviously won't want this ring, but maybe she can sell it. I owe her something for all the help she has been. I don't think I could be doing any of this without her. I don't have a backup plan. I am all in on Nikki getting me out of my marriage to Karen. I need to go way out on this limb with Nikki, far enough that in her mind Karen could never have me back, and so she will have to snap me off.

So I go all in and lift my hundred pound arm and drop most of what little money is left in our bank account on a Tiffany T square ring. We only use Wells Fargo because Karen made us switch from Chase after the Chase teller in Irvine greeted her in Spanish and she took offense. Lots of people struggle with her olive skin, chubby cheeks, and squinty eyes. Is she Hispanic? Asian? Native American? She even gets aboriginal Australian sometimes.

I make sure Karen can still see where I am with the Find my Friends app. I know she is tracking me right now. She's called a few times this week, but I don't answer. I need to stay away from her because she will use the boys to guilt trip me into not getting a divorce and staying together for the kids. I know I am emotionally unstable and can't risk these conversations. I'm not talking to her until it's to tell her we are getting divorced tomorrow morning. She's sent me text messages asking for money. She emptied the bank account; I have no idea what she expects me to send. When Karen first read my emails with Nikki, she got Nikki's address. I need her to know I am at Nikki's house later.

We are at Nikki's house less than ten minutes when Karen sounds the find iPhone alert on my phone. Nikki and I are sitting on the floor playing a quiet game of Scrabble, and the alarming noise jolts us both to our feet. Here I am the night before I end my eternal marriage calmly playing Scrabble and sipping water to the sound of soft music. My thoughts revolve around which letters will make the best next word. Karen never plays Scrabble with me. The few times she did, I tried to let her win, but she can't do words longer than about three letters. I silence the sirens on my phone and quickly glance at all the text messages from Karen filling up the screen.

One of them she wrote to Nikki: "You are with a married man. He is not yours." Reminding us both I am Karen's property. I don't relay the message.

Another one says she will call the cops on us.

I am looking for a certain text message that should be here by now, but I don't see it yet. More "where are you?"s and "please come home"s but not the one I want to see. I scroll down the lock screen just a little more . . . come on . . . come on . . . there it is! A screenshot of our checking account transactions showing the $2000 debit from Tiffany's. Well, Doctor Adams, it turns out I have learned to speak Karen quite well, and just in time, too. I know just where she will look and just what will disturb her the most. How's that for using my Karen brain? These text messages are her last futile attempts at getting me back. I am almost done now. Everything is finally going according to plan.

Nikki tells me she and her best friend, who's also dating a married guy, just went to Denver so they could get a bunch of legal weed. Her friend left her purse in their Uber and chased it down the middle of the street in heels until she caught it at a stoplight. They bought a bunch of marijuana gummies and she brought some home and they are still in her kitchen cabinet. Wouldn't I like to try one? Why not! I have one last night as the old me, so I can do whatever I want. Except sex. Nikki knows I will not have sex outside of marriage. Lots of LDS people break their chastity covenant with God when they get divorced, but not me. But the little things, like not getting high, I honestly just don't care.

At work, only Matt Kennedy knows what I am going through. He hates drama the same way I do. I know he won't judge me or tell anyone. Karen and Matt's wife, Melanie, are still connected on Facebook. Karen told Melanie everything about Nikki and me and asked her to make Matt fire Nikki. Karen sent all of mine and Nikki's emails to Matt Kennedy, but he doesn't care. We have one conversation about it where he expresses love and support, and we are back to business as usual. I still feel like I might be jeopardizing my career. But I don't think so. Nikki keeps everything a secret and I keep everything a secret and nobody else knows anything. So Karen starts calling other people.

She calls my old friends and tells them that I left the church and am having an affair. Why would they even care? I'm not allowed to be friends with any of them anymore anyway. She can say whatever she wants.

She deletes our blog and our Facebook account. Everything we have, we have together. That's how it works when you marry a controlling person. Joint bank account, joint credit cards, joint Facebook, joint everything. She uses them and makes us look a certain way, and I play along. Happy wife, happy life. As she takes us dark, a lot of people know something is wrong. Kyle has known for days now, he feels it. My sister Kelly knows. They have been calling, but I don't answer any of their calls either. I won't talk to a soul until I have Karen on the ropes. I need focus to deliver the death stroke in the morning. Then I will call them.

Nikki brings out the can of marijuana gummy bears. I eat just one. I am evidently a hyper-aware type of high. I start looking closely at the veins on the back of my hands and the pores in my skin and I watch the hairs move and bristle. I blink slowly and notice how my eyes open and shut, but even when they shut I can't stop thinking super analytically about every sound in the room, every smell, every source of light. Everything starts to annoy me. Especially Nikki. I need the lights off and the music off and for her to stop laughing at me! She calls me skinny boy and I yell back, "Yes, but I'm strong!" and we both laugh as my high wears off.

I will finally talk to Matt Kennedy in person about everything next month on a work trip to Tampa. He will say, "Wow, Matt, you're really strong."

I am a different kind of strong now. Not the strong that gets you muscles to be recognized on Instagram or make your wife happy. Not the strong that calms things down every time said wife throws a dish or bites you to extend your roommate relationship of abuse and misery. I'm a different kind of strong now. The resilient kind of strong that gets you divorced because without a divorce, you will die.

After we eat the gummies from Denver, Nikki wants to watch an old movie and drink more wine. I have a sip of her wine. It tastes like sour grape juice. I don't even like it. By now Nikki is really drunk and really high and completely incoherent. It's close to midnight, and we are sitting on her couch right next to the front door. Someone knocks loudly, and she would have spilled her wine, but I catch the glass. We obviously don't answer. Karen did call the cops! No chance

I am answering, who knows what story she told them. They knock again and stay awhile, but then they leave. Nikki thanks me for catching her wine glass and tells me stories about all her other boyfriends while she walks into her bedroom and passes out on her bed and loudly snores herself fast asleep.

I sit on Nikki's little couch and write notes in my planner before I go to sleep. In the morning I will call Karen around seven a.m. and tell her we are getting a divorce. She will threaten me on three fronts. First, she will say I will never see the boys again. Not up to her, and I will win custody, because she is mentally unstable, hates being a mom, I have medical records, and we can subpoena her GSU psych eval to prove it. Next she will say she is going to get all my money. Cool with me. Take it. And then she will say that she will ruin Nikki's life like she has ruined so many others. I can live with that. I gave Nikki a ring for all her trouble. That will have to work as payment for whatever Karen wants to do to her. One threat, two threat, three threat. Guarantee it. I am ready. In the morning I will have my divorce.

We wake up around five a.m. and go to Nikki's gym. She runs really funny and with lots of agony on her face. I glance over at her a few times during my deadlifts. I see a guy on the bench press I recognize from BYU. Utah Valley is really small, only around a million people total. I get my heart going as fast as I can. I push the sled. I do a bunch of burpees. Pull ups until I can't hang on anymore. I have so much adrenaline and emotion in me and need it gone so I can be calm. I push and pull and press until I am dizzy and the nerves are long gone. We drive back to Nikki's, and I shower first. While Nikki showers, I go to my divorce office on her little couch and call Karen. She sounds apologetic and croaky and hoarse, but no matter how pathetic she sounds, she will not win me back.

She uses her fake nice voice for a while and I just listen. I will never have to listen to her like this ever again. I am so excited. Her words have zero meaning. I know mostly I am hearing regurgitated lessons from Brian, so I don't feel bad about not listening. She can finish, and my turn will be short. Finally she says I should come down to Twin Peaks and we can start over, and then I get my long-awaited pause where I get to be the obedient husband and do what she wants me to again. Instead I swear at her for the first time ever and end it with just six words.

"We are getting a fucking divorce." I sound exactly like I need to. I deliver the best line of poetry of my life. She finally hears me, too.

She threatens me exactly how I knew she would. She tells me about the courts and she already has a lawyer and she already has a new apartment and I am paying for everything and on and on and on. This woman can talk forever. I enjoyed it so much a minute ago, I jump in at another rare pause and swear at her one last time, in honor of PJ, and hang up.

"You can fight me, and I will win. Do your worst, bitch."

I cannot believe how well I did. I ended it! I am free! I finally spoke the truth to the woman who made me a liar. I am so happy.

But not everyone will be this happy. Time to call my family. Time to see what Kyle says. I call Kyle first.

"I just told Karen we are getting a divorce. I'll get a lawyer and file in the next few days." I come right out with it to my brother, who just got married and does not need this crap from me. I choke back tears and feel like I've let him down.

"I don't have a clue how you made it that long and I am so proud of you," he replies. "I love you, bro."

He says it, and I feel it, and the tears flow freely down my face. This is what love feels like. I have never felt loved before. All the holes Karen left in me open up again, and I cry from my whole body. Thank goodness Nikki is still in the shower. My brother's words heal me. I don't deserve the love he freely gives me, but I know it's been there all along.

Next I call Gramalisa and PJ. They know something is up with me too. They have been sitting by their phones for days waiting to hear something from someone about me.

"I am getting a divorce."

"Woohoo!" says my mom without a moment's hesitation, like we just decided to go to the beach. I hear PJ sniffling tears of joy. "Can we come get you? Where are you?" they ask me excitedly.

I did not expect such supportive responses to my decision to get a divorce.

I still don't know anything about the legal counsel my parents have sought multiple times to have the opportunity to see their grandsons. Don't know about the many therapists they have seen trying to do the right thing for me. Don't know that in the midst of all the trials these two pioneer Christians have faced in their entire lives, I just dragged them through the most trying of them all, and they have been praying for me to get divorced from the month I got married.

I call my three sisters and Tanner and a few other old friends. Karen already called them to get them "on her side." I tell them I love them and I am sorry and they all forgive me. I call my bishop, who asks me to come see him tomorrow, which I will. Karen already called and asked him to kick me out of the Church. It doesn't really work like that. Someone tried to kick me out before. The Kanab mayor. After I condemned him in my Cowboy Currents column for outlawing gay people. Lots of people told me he has "little man syndrome." I am finally making people mad again for being mean again and I am finally being me again.

Nobody even asks me if I really am having an affair. Because Matt Livingston isn't a liar anymore.

Sneak Preview of the Sequel to

Matt Livingston, You Liar!

Our first morning in Bastimento, Mom opened up about their relationship.

"Mom didn't want me when I was born," she told me. "My mom just didn't want me. She already had her kids, and when I was born, she wished I would die. She actually told me that, that she wished I would die."

I felt Mom's pain as she cried on. I held her hand and listened lovingly and silently.

"Since she didn't want me, the only purpose I had was to serve her. I was a big inconvenience to her, so if I didn't make her life better, I was worthless."

I had no idea about any of this. I knew Mom had a strong sense of duty and that she always thought she didn't do enough for us. She got a job as a college recruiter just so she could offer us reduced tuition and hang out with us at high school. Everything she did was for her kids. I didn't know this was in polar opposition to the way she was treated as a daughter.

It was hard to listen to. I knew as I heard what my mom said that what she believed was false and yet deeply ingrained in her. How could she unlearn lies told to her over and over again by her own mother during her most formative years? I knew how hard it was for me to try to un-learn the lies I told myself and others during a handful of adult years. It seemed almost impossible. Her task was even more so.

"I love you, Mom," I said. "Thank you for sharing that with me."

Her truth healed a big part of my heart in that moment we shared. I had spent so much time being so severely dishonest with myself that even after two years of divorce, the best I could do in a book was to write myself as the female character and live the entire marriage through one day of stream of consciousness as if the whole thing had been a dream. I didn't know how to face my own reality and be honest with myself. I worried so much about making other people happy and not letting them down, I had lost myself in that shuffle. And I was still lost.

Mom's honesty that morning taught me a lot. She was emotionally abused and abandoned by her own mother her entire life. She was so brave to face that reality.

I wasn't there yet. I was still floundering in the bowels of anger and blame. But her honesty brought me closer to emerging from that awful place.

We walked to the cacao farm and played Scrabble. We walked to the beach and played in the waves. We got lost in the jungle and howled with the monkeys. We went back to our sacred dock for sunrise and sunset, for prayers and meditation, for breakfast and reflection.

I asked my on-call love interest if she could help us get a private boat rental to take us around. My buddy Francesco knew this place like he knew a good avocado from a bad one, and he had already given me a handful of places to visit: to see dolphins, to be surrounded by starfish, to swim with turtles. Her cousin had a private boat and could take us the next morning, our last full day, Saturday. Perfect!

We started with dancing dolphins in a bay surrounded by tall trees coming straight out of the water. Most of the little islands seemed more like trees coming up out of the ocean than actual land masses. It was beautiful. The colors were striking. The dolphins were happy and free. We found the starfish, hundreds of them, so plentiful we could lean over the side of the boat and scoop two or three of them out of the water at once. Orange, red, yellow, white, all the colors of the sun.

We were having a blast. For our last snorkel our guide told us he had a treat for us, the best secret spot in Bocas, where we could swim the last few hours. We beamed at each other in anticipation and excitement. I knew Mom was tired, but she was hanging in there and letting her adrenaline carry her. I was a little worried that we were over-doing it. But how could we say no to a private snorkel in a secret spot!

We veered off to the south of the cove we would soon head to spend our last night in the treehouse. Around a bend we glided in toward a beautiful and miniature beach with deep water and lots of submerged rock and concrete that would yield some great snorkeling. Long and gangly tree branches shaded the pristine sands. The beach was so small our driver said he wouldn't beach his boat; rather, he would stay out in the bay and we could snorkel in.

"You two go on in and I'll stay here," he said, chill as ever as he killed the engine.

"Great! Can we just leave our stuff with you?" I asked. He nodded.

For safety purposes Mom and I had decided to keep our phones and passports on us at all times. They would be safe with our driver. After all, he was my new girlfriend's cousin.

"Enjoy yourselves! There is the most marine life down there of any beach in Boca," he boasted with flare.

"Great, see you in a little bit, thanks again!" I mirrored his excitement, and Mom followed suit.

We grabbed our snorkel gear and swam ashore. We heard the boat engine roar back to life and turned around to see our phones and passports and transportation disappear from sight. I pretended this was part of the plan. I was a great pretender, after six years of pretending happiness in an unhappy marriage and then two years of playing make-believe games with my two boys since then. Pretending was easy. But that wasn't the only thing that threw us off.

The beach had only one other occupant, who looked fine from a distance, but now that we were up close and personal, appeared menacing. There was a sign in the ground that I can't find on Google, which doesn't make any sense. It should be on the Google page for that beach, but it's not. It was a very prominent sign, one of the first things you'd notice. I can still feel the eerie sensation that came over me as I read it that day. It was probably two feet square and made of cast iron, written in English, and it was scary. I do not remember the exact words, but it said something to the effect of, "This beach is a place where pirates come to steal your things. Beware!"

I wanted at first to think it was a joke and laugh it off. I walked past the man sitting on a fallen log so as to get a better look at him without staring. He wore a wide-brimmed leather hat such as pirates wear. He had on several layers of loose-fitting leather clothing such as a pirate would have on. He had a few bags of what I can only assume was loot from traveling snorkelers, because pirates are in the business of amassing their treasure. What looked like a sword lay next to him on the log. Tattoos on his face and arms jumped out at me, including one that looked a lot like a black spot on his wrist.

We didn't have anything for him to steal. I whisked past him briskly, pretended to examine something past him on the shore, and then circled back to my mom.

"Let's check out this reef!" I pretended a carefree attitude.

I got lost exploring the large concrete pipes and huge coral boulders on the ocean floor. I bobbed my head up every so often to examine the beach and my mom. The pirate left. Then Mom was gone too. I swam back to the beach and found her on a little raised outcropping covered in spiky green grass.

"He's still gone," she lamented as I plopped down next to her. "Do you think he's coming back?"

It was now nearing sunset, and though the bay looked beautiful and triumphant in the fading orange light, it looked equally vast and defeating.

"Honestly, I do not know," I replied.

"Looks like a pretty far swim," Mom continued. "Could we make it?"

We could see our treehouse off in the distance, probably around two miles away. Maybe half a mile out was the waterway where most boats were passing by us. There were still boats every fifteen minutes or so. But time was running out with night fast approaching.

"I don't think we could make it," I replied, choosing honesty over reassurance. "But I do think we could make it to where the boats are passing and flag one down!"

Mom laughed uproariously at our predicament and my proposed solution. I joined her.

"Hahaha! Could you imagine!" she croaked, already hoarse from the high pitch of our laughter. "Help us! SOS! Our boat left us to die!"

"He hustled us and fed us to the pirates!" I added, and she laughed even more.

We were free. Starving, destitute, lost, forgotten, whatever we were, we were happy. I knew our freedom came from the connection we shared from Mom's honesty. We had read several chapters in *Emily Rose* and while it was okay in parts, it was a rough read. But it was bringing us together too. The truth had made us free.

I felt in that moment I had finally found what I was looking for. Waiting for. Yearning for. With everything stripped away from me, with nothing but the love of my mother between me and life and death, I found everything. The peace and happiness I felt with my mom in that still moment on a destitute beach was everything I needed.

About the Author

MATT GREW UP THE OLDEST OF FIVE KIDS TO TWO PARents who made great sacrifices for each other and for their family. His dad was an avoider and his mom an enabler, and Matt picked up on the best of both.

During Matt's childhood, the family bounced around from living down the hill from Grandpa's cattle ranch, to living with cousins, to staying in the rental houses near the schools where Matt's dad ended up teaching. Then they got to Utah where BYU and marriage called out to Matt loudly through his adolescent years. He avoided and enabled through seven years of marriage and then, at the encouragement of his therapist, turned back to writing to process the pain of divorce.

Matt now lives in Mesa, Arizona with his wife Alissa and their four boys. Matt and Alissa both view this time in the world as one of awakening, healing, and reconciliation. We all have the opportunity through facing and hearing our own pain to heal the pain of the universe. We can always face our pain as an ally, we can always forgive ourselves, and we can always choose love. For more information, you can reach them at kundalinicobras@gmail.com.

CPSIA information can be obtained
at www.ICGtesting.com
Printed in the USA
LVHW031743111221
705948LV00005B/79

9 781947 966505